The Accountant Beside You

presents

Using QuickBooks ® Online

For

Small Nonprofits & Churches

Books by Lisa London

The Accountant Beside You series

Using QuickBooks® for Nonprofit Organizations, Associations, & Clubs
QuickBooks® for Churches and Other Religious Organizations
QuickBooks® para Iglesias y Otras Organizaciones Religiosas
Church Accounting—The How-To Guide for Small & Growing Churches

Historical Fiction

Darker the Night

The Accountant Beside You

Presents

Using QuickBooks® Online

For

Small Nonprofits & Churches

Lisa London, CPA

&

Eulica Kimber, CPA

Deep River Press, Inc.
Sanford, North Carolina

The Accountant Beside You Presents
QuickBooks Online for Small Nonprofits & Churches
ISBN 978-1-945561-02-3
Library of Congress Control Number 2016946413

Published by Deep River Press, Inc. July 2016
Copyright 2016 Deep River Press, Inc.

Reasonable efforts have been made to assure the information in this book is reliable and complete. No representations or warranties are made for the accuracy or completeness of the contents of this book. Any responsibility for errors or omissions is disclaimed by the author.

This book is to provide guidance in using QuickBooks ®. No information in this book should be perceived as tax or legal advice.

QBO®, QuickBooks®, Quicken®, and all Screenshots ® are registered trademarks of Intuit, Inc.
Microsoft Excel ® is a registered trademark of Microsoft, Inc.
PayPal® is a registered trademark of PayPal, Inc.
Intuit, Inc., Microsoft, Inc., and PayPal, Inc. are not affiliated with this book or Deep River Press, Inc.

©Boy Scouts of America, ©Girl Scouts of the United States of America, ©North American Montessori Teachers' Association, and the American Society of Association Executives™ are owners of their respective marks and are not affiliated with this book or Deep River Press, Inc.

EDITED BY Susan Sipal
COVER DESIGN BY Greg Schultz

Dedication

To our parents,
Jim & Jane VanLeeuwen and Eulis & Patricia Beasley.
Your love and support has been greatly needed and appreciated.

Contents

Introduction

When I helped my church convert their accounting system a few years ago, I was surprised how few resources there were to explain how church accounting works. This led to the first book of **The Accountant Beside You** series, *QuickBooks for Churches and Other Religious Organizations*. Now, less than three years later, there are four books in the series helping over 10,000 organizations.

As time moves on, so does technology. More and more organizations want the convenience of an internet-based accounting system. I'm Lisa London, and alongside CPA Eulica Kimber, we'll be **The Accountant Beside You** guiding you through the process of setting up QuickBooks Online and maintaining a streamlined accounting process for your nonprofit or church.

As a CPA for several decades, I have helped many small, medium-sized, and start-up companies establish accounting systems to streamline their businesses. As a person who finds it hard to turn down requests from organizations I volunteer with, I have served on boards of various nonprofits, on the audit committees for several churches, and as church treasurer. My accounting career started as an auditor with Deloitte, one of the world's largest accounting firms, where I learned the importance of internal accounting controls.

Eulica Kimber, a CPA from Virginia, operates Firm Foundations Accounting Solutions and specializes in providing accounting services to churches, small businesses, and nonprofits. Her background as a federal auditor and a QuickBooks Certified ProAdvisor has given her a strong understanding of both controls and accounting systems. Her clients use QBO almost exclusively. Her extensive experience enabled me to bring this book to life.

Keep it simple is our motto. We are going to walk you through the nonprofit specific terminology you need to know, teach you what the QuickBooks limitations are for nonprofit organizations and provide work arounds, and help you design internal accounting controls. Then, you'll learn how to set up your organization's accounting system, pay bills, and receive money through the system. Month and year-end reporting and review will be covered, and finally, you'll learn some unusual and non-frequent items that you need to consider.

Our approach is designed to quickly and easily get you up and running on the processes nonprofits use frequently and find the most important. This book is not meant to be read once and forgotten. Keep it close to the computer, use what you need, and check my website, www.accountantbesideyou.com, for additional tips, videos, discussions, and updates.

Now, remember, Eulica and I are with you all the way. Let's get started.

1. QuickBooks Online & Nonprofits

A. Will QuickBooks Online Work for My Organization?

Note: For simplicity sake, all nonprofit organizations, churches, associations, and clubs will be referred to as **organizations**, and QuickBooks® will be **QuickBooks** or **QuickBooks Online (QBO)**.

The QuickBooks programs are not designed for nonprofits but can work up to a point that is acceptable for most organizations. This book is designed to show you how to make it work for your nonprofit needs.

QuickBooks is available in a desktop version for PCs, a desktop version for Mac computers and an online version. Each are similar, but independent programs. This book will cover only the online version. If you are running QuickBooks desktop, I recommend reading *Using QuickBooks for Nonprofit Organizations, Associations, & Clubs* or *QuickBooks for Churches and Other Religious Organizations*.

There are three basic QuickBooks Online (QBO) subscription levels: Simple Start, Essentials, and Plus. Payroll and merchant services can be added to any of the subscriptions.

Each of the online levels offers most, but not all, of the features of the desktop versions. Your data is automatically backed up, and up to two accountant users can be invited at no additional charge. As of the printing of this book, the monthly subscription cost for Simple Start is $12.95, Essentials is $26.95, and Plus is $39.95. Each subscription includes a 30-day free trial, or discount pricing for 6 or 12-month commitments (depending on the subscription level).

Qualified nonprofits and churches may be able to purchase a one-year subscription from Techsoup.org for $50.00. Techsoup is a nonprofit dedicated to matching other nonprofits with technology solutions. They receive donations from technology companies and give them to qualifying nonprofits for a small handling fee. It is a wonderful resource, and I highly recommend that you check out their website, www.techsoup.org, for all your technology needs. (Please note, neither my co-author Eulica nor I have any affiliation with Techsoup. It is simply a valuable resource we want you to be aware of.)

To help you see the differences in the versions, here is a chart listing the features of each QBO subscription level.

QuickBooks Online Subscription Levels			
Features	Simple Start	Essentials	Plus
Monthly cost	$12.95	$26.95	$39.95
Number of users	1	3	5
Number of built in reports	20+	40+	65+
Track income and expenses	√	√	√
Create and send invoices	√	√	√
Print checks and record transactions	√	√	√
Download bank and credit card transactions	√	√	√
Backup data automatically	√	√	√
Import data from Excel and QuickBooks Desktop	√	√	√
Invite up to two accountant users to access your data	√	√	√
Access data from a tablet or smartphone	√	√	√
Control what users can access		√	√
Manage, schedule, and pay bills		√	√
Create and send purchase orders			√
Prepare and print 1099s			√
Create budgets ***			√
Use class tracking ***			√
Use location tracking			√
Track inventory			√

> *** Class tracking and the ability to create budgets are very important for nonprofits and churches, therefore the only level of QBO We recommend is the **Plus** level. QuickBooks support may tell you the Simple Start or Essentials options will work, but they do not understand the complexities of nonprofit accounting.

If you have employees, QuickBooks offers payroll services that can be added to any of the QBO accounting service levels. I will explain each of the options and how to enter the data in Chapter 10.

B. QBO vs Desktop

Should my organization buy QBO or the desktop version? This is probably one of the questions most frequently asked of Eulica and me. The answer is, "It depends on which features are most important to you."

The main differences between the desktop and online versions of QuickBooks are the pricing and the location of the software. QBO is subscription based, payable with a monthly fee, and its software is located in the cloud. The desktop version is paid for once and resides on a computer in your physical location. Let's go into the advantages and disadvantages of each.

1.   Advantages of QBO

There are many reasons for an organization to move their accounting system to the cloud.

Flexibility and convenience are QBO's biggest advantages. Your organization's accounting records can be accessed from any internet-connected PC or mobile device. The executive director or pastor can review reports even if they are not in the office. The volunteer treasurer can work from home. You aren't tied to working only in the office. A mobile app is available for your phone to see financial data on the go and there are numerous third-party applications to help with specific fun

Multiple users at different locations can use the program or view reports simultaneously. The treasurer can be online reviewing the previous month's financial statements while the bookkeeper is inputting this week's donations. If the members of your board of directors live in separate cities, each can review the reports online while on a joint conference call or Skype session. This is a contrast from the software for desktop versions which is located on a single computer and can usually only be accessed from that location, through a cloud hosting or sharing service is sometimes used at an additional monthly cost.

There is no need to backup data because your work is automatically saved by QBO. The desktop version must be backed up and the files kept in a secure location. If your computer crashes or you are moving the accounting system to a different unit, you can simply log into your QBO account instead of having to restore the data manually.

Bank data is fed automatically, giving you an up-to-date view of your cash situations at all times. The desktop version will allow you to import your bank data, but it will not be automatic.

Your professional accountant can be given access to the system, which can save time and effort for both the organization's staff and the accountant. Your accountant can use QBO's accountants' tools to add to the value of the services offered. In the desktop version, you have to set up a special Accountant's File to send for review, determine a date so you and the accountant are changing data in the same accounting period, and then restore the Accountant's File.

Intuit, the company who makes QBO, is focusing their development and marketing efforts on the online version instead of the desktop version. Intuit claims they are not going away from the desktop version, but their focus is obviously in the cloud. QBO updates and system improvement are released on a regular basis. With a QBO subscription, there is no need to install updates to receive new features. QuickBooks Online is always current. By contrast, new features for desktop versions are only available by installing updates manually or purchasing and installing new editions which are released annually.

2. Disadvantages of QBO

Just as there are many reasons to move your accounting system into the cloud, there are also reasons to prefer the desktop version.

QBO requires an on-going fee. You pay for the desktop version once and you are finished. Upgrades are available, but you only pay for them if you think you need them. I've seen statistics showing users keep their desktop versions on average 3-5 years. Any longer than that it usually becomes a problem to keep up with the changes in computer technology, and add-on services, like payroll.

If the internet connection is not reliable, QBO is very frustrating. With the desktop version, you don't have to worry about the reliability of the network. Additionally, the QBO system sometimes goes down on Intuit's side. Obviously, Intuit is highly motivated not to let this happen often, but it does happen. This is aggravating, but usually not as disruptive as it is for a business trying to check out customers. You will need to have procedures in place for when this occurs.

QBO does not have the desktop version's intuitive feel. This is another area that QBO has improved in the last few years, but the desktop is still more user friendly, especially if your bookkeeper/treasurer already has experience with QuickBooks.

Reporting is more limited in QBO than the desktop version. If you don't purchase the most expensive Plus version of QBO, you will not be able to track fund accounting or prepare budgets. Even with the Plus subscription, the reporting is not as robust as the Pro or Premier desktop versions.

With QBO, your organization's data is in the cloud and more susceptible to hacking. This is a low risk, as Intuit is doing everything possible to keep the data safe, but organizations should acknowledge the possibility. I am not aware of any breaches that have occurred as of the writing of this book.

> **The Bottom Line:** You need to weigh the need for flexibility and convenience against your organization's internet access and reporting needs.

C. Fund Accounting

Not-for-profit organizations do not work the same way as for-profit organizations; nor do they account for revenues and expenses the same way. Historically, the accounting for nonprofit organizations was called Fund Accounting because each designated "pot of money" was accounted for in a different fund. Currently, organizations are using a "net asset" model based on what restrictions were placed on the donations when they were received.

The Financial Accounting Standards Board (FASB) has proposed new accounting standards for nonprofits which will take effect over the next several years. These are primarily reporting changes and should not affect your organization's chart of accounts. If you are large enough to require financial statements presented with Generally Accepted Accounting Principles (GAAP), you will need to work with a CPA to see how these changes affect you. For the purposes of this book, I am going to assume you need an accounting system that will generate financial reports to help manage your organization and be a good steward of the donors' gifts, but I will not be addressing the accounting standards.

An organization may receive donations from many different areas: membership dues, pledges or tithes, general support of the organization, an outreach program, a capital campaign, or maybe an endowment. Some of the money given, like the dues, is considered unrestricted. It is assumed the organization will use this money as needed, and the donor has not requested any particular restrictions on the use of the funds.

Other times, money will be received for a very specific purpose—an outreach program or a capital campaign, or for a specific time—say next year's dues. Then the money is considered temporarily restricted. This means it can only be used for the purpose or time period the donor has specified. When the restriction is met, i.e. the building is built or a new year has begun, then it becomes an unrestricted asset. If an endowment is established allowing only the investment earnings to be spent, a permanently restricted fund must be set up.

In accounting jargon, nonprofit organizations are required to keep their accounting records using a modified form of fund accounting. **A fund is defined as a discrete accounting entity with its own set of accounts that must balance the cash and other assets against the liabilities and reserves of the organization**. That is a wordy way of saying each significant donation (funds given for particular purposes) should be tracked separately. But as most organizations don't keep separate bank accounts for each fund, you will be using a bit easier system called net assets to track the funds.

For reporting purposes, these funds can be combined by the restrictions placed on them and tracked by net assets. Net assets are the components of equity in the organization. It is what is left over after the liabilities (what is owed) are subtracted from the assets (what the organization owns). In the business world, this would be the accumulated profit or loss of the company and is called retained earnings.

Net assets are currently divided into three categories:
1. Total Unrestricted Net Assets
2. Total Temporarily Restricted Net Assets
3. Total Permanently Restricted Net Assets.

Because it was designed for businesses, which only have one retained earning account, QuickBooks cannot automatically record net earnings (donations less expenses) in each of the three types of net asset accounts. You will have to create the net asset equity accounts and use journal entries to move the balances from retained earnings. I'll walk you through how to do this in Chapter 15.

D. Reporting Differences

Financial reports for organizations also have different names than those for a business. The *Income Statement* or *Profit & Loss Statement* that tracks income and expenses for businesses is called **Statement of Activities** for nonprofits and churches. Assets, liabilities, and equity are tracked by companies in a *Balance Sheet*. A nonprofit uses a **Statement of Financial Position.** This is important as most versions of QuickBooks will list the reports using business terminology by default. For purposes of this book, I'll refer to these reports as Profit & Loss Statement and Balance Sheet, to make it easier to find in the report menus. Although there are numerous limitations to the standard reporting that QuickBooks offers as it relates to organizations, Chapter 13 will go into detail on how to work around these limitations as you set up your reports.

By default, QuickBooks also refers to the people you receive money from as "Customers." Under company settings in QuickBooks Online, you may change the customer labels to one of the following: Clients, Donors, Guests, Members, Patients, or Tenants. The term selected will replace "Customer" wherever it's shown in QBO. I will explain how to change this label in Chapter 3.

Grants received will be tracked as "Sub-Customers," and designated monies and programs will be referred to as "Classes." Sub-customers and classes are ways the system tags information so reports can be run—pulling all the related data together. This terminology may sound strange, but it will become more clear as you go along.

Other packages may offer a 13th accounting period so you can record year-end adjustments and entries separate from the normal transactions of the organization. This allows you to have one time period that contains only end-of-year transactions. A way to get around this in QuickBooks is to enter all of your December transactions dated on or before 12/30. Then use 12/31 as the date for your end-of-year adjustments. (If your accounting year ends in a different month, use the last day of that month.)

E. Differences in Terminology

On the facing page is a table showing the different terminology. While learning to use QBO, you may want to make a copy to have by your desk or to bookmark it for easy reference. A PDF version is available for free at www.AccountantBesideYou.com.

F. The Case for Internal Accounting Controls

I know it's easy to think, "Why worry about accounting controls? Our employees and volunteers would never steal." With Eulica and my experience as auditors, we would beg to differ. As much as you would like that to be the case, it's not unusual for a donor or employee to steal from a nonprofit. Do an internet search on "money stolen from nonprofits," and you will get over 3 million hits. Some of these were perpetrated by outsiders, but many of the news accounts mention administrators, bookkeepers, volunteers, and even pastors stealing.

Description	Nonprofit Terminology	Church Terminology	QuickBooks Terminology
Your organization	Organization	Church, Parish, Synagogue, Temple	Company
People or organizations you receive money from	Donors, members, grantors, etc.	Parishioners, members, donors, etc.	Donors or members
People you pay money to	Vendors, suppliers, or people you reimburse	Vendors, suppliers, or people you reimburse	Vendors
People who are employed to work at the organization	Employees (payroll)	Employees (payroll)	Employees (payroll)
Report to show money in versus money out (track income and expenses)	Statement of Activities	Statement of Activities	Income Statement or Profit & Loss Statement
Report to show assets (cash, property, etc.) against liabilities (amount owed) to track the accumulated net wealth	Statement of Financial Position	Statement of Financial Position	Balance Sheet
Accumulated net wealth/profit	Net Assets	Net Assets	Net Worth
Grants received that need to have the expenses tracked	Grants	Grants	Sub-Customers
Monies received for programs or that need to be tracked	Funds or programs	Funds or programs	Classes

Internal controls are not only in place to protect against fraud, but to keep errors from occurring and to make them easier to catch when they do. A good bookkeeper will require strong internal controls to keep themselves above suspicion. Additionally, you know that you wouldn't steal, but having controls in place gives you reassurance that the person who takes over after you will not either. The smaller the organization, the harder it is to have separate people in the required positions to maintain strong controls. But don't worry, this book will highlight options and ideas to put controls in place in even small nonprofits.

The most basic start for establishing internal controls begins at the governing body level (the board). A strong board with transparency, stewardship, and accountability sets the tone and is the first defense against fraud.

Because QuickBooks Online is accessible from any computer logged on to the internet, access controls need to be carefully thought out. Secure passwords are a must. Also, QBO allows for the setup of user profiles to create a segregation of duties. The master administrator of the company file can create limited user profiles that keep the user who is responsible for recording donations from accessing bill paying and vice versa. I will explain user profiles in Chapter 3.

G. Advice for the Governing Body of the Organization

Members of the governing body have a fiduciary responsibility to the donors and employees. It is in their best interest to understand the internal controls of the organization. There are a few basic starting points for the board to consider.

1. Financial statements should be reviewed by the board on a regular basis (monthly or quarterly).
2. Annual budgets should be prepared and variances reported on a regular basis.
3. There should be a designated treasurer who is NOT the bookkeeper.
4. A conflict of interest policy needs to be established. (This does not mean donors or board members can't do business with the organization. It simply limits the level of related party transactions and determines steps to make certain the most appropriate price is paid.)
5. An annual audit must be performed. If the organization cannot afford an outside auditor, designate an audit committee composed of volunteers or board members not associated with the accounting part of the organization.

Within the chapters of this book, there will be recommendations for setting up the internal controls for each process of dealing with the finances. On my website, www.accountantbesideyou.com, I offer a companion handbook to assist you in organizing your data with areas for you to detail your accounting controls procedures. If you have a CPA in your membership, you may wish to ask for additional advice as well.

H. Tips, Hints, and When to Let Someone Else Do It

Throughout this book, you will notice symbols with additional information.

These symbols and scrolls are to alert you to tips and hints to make the work go easier or items that need special attention.

If you'd like to save time, you can go to www.accountantbesideyou.com and purchase a QuickBooks Online file with the chart of accounts I recommend in the appendix of this book. You then simply edit them for your particular organization and you won't have to start from scratch. Please read over the book first, evaluate the amount of time you have to set up the system, and then you can decide if it makes more sense to spend a few dollars on the file or to input the information yourself.

For the record, I hate sales pitches, but in areas where I have already done the tedious part (like creating the chart of accounts), I'd like to save you that time. So, periodically check my website to see what downloads or files are available for your convenience. Please note: The book will explain how to do any of these processes, so the downloads are simply time-saving options. Now let's take a look at QBO.

2. Acquainting Yourself w

A. Layout of the Program

Before creating your company file or starting to enter data for your organization, I recommend you spend some time seeing how QBO is laid out and how to move around the program efficiently.

Fortunately, QBO has one sample "test drive" company called Craig's Design and Landscaping Services at https://qbo.intuit.com/redir/testdrive. This is a fully functioning practice company file with transactions already entered. I suggest you open the test company and follow along with the chapters to put what you are learning into practice.

You don't need an account or sign on to access the test drive, just a simple captcha code. Once accessed, you can add transactions, review reports, and explore functionality. This test drive is a place for you to explore and try out new things without the fear of breaking something or making a mistake. The practice company does not retain any of the changes you made. Please keep in mind, this test company is a for-profit company. Though the transactions and labels may be different than for nonprofits or churches, but it will familiarize you with the system's functionality.

QBO is a database of tables and data fields. As you enter transactions, the system organizes your financial activity into financial results, so you can utilize what you've learned to make sound decisions for your organization. I know this can seem overwhelming, but I like my co-author Eulica's advice to her clients—*always take your bookkeeping one transaction at a time*. This book will do just that, let's get started with the basics.

B. The Basics

First, think about the money received and paid out. You *receive* money from **donors** or **members**, and you *pay* money to **vendors** and **employees**. Each transaction is grouped with similar transactions into a category, or **general ledger account** (which you will refer to simply as an **account**). For example, power bill or water bill payments may be grouped in an account called *utilities*. All of the accounts are compiled into a list called the **Chart of Accounts**. The money may be physically kept in a **bank account**, but it is recorded in a **general ledger account** in your organization's accounting system.

The names and information about donors, vendors, employees, and accounts are each stored in their own lists. **Lists** are the foundation of the QBO program. Accurate

depend on your understanding how lists work and how to set them
up correctly. This isn't nearly as confusing as it may sound.

When you go to the QBO **Home** screen, you will see something like this.

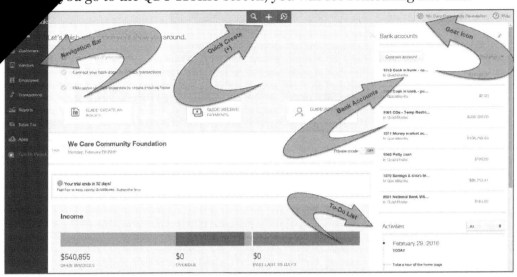

To the left is the **Navigation Bar** where the **Customer**, **Vendor**, and **Employee** lists are found in addition to **Reports** and **Transactions**. At the top center are buttons for **Search** (magnifying glass), **Quick Create/Plus** (+), and **Recent Transactions** (clock face). The **Plus** will be the starting point for most of your day-to-day transactions. Click on the **Gear** icon at the top right to access any of the lists: **Chart of Accounts, Products and Services, Classes, Payment Methods,** etc. Just below the gear icon is the list of **Bank accounts**. The **Activities**, in the lower right hand corner, will remind you of bills or payroll tax payments that are due and other tasks that need your attention.

I will cover these lists, preferences, settings, and functions in detail as you set up the company file and learn how to enter transactions. But for now, let's understand how the lists work. **Donors** (customers in for-profit terms) and **Vendors** menus have a similar layout and functionality. I'll use the Vendors list as an example. To access, go to the **Navigation Bar** on the left of the home screen and click on *Vendors*.

From this screen, you can click on the clock icon at the top to see the most recent transactions, or select *New vendor* to create a new vendor or prepare 1099s. The colored blocks show you the total amount due, the amount overdue, and the amount the organization has paid for all vendors in the last thirty days. Please note, you may also have a box for purchase orders.

In the appendix is a list of keyboard shortcuts to get you through the system.

> If you get ever get lost in the system, you can always go back to the main screen by clicking on the *Home* icon in the left **Navigation Bar**.

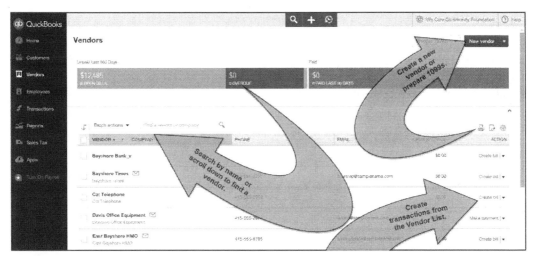

Below that, all the vendors are listed in alphabetical order with their contact information and open balances. You can locate a specific vendor simply by scrolling down the list or entering a name in the search box at the top of the screen.

C. Find and Correct Posted Transactions

Finding previously posted transactions is easy in QBO. Notice the icons to the left and right of the **Plus** menu icon the top center of the screen.

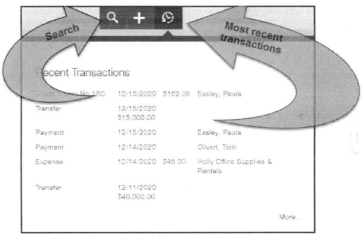

The left icon is a magnifying glass that allows you to **Search**. The right icon looks like a clock and displays the most **Recent Transactions** entered. Let's start by looking at this right clock icon.

Click on the *clock icon* to view the 10 most recent transactions. Double click any listed transaction to view the original entry where any corrections can be made. Remember to save any corrections made to the transaction. To view more transactions in posting order click on *More* in the bottom right of this window.

Clicking the magnifying glass icon to the left of the **Plus** icon allows you to search transaction by key word (donor or vendor name), check or deposit number, transaction date or by dollar amount.

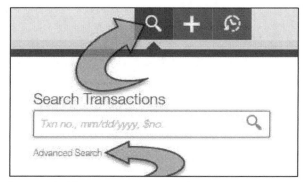

Click *Advanced Search* if you want to perform a more specific search by more than one filter.

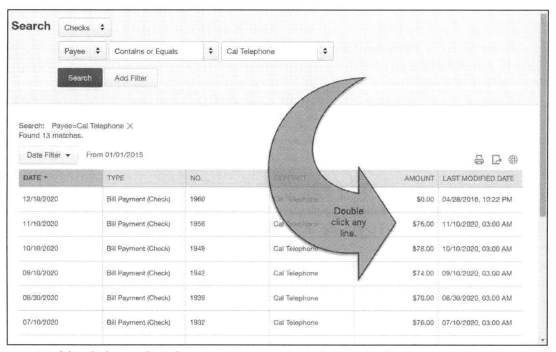

Double click any listed transaction to view the original entry. Corrections can then be made. Remember to save any adjustments.

You can also get to original transactions by running reports (see Chapter 12). From any report, double clicking on a number to get to the entry screen.

D. Using QBO Help

In the top right corner of the QBO screen, you will find the help icon.

Click this icon and enter any phrase to find answers and "how to" instructions on the fly. This is a great resource, but you may need to reword your request a few times before getting the answer you need. You can also call QBO or a ProAdvisor accountant/bookkeeper for help.

E. Transaction Entry Screens

Each time you enter a donation or pay a bill, you will see a **Transaction Entry Screen**, so I'd like to familiarize you with the format of the system before you get into the details.

The lists are important because they tell the system what each transaction is about. For example, when you receive money from a donor, you will have a cash receipt transaction. You have to let QBO know who the donor is via the **Customer List** and what revenue and bank accounts it should go to via the **Chart of Account List**.

The transaction entry screens are designed to look like the forms used in businesses. The fields in these forms are populated by the information set up in the **Lists**. To open a transaction screen, click on the *Plus* **(+)** at the top center of the home screen.

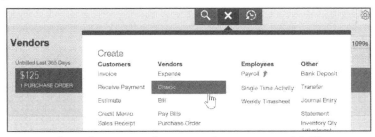

Now you can select the type of transaction you would like to enter. We'll use a check for our example.

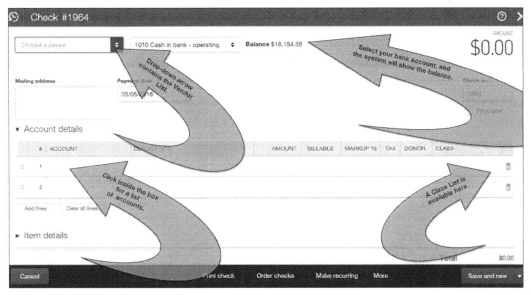

In the check example above, there are drop-down menus for **Payee, Bank Account, Expense Account,** and **Class** (though if you are in the test drive company, you probably won't see the **Class** column). You can also begin typing a name in the respective field, and QBO will automatically populate the field from names found in that list. Finish the transaction by entering the dollar amount and *Save and new*. Close out this screen by clicking on the *X* in the upper right hand corner.

All transaction entry screens in QuickBooks work in the same basic way. There are fields with drop-down menus for every transaction. As you read this book, play with the test company to become more comfortable with the relationship between lists and transaction entry.

> Now you have the basic layout of QBO. In Chapter 3, you will be setting up the files and settings to make QBO work most efficiently for your organization.

3. Setting up Your Organization File

A. Required Information

It is time to set up your nonprofit or church with QBO. (Note: If the organization is already set up, you can skip to Chapter 5 to learn to work with transactions, but you may want to review this section to see if you can improve your current system.) To get started, you'll need to pull together some data. Below is the basic information you will need to design the data file. A complete list of information needed to set up the system is in the appendix.

1. Nonprofit's legal name and address
2. Federal Employer Identification Number (EIN)
3. First month of accounting year—usually January
4. Type of tax return—990, 990 EZ, or 990-N, if any
5. Chart of accounts—from the appendix or the one you are currently using

B. Creating a QBO Account

To create and set up your QuickBooks Online account, go to http://quickbooks.intuit.com/online. This will bring up a screen similar to this one:

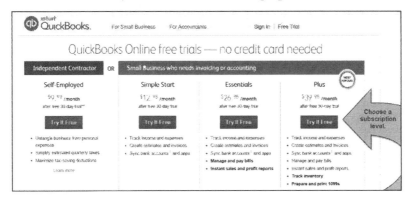

Click the *Try It Free* under the Plus option. The less expensive options will not suffice for nonprofit use. The *Try It Free* option is also nice for you to play with if you are trying to decide between the desktop and online versions. If you purchased your subscription to QBO from TechSoup.org, follow their instructions to bring up the system.

You will be directed to create your user ID and password using an email address.

> The email account used to create the account will be designated as the **master administrator**. If possible, use an email attributed to the organization (i.e. treasurer@yournonprofit.org) that can be used by others if you leave your position.

Don't worry about the other users yet. I'll explain how to set them up in a later chapter. Once you've filled in the required information, QBO will create your account. Check your email for a confirmation notice.

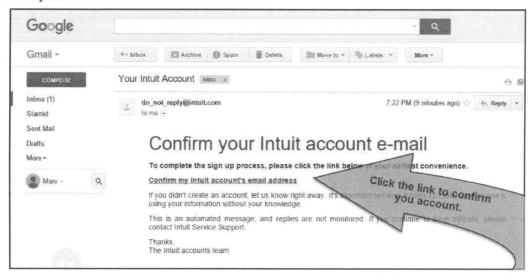

Click *Confirm my Intuit account's email address* to complete the registration.

Now you are ready to follow the company set up screens. The ***Company Name*** is the name you would like on correspondence generated from the system (donor statements, financials, etc.), not necessarily the legal name. Entering your organization's address and phone number in addition to uploading your company logo is optional at this point. I'll show you where to do that later. The company name is the only required field on this screen. Click *Next* when done.

> Some of the screens shown throughout the book may look different than those you will see on your computer. Intuit (the company that makes QBO) frequently changes the look of the screens. The information required will still be basically the same.

Another screen will appear asking for more information about your organization.

Under **Your industry**, start to key in *Non-Profit (or Church)*. As you type, a list of industries will appear. Click on the one most closely related to you. Next go to the **You sell** box and select *Product and services* from the drop down menu. Choose *Non-Profit* in the **Company type** box.

Ignore the rest of the questions. You will set them up later after I've had a chance to fully explain the impact of each.

QBO will populate your chart of accounts based on your industry and company type selections. These are names of accounts, not account numbers, which I will discuss in great detail in the next chapter. QBO also tends to add many more accounts than is actually needed.

You did it! You have created your QBO account and are ready to get to work. In the next section, I'll explain how to move your existing QuickBooks desktop data to QBO. If you are brand new to QuickBooks and will be starting your accounting fresh from this point, grab a cup of tea, and I'll meet you back in Section D.

C. Exporting Existing QuickBooks Desktop Data to QBO

If you are a currently using a QuickBooks Desktop (Pro, Premier, or Nonprofit versions, 2008 or later) company, you don't have to start your accounting from scratch to move to QBO. It only takes a few steps to export your historical company and transaction data to QuickBooks Online. Before exporting your data, however, you must do some preparation.

1.   Run Reports in Desktop Version

Before you start the exporting process, it's a good idea to run and print some basic reports. You will use these reports to verify that your data converted correctly. I suggest you run a year-to-date Profit & Loss (income) statement and a Balance Sheet dated as of the day of the conversion. I'd also run a general ledger report for the last fiscal year and save it as a pdf file instead of printing it, as it will probably be a very large file. The general ledger can be found in the desktop versions under **Reports, Accountant & Taxes, General Ledger.**

It's also good to know where you left off with your transaction entry in the desktop version. Write down the last check number, the last bill, the last donation, and the deposit you entered. This keeps you from getting confused and duplicating entries into the new system.

2. Identify Targets

The existing QuickBooks Desktop file can have not more than 350,000 data points, which the system refers to as targets. To find your organization's number of targets, go to the **Homepage** of the desktop. Press *F2* (usually along the top of your keyboard), and the **Product Information** screen will open.

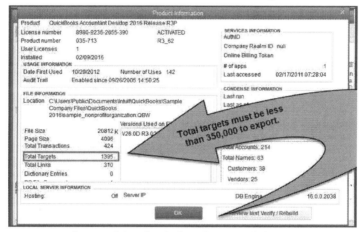

The total targets are located in the left column of this screen. If your targets are under 350,000, click *OK* to close the screen, and I'll show you what to do next.

If your existing company file is larger than 350,000 targets, you can still import lists from your desktop company, but not transactions. This will be discussed in Chapter 7.

3. Verify Data and Backup

Next, you will need to verify your desktop company file. Verifying will ensure there are no errors in your data. From the **Home** screen's top menu bar, choose *File, Utilities, Verify Data.*

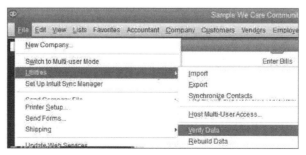

Depending on the size of your file, this process may take some time. Once the system is finished, you should receive a pop-up box stating, "QuickBooks detected no problems with your data." Click *OK* to close the box.

If there are problems with the file, you need to contact a ProAdvisor or an accountant with expertise in QuickBooks to fix the file before continuing.

Now back up your company file. I am going to assume if you have been using QuickBooks, you know how to back up. If not, check out my video tutorial at http://accountantbesideyou.com/video-tutorials.

4.   Export Desktop Company File to QuickBooks Online

With your verified data backed up, you can now export the desktop company file to QBO. Keep in mind that the computer where your software is located must be connected to the internet to perform this task.

From the Home screen's top menu bar, choose *Company, Export Company File to QuickBooks Online*.

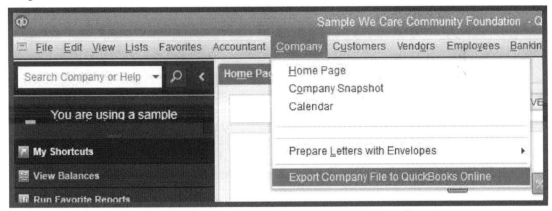

A QBO sign-in screen appears. You probably already created a QBO account at the beginning of this chapter. If not, you can create the QBO account during the export process.

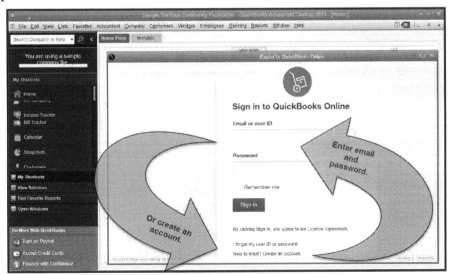

Sign into your account, and the system will handle the rest. It will take a few minutes for the desktop data to be exported to QBO. The system will email you once the transfer is complete.

From that email, click on the *Continue to account setup* box. You will be prompted to login using your user id and password.

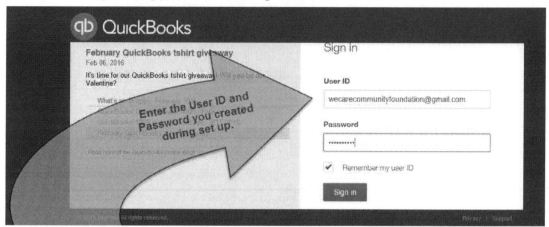

The QBO home screen will appear. Before adding any new data, you need to run a few reports to make sure the totals and balances match the reports you ran in the desktop version before the transfer. Select reports in the left menu bar of the home screen.

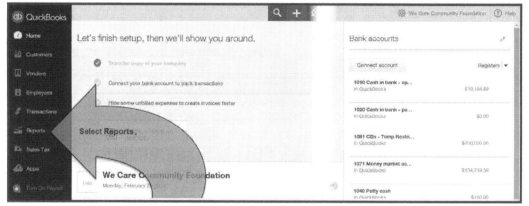

From the list of recommended reports, run the Profit & Loss and Balance Sheet for the exact same period you ran the reports from the desktop version. Now compare the sets of reports. Neither Eulica nor I have ever experienced an issue with the reports not matching. However, if they don't match, it may mean that some transactions are missing or are duplicated in the new system.

You've got your historical data in the system, so it is time to review and customize the settings.

D. Account and Settings

Settings determine what information will show up on various screens and allow for the flexibility of the system. Due to this flexibility, it is important to understand what each of these options do. In order to access **Settings**, select the *Gear Icon* in the top right of the home screen. Under **Your Company**, select *Account and Settings*.

Account and Settings will take you to a list of settings categories on the left side of the screen.

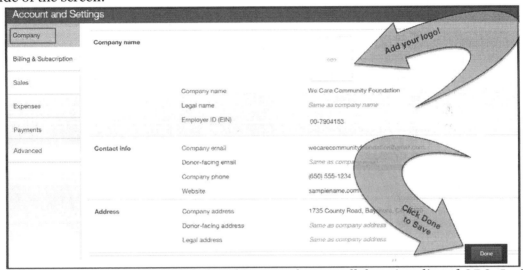

The settings found here are global and impact the overall functionality of QBO. I will walk you through the options in many of these categories, and we'll skip the ones you are less likely to use.

1.   Company Settings

Let's start with *Company* settings located first in the list. Here is where you will add or make updates to your company name, legal name (if different), federal ID number, contact information, and logo. Click on the **Pencil** icon or on the line of any of the areas you wish to edit to key in additional data.

Upload your logo into the system by clicking on the *Company name* section, + sign and pointing to the file on your computer. The **Company name** box should be populated with the name you want to show on report headers and forms produced by QBO. If the organization's legal name is different, unclick the **Same as company name** box and enter the legal name. This will be used by the system on payroll and tax forms.

The **Employer ID (EIN)** is your Federal Identification Number. You should be able to find this on your payroll or other reports. You must select *Save* before you can go to the next section on the page. Continue down this screen and enter your contact information and email preferences.

The next block down is the **Tax Form**. Using the pencil to the right, you can change it to *Nonprofit organization (Form 990)* or, if you don't need to file a return (i.e. some churches), select *Not sure/Other/None*.

Categories block includes the options to track classes and locations.

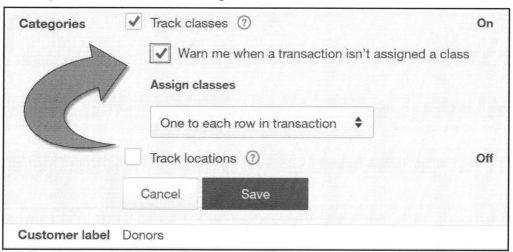

It is crucial you select *Track classes* in order to account for nonprofit programs, funds, and grants. I also recommend *Warn me when a transaction isn't assigned a class* and to select **One to each row in transaction**. Select **Track locations** only if you have more than one office or church campus that you need to account for.

The next block is the **Customer label**. This is where you select what you call the people who give you money. There is a drop-down option to select Donors, Members, Guests, etc.

If you click on the **Done** box in the lower right hand corner, you will be taken back to the home page. Click on the *Gear* box and select *Account and Settings* to return back to the **Settings** options.

2.   Billing & Subscription Settings

The next screen in **Account and Settings** is **Billing & Subscription**. If you do not see this option, don't worry. It may not appear in the trial mode, but the information will be available if you decide to purchase the subscription.

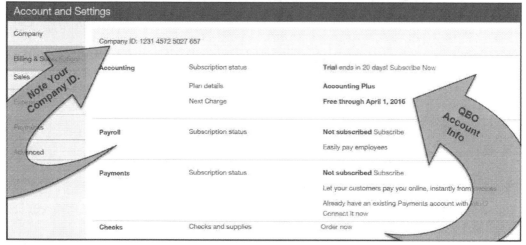

Here you will find details and options about your QuickBooks Online account to include your **Company ID**. Use this number anytime you contact QuickBooks customer support. This also shows you any additional services you have enrolled in, like **Payroll** or **Payments** (to accept credit cards and bank drafts from donors).

3.   Sales Settings

The next item on the left-hand menu is **Sales**. This screen allows you to customize options related to how the money your organization receives is recorded. Just keep in mind that, for our purposes, sales are actually donations, dues, and contributions for your organization. You won't change much here, but pay attention to **Customize** and **Messages** for sales (donation) receipts and membership dues invoices.

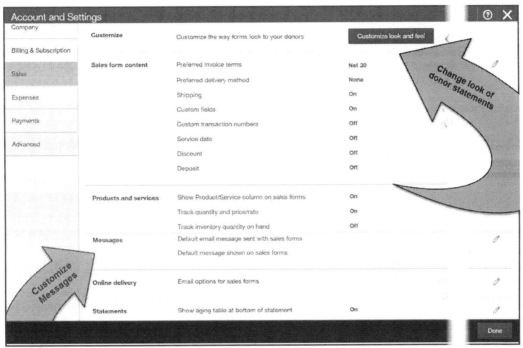

Click the *Customize look and feel* button to view and customize form templates. You will arrive at the *Custom Form Styles* list which allows you to create customized invoices and receipts. You may want to create a *New style* (form template) for each type of collections to make, like dues, donations, or pledges.

Select *Edit* to reach a form template. As you have seen on the other QBO screens, the left side will have the menu tabs. Each template allows you to edit the **Style,**

Appearance, Header, Activity Table, and **Footer** for an invoice or receipt. You can set the color scheme, rename fields, and change the layout of your forms. Select *Save* to get back to Home page.

Let's go back to the **Settings**. Click on the *Gear, Your Company, Account and Settings*. This time you are going to *Expenses* settings.

4.   Expenses/Expenditures Settings

The **Expenses** screen under **Account and Settings** allows you to customize options related to how money paid out is recorded. Here you will make choices about what fields are available on expense and purchase forms.

Account and Settings			
Company			
	Bills and expenses	Show items table on expense and purchase forms	On
Billing & Subscription		Track expenses and items by donor	On
		Make expenses and items billable	On
Sales		Default bill payment terms	Net 10
Expenses			
	Purchase orders	Use purchase orders	Off
Payments			

Turn the **Bills and expenses** options to **On.** I'll explain how to track by donor and the use of items in Chapters 5 and 8. Turn **Purchase orders** off unless your organization currently uses them. Now, let's look at **Payments** settings.

5.   Payment Settings

The payment settings screen is only used if you choose to sign up with Intuit to accept payments directly through emailed invoices or mobile devices. There is an additional cost for this service. In Chapter 10, I'll explain the cost and benefits for these.

6.   Advanced Settings

The last tab is titled **Advanced**. I want you to understand these options as they have a significant impact on the accounting.

As you have done previously, double click on any section or click the pencil to make edits. Remember to select *Save* after your changes to each section and *Done* when you are completely finished with **Advanced** settings, as shown on the following page.

In the *Accounting* section, you will select the first month of your organization's fiscal year and accounting method. Usually the fiscal year and the calendar year are the same, but if your organization closes its books on June 30 each year instead of December 31, use July for the **First month of fiscal year.** As a small nonprofit or church, you probably don't really have to worry about the income tax year.

Accounting method determines when you record income and expenses. For small organizations, the **Cash** method is more common. Larger organizations and those who have to submit their financial statements to large donors usually use the **Accrual** method. QBO allows you to change the accounting method on reports easily.

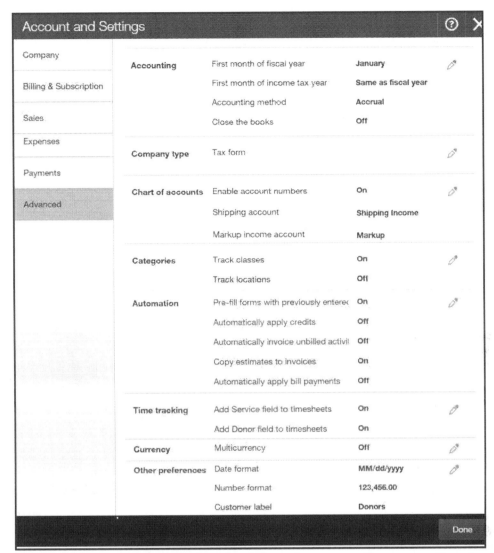

You can also set a **Close the books** date to keep users from recording data in a previous accounting period. I'll show you how to use this in Chapter 15, but for now, let's leave it off.

In the **Company type** section, you will choose the tax form for your organization, most likely Form 990. If you are a religious organization, you may not have to file any tax return at all.

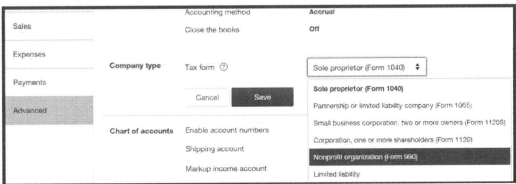

For the **Chart of Accounts** section, it is important to **Enable account numbers**. I will go into great detail about that in the next chapter. Ignore the other two options in that box.

The **Automation** section has more flexibility based on your preferences. Turn on the **Pre-fill forms with previously entered content** if you enter the same type of transaction frequently. You can always turn it off if you find it a hindrance later.

Let's skip the **Time Tracking** and **Currency** sections, assuming you aren't billing hours or working in multiple currencies. If so, please explore these options, but they are beyond the scope of this book.

In the **Other preferences**, the important areas are to change the **Customer label** from "customer" to "donor" or "member" depending on the main group your organization receives money from. Also, turn on the **Warn if duplicate check number is used**.

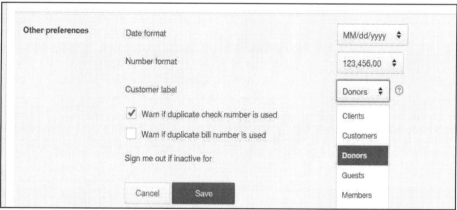

Select *Save* and *Done* when you are finished.

> Take a well-deserved break and be ready to learn how to set up a Chart of Accounts that will be useful to you, your pastor, executive director, donors, and any governing boards.

4. What is the Chart of Accounts?

A. Designing the Chart of Accounts

Now it is time to determine our chart of accounts. This is the listing of all the accounts used to record transactions. The accounts are then used for generating your financial reports. For now, don't worry about programs or grants; you only want to concentrate on the individual accounts where you will be posting transactions.

If you are currently using a chart of accounts that works for your organization, you may wish to design something very similar, but first, read through this chapter so you understand how QBO uses the information for both transactions and reporting. I'd also recommend that you have an accountant or member who knows accounting requirements review any chart of accounts you are planning to use to make sure it will work for your organization.

The best way to design a chart of accounts is to first consider your reporting requirements. If you have to file a tax return (990 or 990EZ), you will want to be certain you are tracking expenses that can easily be summarized in those categories. If you have a national or parent organization you report to, look at their reporting requirements to see what should be included.

And try to keep it as **simple** as possible. I don't like to use the QBO recommended accounts unless you scan through the list and delete all the extras. I would discourage you from using the Unified Chart of Accounts (UCOA) for nonprofits unless your organization is large and needs most of those accounts. The appendix has my recommended charts of accounts for several different types of nonprofits and religious organizations. If your organization has similar programs, consider using one of these as your guideline.

In designing your chart of accounts, you need to understand how accountants define the different types of accounts. One of the best explanations I have seen comes from the *Small Non-Profit QuickBooks Primer* by Poppy Davis, CPA. An excerpt is on the next page.

B. Numbering Structure

Eulica and I strongly recommend you use account numbers. QBO does not require account numbers, but you will severely limit your reporting options if you do not use them. The numbers can be anything up to seven digits, but unless you have a very complex system, I recommend starting with just four or five.

Assets stick around
Expenses go away
If you buy a stove for the kitchen, it will stick around, so it is an asset. If the stove breaks and you repair it, that is an expense (the repair man goes away, the stove is back to working like it is supposed to.)

Income is yours
Liabilities belong to others
So if you receive a donation or a grant to serve meals to people, it is income, but if you borrow money from the bank to build a new kitchen, it is a liability.

Net Assets are what is left over for you
QuickBooks does not use the proper non-profit name "net equity," instead it uses **Beginning Balance Equity** (the Net Assets the first time you enter information to set the business up) and **Retained Earnings** (the change in Net Assets over time).

QBO automatically sorts the chart of accounts by account type and runs reports according to this sorting.

Assets are sorted by:
- Bank Account
- Accounts Receivable
- Other Current Assets
- Fixed Assets
- Other Assets

Liabilities are sorted by:
- Accounts Payable
- Credit Card
- Other Current Liability
- Long-Term Liability

A **current asset** or **liability** is due or used within a year. A **long-term asset** or **liability** is available or due in more than a year. For example, a pledge made for the next year is a current asset, but a capital campaign contribution due in five years is a long-term asset.

All the other accounts are sorted by number. Therefore, if you have numbers out of sequence with the type, you cannot view your chart of accounts in numerical order. This will become much clearer in Chapter 13 on reports.

1000s—Assets: bank accounts, receivables, computers, etc.

2000s—Liabilities: accounts payable, due to other organizations, payroll, loans, etc.

3000s—Net Assets: unrestricted, temporarily, and permanently restricted.

4000s—Donations and Support: dues, donations, bequests, capital campaigns, endowments etc.

5000s—Earned Revenues: program service fees, membership dues, fundraisers, interest, fixed asset sales.

6000s—Operating/Functional Expenses: facilities, salaries, program costs, etc.

7000s—Non-operating Expenses: extraordinary repairs, depreciation, etc.

8000s—Ask My Accountant: a place to record transactions you don't know what to do with. This is then reviewed by your accountant on a regular basis and cleared out.

Within the above, consider using the ranges below as a basic recommendation for the balance sheet asset accounts:

1101-1199	Cash and investments
1201-1299	Undeposited monies (I'll explain this in Chapter 9)
1301-1399	Receivables—amounts owed to you
1401-1499	Prepaid assets—this can be insurance, postage, etc.
1501-1699	Available for current assets categories in the future
1701-1799	Building, real estate, and the related depreciation
1801-1899	Available for long-term assets categories in the future
1901-1999	Other long-term assets.

As you can see, this gives you at least 99 accounts under each of the categories. Use the same concepts for the Liability accounts in the 2000 level and Net Assets/Equity accounts in the 3000 range.

Consider how you would like to see your expenses grouped together. Using the ranges in the blue box on the previous page, you may also wish to have sub-ranges.

For example, the facility costs may be in 6000-6399, personnel expenses in 6400-6599, and program expenses from 6600-6999. As you need to add accounts within a range, consider adding them by 10s so you will have space between accounts. For clubs and smaller organizations, using four-digit account numbers should be sufficient.

Any reporting requirements will determine how to set up your income and expenses accounts. The first thing I want you to look at is the tax returns or annual reports your organization filed last year. If your organization did not file a return and you wonder if you should, please contact your local accountant or go to www.irs.gov for filing requirements. Due to the myriad of laws and the differing types of organizations and organizations, this book does not offer any tax advice.

If you will be filing IRS Form 990EZ, the income requirements as of the writing of this book are:

1. Contributions, gifts, grants, and similar amounts
2. Program service revenue
3. Membership dues and assessments
4. Investment income
5. Gross amount from sale of assets other than inventory
6. Gaming and fundraising events
7. Gross sales of inventory
8. Other revenue.

The expense requirements are:

1. Grants and similar amounts paid
2. Benefits paid to or for donors
3. Salaries, other compensation, and employee benefits
4. Professional fees and other payments to independent contractors
5. Occupancy, rent, utilities, and maintenance
6. Printing, publications, postage, and shipping
7. Other expenses.

This would be the minimum number of income statement accounts required for Form 990EZ. If you were filing Form 990, a Statement of Revenue and a Statement of Functional Expenses will also be required. You will therefore need a few more accounts:

1. Federated campaigns
2. Related organizations
3. Government grants (contributions)
4. Noncash contributions.

All of the income will have to be designated on the 990 as Related function revenue, Unrelated business revenue, or Revenue excluded from tax. In Chapter 5, I will show you how to set up programs to assist with that information.

There are additional expense-reporting requirements on Form 990.

1. Grants paid must show payments to government and organizations separate from individuals.

2. Grants paid to organizations, governments, or individual outside of the US are accounted for separately.

3. Compensation to current officers, directors, trustees, and key employees is listed separately, as is pension plans and contributions and other employee benefits.

4. Expenses are broken out in more detail.

5. All expenses are then designated into one of three categories:
   a. Program Services
   b. Management & General
   c. Fundraising.

The National Center for Charitable Statistics supports the UCOA, the Unified Chart of Accounts, for nonprofit organizations. If you are large enough to file a 990 and report to outside organizations, this may be a good option for you. But because the chart of accounts was designed for large nonprofits with numerous activities, there will be many excess accounts you probably won't need.

In the appendix, I have included several sample charts of accounts for various types of nonprofits. The first one is a simplified version of the UCOA geared toward less complex nonprofits, but still has sufficient accounts to handle the 990 or 990EZ. Next, I have included a chart of accounts based on the ASAE (American Society of Association Executives), standard for an association's records. There are also sample charts for PTAs, civic clubs, scouting groups, and private schools. Many deviate from the numbering system I show below, but they are based on their specific industries' recommendations. My recommended chart of accounts for churches and other religious organizations is designed for small and growing churches as a starting point.

Look through these and see if one is close to your organization's needs. Then add any additional accounts you may need and delete any you don't. Downloadable files of these charts, ready to be imported directly into QBO, are available for sale on www.accountantbesideyou.com. They are the same as the data in the appendix, so you only need to purchase them to save data entry time.

C. Naming the Accounts

Once you have figured out your numbering system, you need to determine how you are going to name the accounts. This sounds very basic, but if you aren't careful, you may have accounts called "Postage and Mailing," "Postage," "Post," etc., which should all be combined. In order to keep things simple, have a policy that significant words are written out with no punctuation marks, and ampersands (&) are used instead of the word "and." If you already have a naming protocol, by all means use it.

> For now, don't worry about setting up accounts for individual programs or grants. I'll explain how to set those up in Chapter 5.

D. Building the Chart of Accounts

It's time to input your chart of accounts. Here I'll show you how to set up the accounts from scratch, but if you like the list in the appendix and want to save time typing, go to www.accountantbesideyou.com and purchase a download of the chart of accounts file. Instructions on uploading the file into QBO are in the appendix. You can also start with the QBO default chart of accounts and delete any accounts you don't need and rename the others. You'll simply upload the file and merge or delete any duplicate accounts. I'll explain how to merge and delete an account on page 39.

You can locate the **Chart of Accounts** in one of two ways. Either go to the *Gear* icon at the top right corner of the screen and click on *Chart of Accounts* under **Your Company** or select from the left *Menu Bar* under **Transactions**.

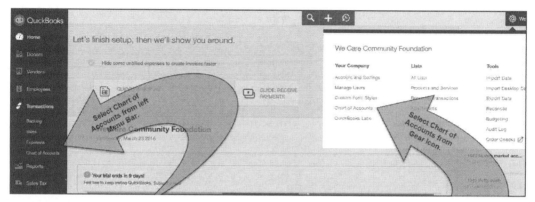

Arriving at the Chart of Accounts, you will see a list of accounts QBO has created based on the industry choices you made during company creation. Because you selected **Enable and Show Account Numbers** under the **Chart of Accounts** section of **Advanced Settings**, the system automatically inserted a blank number column of fields for each account. Note that account numbers are limited to a maximum of seven digits.

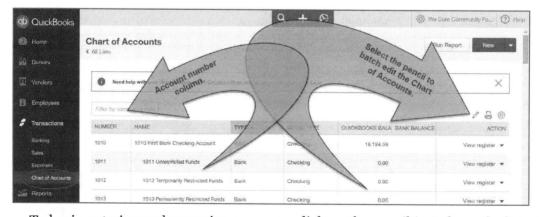

To begin entering and renaming accounts, click on the pencil just above the list of accounts. The batch edit function allows you to change only account numbers and rename accounts, not to add or delete.

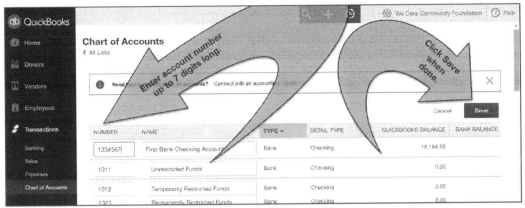

Remember to click *Save* when done. Next, you will learn how to add and edit accounts.

E. Adding New Accounts

You can add one new account at a time by going to *Gear, Your Company, Chart of Accounts* and selecting *New* at the top right corner of the screen.

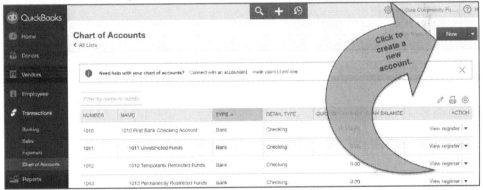

This will take you to the account entry screen.

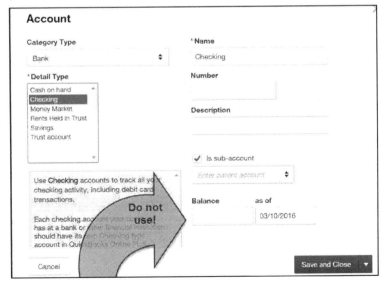

The first thing you need to do is determine the **Category Type** which defines each account's purpose. As I discussed earlier in the chapter, QBO needs to know what the account's purpose is in order to use it properly. If you change the **Category Type**, there will be the corresponding changes in the **Detail Type**.

The account **Detail Type** allows you to further define the account. In this example, I am adding a bank account. As you know, there are different kinds of banks accounts. QBO needs to know if it is a checking, money market, or savings account. Also notice the grey box below the Detail Types window. This box explains how QBO uses each account.

By default, QBO will populate the **Name** field with the Detail Type selected, but you can change it by typing the account name in. When adding bank accounts, I'd recommend calling it by the bank name and account type, i.e. First Bank Checking. It will have a number between 1100 and 1199 so that it stays sequentially with its parent account.

Enter an Account **Number** in the appropriate field. Remember they are limited to a maximum of seven digits. Under **Description**, you may wish to add a note to remind you what this account is used for.

The **Is sub-account of** checkbox allows you to assign subaccounts to any of the accounts. For example, if you use the chart of accounts in the appendix, you will notice that most categories have a "Parent" account with one or more subaccounts. Some even have subaccounts of subaccounts. Subaccounts allow you to track your accounts with more detail and give you more reporting flexibility.

For example, if you would like to easily pull up your electricity costs separate from your gas costs, you may have a parent account called **Utilities** and subaccounts named **Electricity** and **Gas**. You could then run reports summing up all utilities or a more detailed report on each of the subaccounts. In order to use QBO correctly for fund accounting, you need to use subaccounts, as you will see later in this chapter.

There is a box labeled **Balance**. ***Do not use this!*** You will be putting the opening balances in as a journal entry. In accounting, every journal entry must balance the left side of the entry with the right side. Using a journal entry to record your beginning balances is an important way to make certain that your system balances correctly from the start.

Select the drop-down arrow next to **Save** to select *Save and New* and continue adding accounts.

> When you are inputting the account numbers, you can select **Save and New** to bring up a new **Add New Account** screen with the **Account Type** filled in based on your previous entry. Be VERY careful to change the type when you are inputting other accounts. For example, if you were inputting three different bank accounts and then Dues Receivable, the first three times you would not have to change **Type** as it would stay on **Bank**. But when you enter dues receivable, you would need to change the type to **Accounts Receivable.**

F. Tracking Restricted Cash

As was discussed in the first chapter, one of QBO's limitations for nonprofits is that it does not handle fund accounting by separate funds. If your organization uses separate bank accounts for restricted versus non-restricted cash, then the cash will be tracked by bank accounts. But most organizations have one checking account that all transactions go through.

1. Using Custom Reports to Track Restricted Cash

There are two different ways for you to track the restricted versus unrestricted cash in a single checking account. The first approach is to set up your general ledger account for checking based the individual bank account (i.e. Account number 1010=Checking Account). You will then design a report to show the amount of restricted cash versus unrestricted cash within the account. This approach works as long as you use classes for your programs and funds. Chapter 5 will explain the use of classes, and in Chapter 15, I will walk you through the process of setting up the restricted cash report.

2. Multiple Subaccounts for Cash

In the second method, you will need to set up subaccounts for any bank account that has both restricted and unrestricted cash. For this approach, set up three subaccounts under each of your checking and investment accounts: Unrestricted, Temporarily Restricted, and Permanently Restricted. When you record payments or receipts, you will always use one of these three, not the parent account. The reconciliation will be done in the parent account, which will have all the transactions. I don't recommend this approach as you have to be very conscientious to get the right subaccount each time you write a check.

Once you have set up the cash and money market accounts, your chart of accounts list may look something like this (but you may have to scroll through the screen):

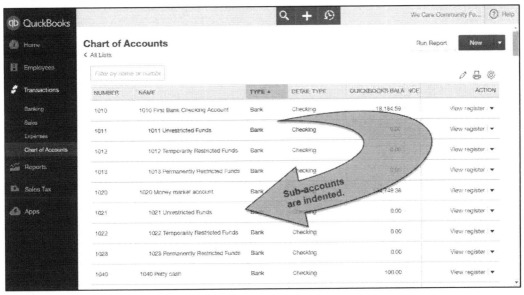

You must be careful about not accidentally posting items to the parent accounts. This is important as any cash posted directly to the parent will not be reflected in either the restricted or the unrestricted cash.

This approach allows you to see unrestricted versus restricted cash balances anytime you open the account list, but requires more attention as you enter transactions. Each time you enter a bill, deposit money, or transfer cash, you will need to assure you have selected the correct subaccount.

G. Enter Chart of Accounts

Now, take your Chart of Account list and start entering each account. It is easiest if you go down the list so the parent accounts are input before the subaccounts. Don't worry about messing something up with your chart of accounts. After you've input all the accounts, I am going to show you how to edit, delete, or deactivate.

> Plan on an entire afternoon for this process.
> This is the most tedious step.

H. Editing, Deleting (Deactivating), and Merging Accounts

1.   Edit Accounts

You have very carefully input your chart of accounts or have uploaded the file from my website, and now you need to check your work. The easiest way to edit your account list is to print it out. Go to *Gear, Your Company, Chart of Accounts* and select the printer icon to print. Now you will see a listing of all accounts and their types.

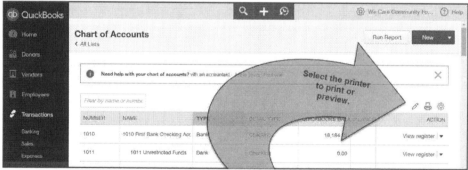

If you find anything you would like to change, editing an account is very easy with QBO. Go to the chart of accounts list, click on the downward arrow found to the right of the account you are editing, and select *Edit* under the drop-down menu.

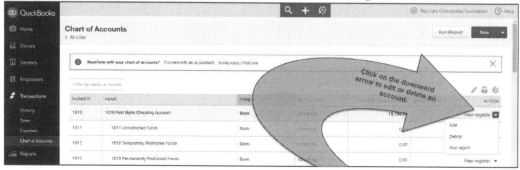

This will bring up a screen that looks just like the one you used to set up the account. Choose the field you need to edit and make the changes. The only exception relates to the account type. *Save and Close* when finished.

2.   Change Account Type

When QBO creates an account automatically, like Payroll Liabilities, Accounts Receivable, or Accounts Payable, the system will not allow the type to be changed. So if you accidentally made an account as an Accounts Receivable type, but it shouldn't have been, you will need to delete the account and reenter it with the correct type. Don't feel bad, however. I do it far more frequently than I care to admit.

If you need to change the type for a parent account with a subaccount, you will first need to unselect the *Is sub-account of* option.

The account is then no longer a subaccount, and you can change the type, first in the parent, then the subaccount. After you've changed all the types, you will then want to go back and replace the subaccount option in each of the appropriate accounts.

Let's say you accidentally set up a prepaid insurance as an *Other Current Liabilities* instead of an *Other Current Assets*. There are two subaccounts under prepaid insurance—one for property insurance and one for general liability. You will need to go to both the property insurance subaccount and the general liability subaccount and unselect the *Is sub-account of* box. Then go to the prepaid insurance account and change the type to *Other Current Assets*. This corrects the parent account. Bring the property insurance back up, change the type to *Other Current Assets,* and then select **Is sub-account of**. Choose *Prepaid Insurance* and save. Now do that for the other subaccount.

3.   Delete (Deactivate) an Account

Deleting or deactivating an account is just as simple. QBO does not actually delete the account but makes its inactive. Click on the downward arrow found to the right of the account you are deleting, and select *Delete* under the drop-down menu.

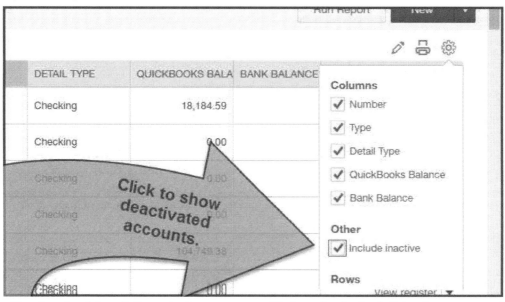

You will then be asked to verify that you really want to do that. If you press **Yes**, the account will be deleted (deactivated) unless it has already had transactions posted to it or has subaccounts. You will need to delete any subaccounts first and then the parent account. A warning will pop up if you try to delete an account that the system automatically generates. It informs you that the system will add that account if it needs it in the future.

I should tell you that deleting an account does not delete the transactions posted to that account but only removes it from the Chart of Accounts list. What QBO calls **Delete** actually only hides it. You can return the account back to the Chart of Account list by selecting the *Gear* icon on the Chart of Account screen, *Include inactive*.

Previously deleted (inactive) accounts will then be included in the account list. You will recognize these accounts by the word "deleted" in parentheses after the account name.

Click *Make active* to make the deleted account active again.

4. Merging Accounts

You may have two accounts with similar transactions that really should be in one account. For example, you may have a "Postage" account and a "Postage and Mailing" account. Both of these accounts contain the same type of transactions and can be merged together in QBO.

Go to *Gear, Chart of Accounts*. Make sure that the accounts you want to merge are at the same sub-level and have the same detail type. If they're not, edit one of the accounts to put it at the same level and give it the same detail type as the other. Select the account whose name you **don't** want to use, and click its drop-down arrow under the **Action** column. Select *Edit* and change the account name so that it is exactly the same as the account with which you're merging. Click ***Save*** *and* ***Yes*** to confirm that you want to merge the two accounts.

> WARNING!!! Merging an account is IRREVERSIBLE!!!

I. Beginning Balances

Look how much you have accomplished. You've set up the program, defined your settings, and even now have a working chart of accounts. Now you need to take the beginning balances for each of the balance sheet accounts and put them in the system. If you have an accountant, ask him for this list. If not, you'll need to get them from your previous system or calculate them from bank statements and the like.

The beginning balances will be input as a journal entry.

	Debit	Credit
Checking	$ 1,000	
Money Market	3,000	
Building	100,000	
Payroll Taxes Payable		1,000
Mortgage Payable		70,000
Equity—Permanently Restricted Net Assets		30,000
Equity—Temporarily Restricted Net Assets-Smith		1,000
Equity—Unrestricted Net Assets		2,000

Journal entries are must always balance. This means all of the amounts being coded to assets have to equal the amounts coded to liabilities and equity. In journal entries, accountants refer to these as **Debits** and **Credits**. As you can see, the debits and the credits in the entry above both equal $104,000. This is a balanced entry.

I recommend using the last day of your previous accounting year as the date of this entry. You can start using QBO anytime throughout the year, but will need to input this year's data to catch up. I'll explain how to do that in Chapters 9 and 10.

Let me step you through the above. In chapter 5, I'll show you how to actually record journal entries, but first I want you to understand what the entry is recording. The **Checking** and **Money Market** amounts should net to the reconciled balance as of the start date. The **Building** is based on purchase price or value (ask your accountant), and **Mortgage Payable** is the amount you owe the bank. The **Payroll**

Taxes Payable is any money not yet paid for taxes or benefits on payroll. I haven't listed Depreciation, because many small nonprofits and churches do not pay taxes and therefore, do not need to depreciate their building or assets. If your reporting requirements to donors or the IRS require it, you will definitely want to include it.

You may have **Accounts Payables** (bills you owe people) or **Accounts Receivables** (money owed to you) as part of your beginning balances. If so, you will need to input them separately by individual donor or vendor and invoice, which I will discuss in Chapters 9 and 10. If you try to input these in the beginning balance entry, QuickBooks will require the amount to go to only one vendor or one customer. Additionally, QuickBooks will not let you post a journal entry with both accounts payable (A/P) and accounts receivable (A/R) data in it.

To record the beginning balances journal entry, you will need another piece of information. Your organization probably has several funds, grants, and programs with designated money in the beginning balances. So, in the next chapter, I'll show you how to organize those.

> Great job getting the chart of accounts set up. Let's move onto how to track grants and programs.

5. How do I Track My Grants & Programs?

A. Using Classes

Throughout the year, your organization may have received money from donors with specific instructions. Sometimes these are formal grants (money given by an organization or government for a specific purpose) and other times they are received from individuals who want the money spent on certain programs. These are referred to as restricted funds, and it is important to track how these dollars are used. As discussed earlier, QBO is not designed to handle the tracking of funds or individual programs within the organization, so you will utilize classes. Classes will be used to track expenses into particular programs, i.e. Education, Worship, Admin and to track donations and the related expenses to specific projects like a grant from Health and Human Services or funds for a Mission Trip.

By using classes, you are able to limit the number of accounts in your chart of accounts and expand your reporting capabilities. For example, most of your organization's programs use supplies. Classes allow you to charge the supplies used (via an account) to several different programs instead of having to set up subaccounts under supplies for each program. Classes are used to track both the revenue and the expenses of a grant.

As you work in the system, every time you see classes, think programs or funds. Before you set up your classes, I'd like you to look at any reporting requirements you have. If you have an audit from last year, study it. If you have a board of directors or governing committee that requires annual or quarterly reports, use them as a good source for the kind of information you may need to track. Review the documents to see what information is required. Nonprofits that file a tax return must designate what money was spent on programs versus administration versus fundraising.

Additionally, any funds for special purposes or events will need to be set up as classes. For every program you want to report the related expenses (i.e. supplies, postage, donations), a class will need to be set up. Finally, all money restricted either temporarily or permanently should have a class designated.

If a donor or foundation has given money for a grant with a specific purpose, you will need to track the related expenditures. This is where the use of the **sub-customer** (or sub-donor) option comes in. You learned in Chapter 3 how to change your company preferences from Customers to Donors. From here forward, I will refer to contributors as Donors.

Sub-donors can be linked to only one donor. For those of you familiar with the desktop version of QuickBooks, sub-customers are the equivalents of jobs and allow

> **Classes vs. Account Numbers**
> **Account numbers** are used to show specifics on the financial statements, like donations or utilities.
> **Classes** are used to allocate the dollars to various programs or funds. For example, if you wanted to charge a literacy program for 20% of the utilities, you would code the expense to the Utilities account with 20% to the Literacy class and the remainder to other classes.

you to track specific revenue and expenditures related to a donor. For example, if one of your regular donors, Joe Smith, gives your organization an extra $1000 to be used for building a playground, you would set up Joe Smith as the donor and Joe Smith Playground as the sub-donor. You will not set up programs this way because they tend to have numerous donors and related expenses.

The grant (sub-donor) will also be linked to a fund class. In this chapter, you will be setting up two separate types of classes: program classes and fund classes. The fund classes are necessary to track restricted versus unrestricted funds. The program classes are geared towards understanding program costs.

Here are some guidelines on how to determine which type of class and whether or not you need a Sub-donor.

Description	Program Class	Fund Class	Sub-donors
Is it a program within the organization?	√		
Are there numerous donors?	√		
Do you need to track the expenses with the fund balance?	√	√	√
Is there a single donor?		√	√
Did the donor specify how the money is to be spent?	√	√	√
Will I be required to give the donor an accounting of the funds?			√

If you answered yes to the last three questions, set up a sub-donor under the donor's name in accounts receivable. (More about this is Chapter 6.) If the answer is no, you can simply include those monies with other funds in a fund or program class.

In the next chapter, we will talk about donors and the use of sub-donors to track grants. If you have several grants, you will not want to make a class for each one. Instead you will assign the sub-donors to the restricted or temporally restricted class.

> Remember the *Keep It Simple* rule.
> Start with fewer classes. You can always add more as needed.

B. Naming of Classes

QBO allows for sub-classes, but does not require you to post to the lowest sub-class like you do in the chart of accounts. Therefore, you will want to clearly title your sub-classes so you know which account the sub-class is associated with. For example, if your primary program is teaching literacy at three different community centers, you may wish to designate a class called 100 Literacy. Then set up sub-classes for locations, i.e. 110 Literacy-Library, 120 Literacy-Senior Center, and 130 Literacy-High School.

> QuickBooks shows the classes using a drop-down menu, listing the names in alphanumeric order. I recommend using numbers in front of your class names to keep program classes together and fund classes together. This also allows you to name the program you will be using the most to show up at the top.
>
> For example, you have classes titled Admin, Literacy, and Job Skills, but most of your expenses besides salaries are Admin related. If you were to title the classes *100 Admin, 200 Literacy*, etc., then Admin would always be your first option.

Before you start entering the class information, make a list of all the programs you would like to track. I strongly recommend not making this list too long. Do not try to track more detail than you have the need for. For example, you may have a literacy program with a men's focus and a women's focus. If you are only concerned about the cost of the literacy programs in total, use only one class, but if different people are responsible for the expenses of the men's group versus the women's group, use separate classes or sub-classes under a Literacy Programs class. The more detailed you make the classes, the more information you will need to enter when recording the bills, and the more complex your reporting will be.

As another example, here is a possible class list for a private school.

- 100   Administration
- 200   Preschool
- 210   Elementary
- 220   Middle School
- 230   High School
- 310   Extended Day
- 320   After-School Enrichment
- 500   Fundraising
- 600   Scholarships
- 900   Unrestricted Funds
- 910   Temporarily Restricted Funds
- 920   Permanently Restricted Funds

C. Entering Class Lists

Now that you have compiled your list, let's input your classes in the system. You will find the *Class List* under the *All Lists* option on the gear icon.

Select the **Classes** option in the right hand column of the next menu.

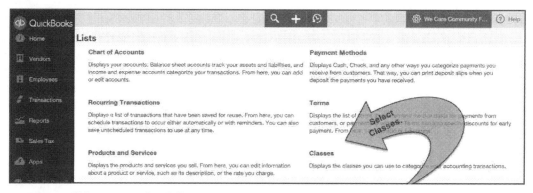

This will bring up the following screen (though yours may be blank).

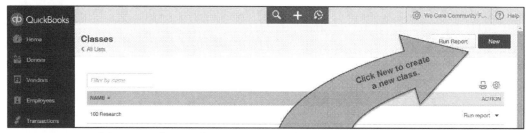

As you can see, this is similar to the screen to add a new account. Select *New* and type in the name of the class you wish to add.

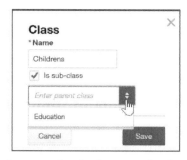

If you wish to set up sub-classes, check the *Is sub-class* box. You can then select the down arrow for a list of available classes. Select *Save* to exit.

D. Editing or Deleting Classes

Once you have your classes entered, you may find you'd like to make some changes. Editing or deleting classes is very simple. Choose *Gear, All Lists, Classes* to open the **Classes List.**

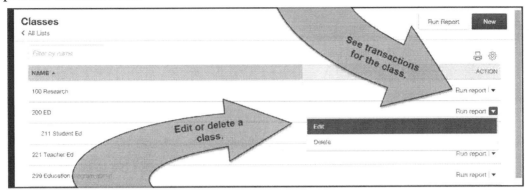

For the class you would like to change, click on the down arrow on that class line to select *Edit* or *Delete*. The **Edit** option lets you change the name or sub-class, or make it a parent class. The **Delete** option does not actually delete the account—it marks it as inactive and hides it from the list. If you select *Delete,* a pop-up box will ask you to verify that you really want to delete the class.

Similar to accounts, you can bring a deleted class back into the list from the *Classes Gear Icon* just above the class list.

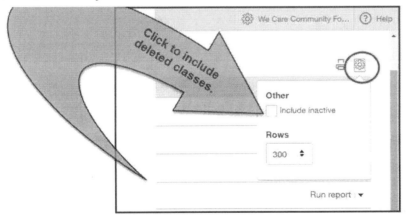

Click *Include inactive* and any deleted (deactivated) classes will appear in the class list. From the list you can use the **Edit** function to make the class active again.

> Once you have transactions entered in the classes, click **Run Reports** to the right of each class found in the **Class List** to bring up a report which includes of all the entries for that class to review or print. Use the *Back Arrow* on your browser to return to the Class List.

E. Recording the Beginning Balance Entry

Now that all of your classes have been set up, let's prepare your beginning balance entry. If you will recall, at the end of the last chapter I shared an example beginning balance entry. To record the journal entry, you will need to go to the **Plus Menu** (at the top middle of your screen) to open the **Create** screen. Select *Other*, *Journal Entry* in the far right column

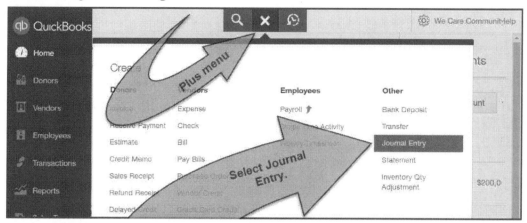

This may bring you to an entry screen with a pop-up warning that QuickBooks automatically numbers journal entries. If so, select *OK* to continue. You will then see a blank screen similar to this one:

Please note the date will default to today, but you will want to change it to the last day of your previous accounting year. Begin entering the account name for the first line item. The system will "guess" what you want and offer a suggestion. If it is correct, tab over to the next field. If not, use the drop-down menu to find the correct account.

Once you select the correct account name, you will need to enter the amount in either the **Debits** or **Credits** side. For your beginning balance entry, the assets should be *debits* (except accumulated depreciation), and the liabilities and net assets should be *credits*.

After you have input the dollar amount, tab across to the **Description** field. This is where you explain why you are making the entry. I've put "Beginning Balance" in the example above. Next, skip over the **Name** field—you will very rarely use it. The final column is **Classes.** If you do not see a column for classes, go back to *Gear, Company, Account and Settings, Advanced* and turn on *Track Classes* under **Categories.** In order to compile a correct restricted funds report, every line must have a class. Unless the line item is specifically for a restricted fund, use the **Unrestricted Fund** class for the balance sheet accounts.

When you enter the account on the next line, QBO will automatically fill in the amount of the opposite side of the entry and the description from the line above. This is because the system requires the entry to be balanced with equal amounts of debits and credits. For multi-line entries like this one, just put the next amount in the correct side, and the system generated amount will be replaced with the correct, balanced amount.

> Put the **bank statement's ending balance** on one line using the checking account number, and enter **any outstanding deposits** on separate lines with the amounts on the debit side of the entry.
> **Any outstanding checks** should be listed separately with the amounts on the credit side of the entry. This will allow you to reconcile your bank account when the previous year's outstanding deposits and checks clear.

If your organization has specific funds, perhaps named after donors or for specific purposes, you will need to enter each one on a separate line with a class specifically dedicated to it. For each of these net asset accounts, I have chosen a class or sub-class to charge them to. If there were several funds under **Temporarily Restricted Net Assets**, each would need its own line. Your previous year's audit or accountant should be able to furnish you with these amounts.

Unrestricted Net Assets is your general fund balance, but it may not yet equal your audit number. The balance of any accounts receivable and/or accounts payable as of the beginning date is still missing. Remember that you should not enter accounts receivables or accounts payables into this entry. In Chapters 9 and 10, you will input the donors and vendors' open invoices so that this data will be recorded.

After your entry balances and you have coded all the net assets to the correct classes, you will press *Save and close.*

You have now posted most, if not all, of your beginning balances. Are you ready to set up your donors and your vendors? QBO groups these together under **Lists.** In the next chapter, I'll go through all of the remaining list options QBO offers and help you determine which your organization should use and which you can ignore.

6. Donors & People I Owe Money To

A. Setting up Members and Other Donors

Probably the most important accounting function for organizations is the ability to receive donations and track them to the correct donor. QBO does this by setting up **Donors**. In Chapter 3, we changed the customer label in the Other Preferences from "customer" to "donor" or "member" depending on the main group your organization receives money from.

The process of setting up your donors is easy in QBO. There is even the option to import your donor list from an Excel file. First I am going to walk you through how to set them up manually in this chapter. This gives you the chance to become familiar with the donor list and also trains you in how to add new donors one at a time.

Technically QBO does not have a limit on name lists, but large lists can impact performance. QBO suggests keeping the combined number of names in your company below 10,000. That would include:

- Donors/Members
- Vendors
- Employees
- Products and Services

So unless you have an exceedingly large donor base, you should have plenty of room.

B. Adding a New Donor or Member

Are you itching to get those donors' names in the system? Start by selecting *Donors* in the left menu bar.

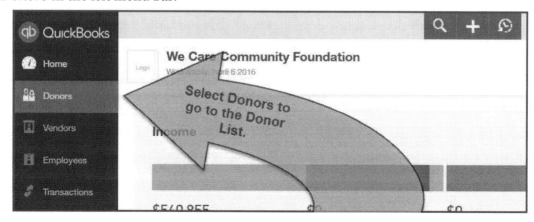

This will bring you to a list of donors and their outstanding balances. You may see a screen giving you the option to upload an Excel file. If so, select *Add manually.*

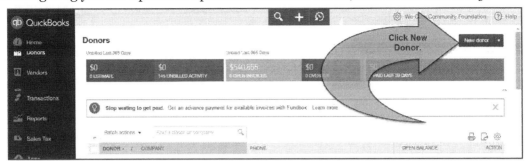

To add a donor, select *New donor*. This will bring up the **Donor Information** screen.

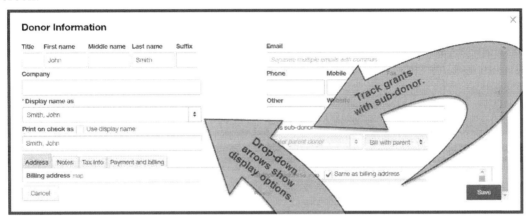

Many times the person collecting donor information is not the same person entering the information into QBO. To make data entry easier and more consistent, Eulica has created a physical form that includes all of the information needed to complete the donor record in QBO. This form would also be used for donor information updates and would be a helpful control to make sure information is complete and entered correctly. It is available for free at www.AccountantBesideYou.com.

Start at the top of the screen by entering the name of the donor. If the donor is an individual, enter the **First name** and **Last name**. If the donor is an organization or company, enter the **Company** name. **Display name as** allows you to determine how the donor name will be shown on forms and reports.

Email addresses for donors are important as they allow you to easily send receipts and statements from within QBO. Multiple email addresses can be entered to the email field and separated by a comma as long as the total characters in this field do not exceed 100. Enter the multiple email address like this: xxx@yahoo.com, yyy@yahoo.com.

The **Phone, Mobile, Fax,** and **Website** fields can be entered as needed.

The **Other** field can be used for whatever you would like, but you'll need to keep it consistent across all donors in order to be useful. You may want to use the Other field for a membership number in a club or an envelope number in a church. Play around and see what use of this field fits your needs the best.

For now, I will skip the sub-donor part and will explain in detail how to use this feature in the next section.

At the bottom of the Donor Information screen are four tabs where you will enter additional information about your donor. Enter up to two addresses, billing and shipping, for each donor under the **Address** tab.

The second tab is **Notes**.

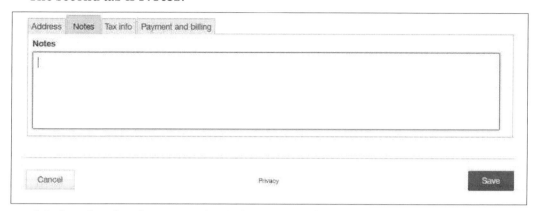

This is a handy place to write information about the donor you might want to have handy, i.e. the donor is related to a teacher in the school or is on a particular committee. QBO allows you to have a maximum of 4,000 characters in the Customer Notes field.

The third tab is **Tax info**.

Most of you will probably not charge sales tax, but if you sell goods through your organization, it may come in handy. As every state has different regulations, you need to check with your accountant to be sure.

The last tab is **Payment and billing**.

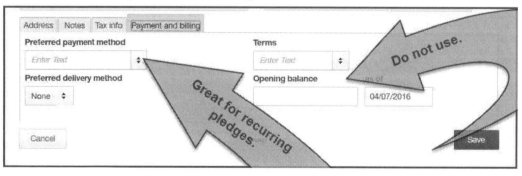

A very handy feature of the system is the ability to hold the donor credit card information. Just be very careful to follow federal guidelines on keeping the information secure. You can enter each donor's credit card information by selecting the appropriate credit card type in the **Preferred payment method** drop-down menu.

If you send out pledge reminders or have some type of membership dues, you may wish to use the **Terms** field. The drop-down arrow offers several payment term options, or you can add your own. **Preferred delivery method** allows you to send out statements via email or print. We'll be discussing online payments in Chapter 9, so you can leave it empty for now.

The **Opening balance** needs to be ignored. If the donor owes the organization money, it must be entered as a receivable, which I'll show you how to record in Chapter 9.

C. Grouping Donors: Parent and Sub-Donors/Members

Before you begin inputting donors, you need to decide how you should organize your donor list. In the business world, this may be wholesale customers or retail customers. If you need data on individual donors' donations versus foundations, you can do this by using sub-donors of a parent donor/member.

Start by making each donor grouping a parent donor, i.e. Granting Agencies, Foundations, Private Donors. If you receive matching funds from employers, make a parent grouping (Employer Name #1, Employer #2, etc.) and then make each donor who is an employee a sub-donor.

Just like the chart of accounts, you can set up sub-donors of any parent grouping you designate. Think about the type of information you will need. For example, if you will want to know about donations by members separate from donations by non-members, you could set up two parent groups: Members and Others. Likewise, if you would like to run reports by size and restrictions of donations, the donor groupings may include: Major Donors, Regular Donors, and Restricted Donors. Each of these could also be sub-donors.

To create a parent group, you will first create a new donor as we learned above. In this example, we are creating a donor called "Major Donors".

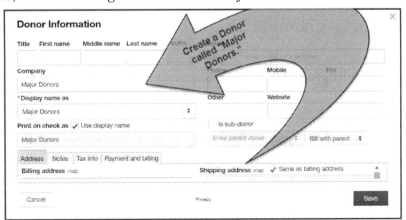

Next for each donor, we will choose the appropriate parent grouping. For this example, we will make John Smith a sub-donor of the "Major Donors" parent group.

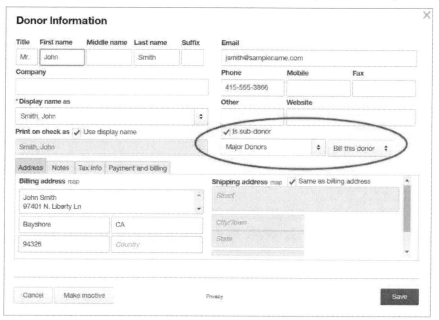

Select **Is sub-donor** box and enter the "*Major Donors*" parent grouping that we just created. Finally, make sure that the option selected is **Bill this donor** not **Bill with parent**. Click *Save*.

For this example, I have moved three donors to be sub-donors of this group, so my donor list looks like this:

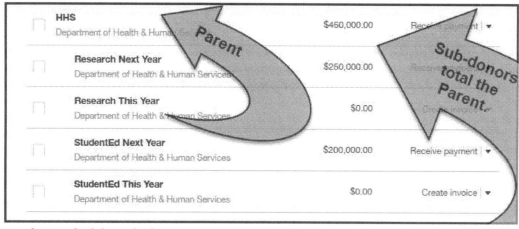

Note the total of the sub-donor amounts equals the parent amount.

D. Viewing & Printing the Donor Contact List Report

The donor/member list is a very important tool to any non-profit organization or church. Many times donor information needs to be shared with leadership for planning purposes. The report can also be helpful as you figure out how to organize your donor list. In chapter 12, we will go in detail about reports, but let's take a moment to learn how to view the **Donor Contact List** you have created.

Select *Reports* from the left menu bar.

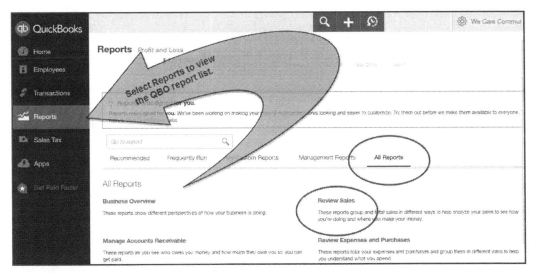

Next, choose the *All Reports, Review Sales*. Scroll down to and double click on *Donor Contact List*. If you are working in the sample company.

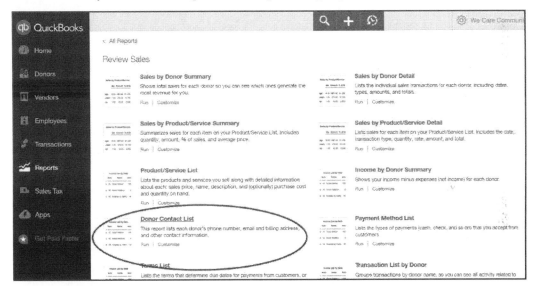

This brings you to the **Donor Contact List** which contains all of the Donors you have entered thus far in QBO.

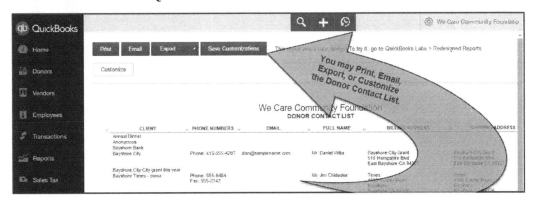

I find it helpful to visit this list while entering donors to make sure that each is categorized correctly, paying special attention to the appropriate parent grouping. Review the list and use the **Edit** function to make any changes.

Great job! Now let's set up vendors.

E. Setting Up Vendors (The People You Pay)

If you select *Vendors* from the left menu bar, you will see a screen like this.

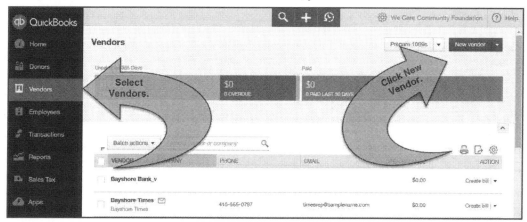

Notice the similarities between the Vendors screen and the Donor screen. To add a new vendor, select *New vendor* from the top of the list.

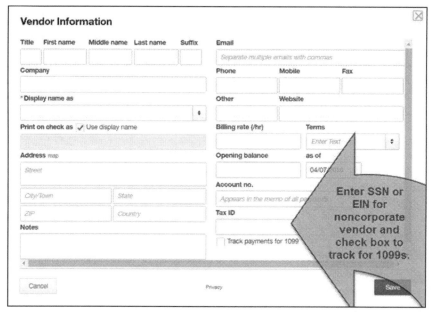

If the vendor is an individual, enter the **First name** and **Last name**. If the vendor is an organization or company, enter the **Company**. Just like the donor entry screen, you will then choose how the donor name is displayed on forms and reports.

If you will need to cut separate checks to the same company (perhaps different insurance plans), you will want to have different Vendor Names. 123 Insurance-Building and 123 Insurance-Liability are possible examples. Like the new donor screen, you can change the titles of any of the boxes with drop-down arrows.

The **Print on check as** is handy when the company name is different than whom they would like the check made out to. If this is the case, remember to uncheck the **Use display name** box.

Similar to the **Donor Information** screen, multiple email addresses can be entered to the **Email** field and separated by a comma as long as the total characters in this field do not exceed 100. Multiple email addresses are entered as follows: xxx@yahoo.com,yyy@yahoo.com.

The **Phone, Mobile, Fax**, and **Website** fields are self-explanatory. You probably don't need to worry about the **Billing rate.**

Do NOT use the opening balance. I'll show you how to enter open invoices in a chapter 10. **Account no** is the vendor's accountant number that is displayed on their bills. It will be printed on the memo line of checks to that vendor. Payment **Terms** aren't often used by organizations, but there are choices in the drop-down menu if you need them.

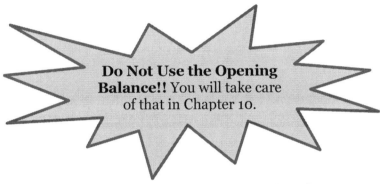

Do Not Use the Opening Balance!! You will take care of that in Chapter 10.

The **Tax ID** is where you will store the Employer Identification Number (EIN) or Social Security number for any non-corporate vendors you expect to spend more than $600 a year with. For those vendors, you will also need to check the box **Track payments for 1099**. If you are unsure whether a vendor should be issued a 1099, check out the IRS publication at https://www.irs.gov/pub/irs-pdf/i1099msc.pdf. If there is any question, go ahead and request their EIN or SSN and check the **Track payments for 1099** box. This will bring up the vendor's information at year end, so you can make the final determination.

I hope you feel like you have accomplished a lot!
The next chapter explains how to import names and addresses from your email contact base or from a spreadsheet. Feel free to skip it if it is simpler for you to enter the data with the method discussed in this chapter.

7. Inputting Donors & Vendors from Files

A. Connecting Your Email Contacts

If you have the names and addresses of your donors and vendors in email accounts or on a spreadsheet, you can save time by uploading this data directly into QBO instead of rekeying the information manually. First I will explain how to import the lists from your Gmail system and then show you how to import from a spreadsheet.

QBO makes it very easy to import your members from a Gmail account and to keep it updated. If your organization or church uses Gmail to communicate with donors, members, or vendors, you can add contact information from Gmail directly into QBO. QBO uses the email addresses to send invoices, receipts, and reports directly from QBO and the physical addresses for printing mailing labels. If you are using a different email program, you will need to export the data to a spreadsheet and update as needed.

Your contact database probably includes people who are neither donors nor vendors. Luckily, connecting your Gmail contacts does not create a donor or vendor record for every contact, but allows you to add them as needed. In effect, QBO creates a holding list. From this list, you can add the new contacts into the accounting system as desired.

If your organization doesn't have a Gmail address (or other designated email address), consider setting one up to be used exclusively by your organization. I suggest that you don't use a personal email address as it will be displayed on any invoices or receipts created in QBO. For these examples, I have created a Gmail address of wecarecommunityfoundation@gmail.com—the name of the sample organization used in this book.

To connect your Gmail account contacts to QBO, you only need to go through the connection process once. First, log into your organization's Gmail account where your contacts are saved. This can be done from any form on the QBO menu (**Invoice, Bill, Sales Receipt**, etc.). Let's use an invoice. From the *Plus* menu, select *Invoice*.

After the invoice opens, find the **Choose a donor** field at the top left of the invoice screen. Click *Add new*.

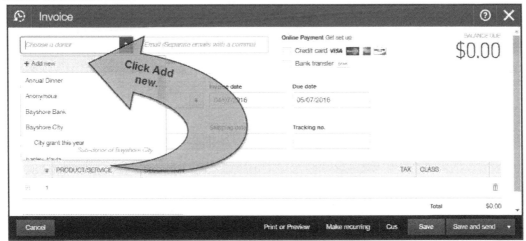

A **New Donor** window will open within the invoice screen. Click on *Connect your Gmail account*.

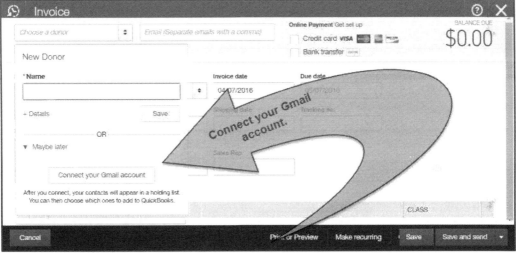

If you are already logged into your organization's Google account, the following screen will appear asking for online access. Click *Allow*.

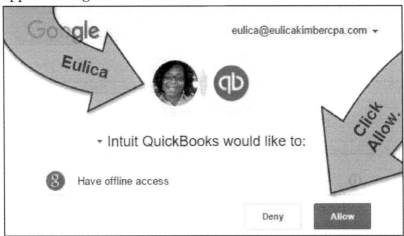

If you are not logged in with your organization's Google account, you can log into it now. QBO will confirm that your Gmail account was successfully connected.

Congratulations! You have completed a great timesaving step. Your donor and vendor contact information is now available in the system as needed. I'll explain.

Let's say you want to create a new donor for someone you have been corresponding with via Gmail, and now she wants to become a donor. To send her an invoice, go to *Plus, Invoice* to open the invoice screen. Search for her name in the *Donor* field in the invoice screen.

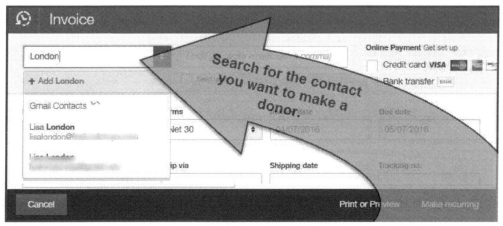

You could also do this from the receipt screen or the expense screen if she were a vendor. Click the email address and add the Gmail contact as a donor (or vendor in the check or expense screens).

Complete or update the **Name** field as you want it to appear in your forms and reports within QBO. Select *Save,* and Lisa London is now a donor.

If for any reason, you want to disconnect your Gmail account from QBO, the process is just as simple. Open an invoice and go to the donor field again.

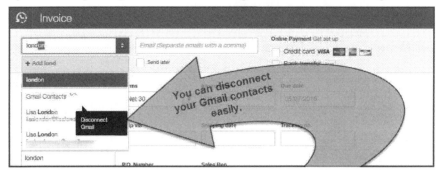

At the top of the drop-down menu, hover over **Gmail Contacts** with your mouse and click *Disconnect Gmail.*

With other email providers, you will need to research their instructions on downloading the contacts to a spreadsheet or CSV file. In the next section, I'll explain how to import this information.

B. Spreadsheet Method—Importing Donor and Vendor List

You may enter the donor or member data by uploading a Microsoft Excel spreadsheet (Excel must already be on your computer). Select *Donors* from the **Home Screen**. Go to the drop-down arrow to the right of the **New donor** button. Click *Import donors.*

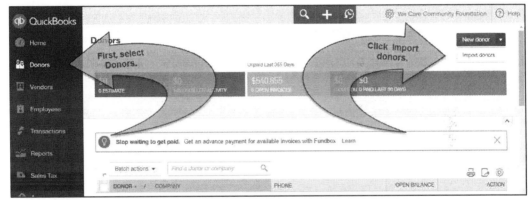

On the **Import Donors** screen, select *Download a sample file* located just below the upload field.

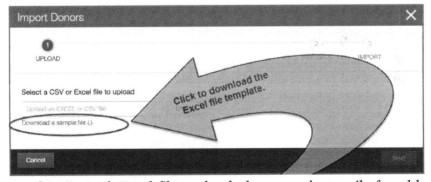

Save the sample Microsoft Excel file to the desktop or other easily found location. It will become the template for your donor or member data.

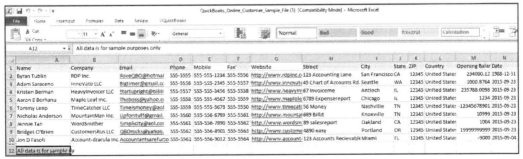

Use the sample data provided as a guide, but you can leave fields blank that do not apply or you don't currently have the information for. Part of the reason I had you set up a donor manually was so you could see which fields you wanted to use and which were okay to leave blank (i.e. leave the company field blank if the donor is an individual).

Each column in your worksheet should be in the same cell format as the example file, i.e. if the date shows year-month-day, key in 20xx-xx-xx, not xx/xx/xx. Enter your donor or member information in the appropriate fields as listed.

If your spreadsheet was downloaded from your contact base with the columns in a different order, move them to mirror the columns in the example file, i.e. A=Name, B=Company, C=Email, etc. Remember that all of the columns do not have to be filled in. Some donors may not have email addresses, a website, or fax numbers for example. You may also delete columns that are not needed for your donors.

> Do **NOT** include the Opening Balance column. These amounts will be input later as invoices.

Unfortunately, you cannot make sub-donors and parent groups during this process. You will have to do that in QBO after the donors are uploaded.

> The more complete you can make the information in the spreadsheet before it is imported, the less you will have to do later.

Once all the data is complete in your spreadsheet, save it to your desktop or other easily found location. Don't forget to delete all of the sample donor information from the template before proceeding.

To import the file, from the **Home Screen,** select *Donors,* click on the drop-down arrow beside **New donor** and *Import donors.*

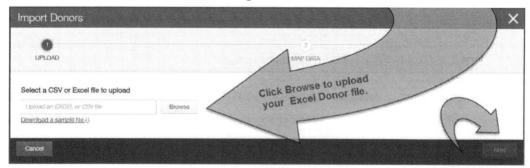

Click on the **Browse** button and locate the donor file you have updated and saved. Click *Next.*

Now it is time to **Map your fields to QuickBooks fields**. This process will point the fields from your spreadsheet to the corresponding field in QBO. The system pulls the column names from your spreadsheet and tries to line it up to the **QUICKBOOKS ONLINE FIELD.**

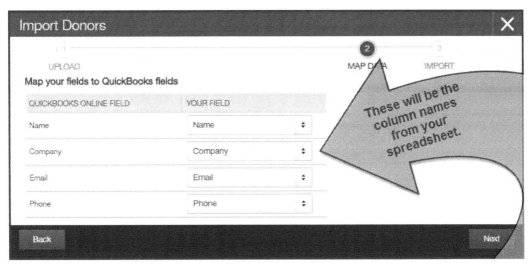

Review each field. If you used the Microsoft Excel template provided, you will probably not have many changes to make. After you have made any necessary corrections, select *Next* to import the data.

You will receive a success message indicating the number of records that have been imported.

The example we just completed was for donors. Repeat the same process for your vendors by going back to the **Home Screen** and selecting *Vendors, Import vendors.*

Once you have added your donor and vendor lists, you are almost ready to input transactions, like donations and checks. In the next chapter, I'll first explain how **Products and Services (Items)** are used to facilitate the process.

8. Products & Services—Tracking the Transactions

Recall in the first chapter how I explained the importance of lists. One of these lists is **Products and Services**. QuickBooks Online uses **Products and Services** to track revenues and expenditures. If you have used the desktop version of QuickBooks, you know them as **Items**. The term "Items" is used in QBO when entering expense transactions, so I will use these terms interchangeably.

By using products and services (items), QBO does the accounting for normal recurring transactions without requiring you to remember the account numbers. In a business, the items would be the goods or services it has to sell or to purchase. For a nonprofit or church, the items will be donations, grants, membership dues, designated programs, tithes, offerings, capital campaigns, etc. This is how you will track the money coming in. You will also set up items for recurring purchases or for tracking volunteer hours.

A. Product and service types

There are three different product and services types.

Service—most of your receipts, including your donations, grants, tithes, and funds collected for other organizations, will be the Service type.

Inventory part—if you sell tee shirts, books, or other things that you buy to resell, and need to keep track of the amount on hand, you will use this.

Non-inventory parts—use this for items you sell but don't need to inventory, i.e. magazine subscriptions.

If you are familiar with the desktop version of QuickBooks, please note the products and services types listed above are used to record the following:

- **Other charges**—used for fines or service charges. You probably won't use this much.
- **Group**—I'll show you how to use this for allocations.
- **Payments**—record the payment received when you prepare the invoice.
- **Sales tax item and Sales tax group**—if you are selling goods that your state requires you to collect sales taxes on, you will need a sales tax item.

B. Types of Services

I'll start with the **Service** type. Your most important service is probably **Donations.** Like the Chart of Accounts, Products and Services can have sub-items. For your **Donation** item, you can establish sub-items such as **Dues, Plate Offerings, Online Giving,** and **Donations.** Don't worry about entering all possibilities. It is easy to add more products and services as you need them.

> There should be an item set up for every revenue line item on your chart of accounts. If you would like to track additional detail use Sub-products/services.

Before we proceed, let's check to make sure you have the correct **Products and Services** settings selected for your organization or church. Go to *Gear, Your Company, Account and Settings.*

The **Account and Settings** screen will appear. Select *Sales.* Under the section marked **Products and services**, turn on the options according to your organization's needs.

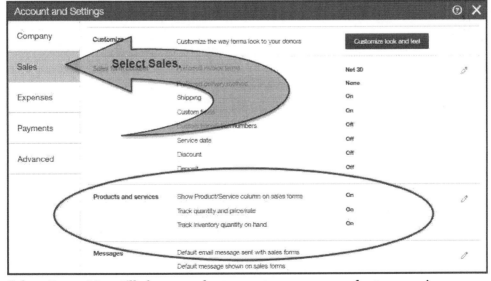

Select *Done.* Now I'll show you how to set up a new product or service.

C. Setting Up New Products and Services

Let's set up a service item. From the gear menu under *List*, select **Products and Services**.

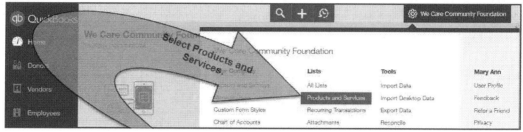

After arriving at the **Products and Services** list, select *New*.

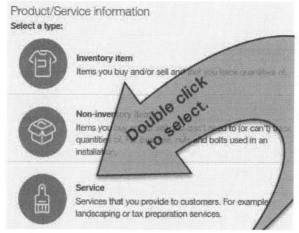

You will start by selecting the **Type** of item. Our example will be a service item.

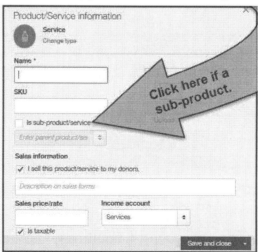

Assign the item a **Name.** The **SKU** (Item number, if you are familiar with the desktop version) is rarely necessary. Just like donors, products/services can have a parent and a sub-item. If it is a **Sub-product/service**, select *Is sub-product/service* and associate it with a parent service using the drop-down arrow, like you did in in Chapter 6 with sub-donors.

The detail you key into the **Sales information** box will display on invoices (donation form), so be sure your spelling is correct and the description would make sense to the donor. This can be overridden when you enter the transaction.

Products and services allow you to designate a flat **Sales price/rate**, say $100 honorarium to speak at a function. If the item you are entering has a standard rate, input it here; otherwise leave it blank. The invoice screens will allow you to override this amount. Any parent item should have a rate of $0.

The revenue recorded for a transaction with this item will go into the **Income account** you designate. The drop-down menu allows you to select from the chart of accounts.

Once you are happy with the description, amount, and the account the product will go to, select **Save and close** to exit the **Product/Service information** screen or click on the drop-down arrow to select *Save and new* to continue entering other items.

> You will notice a redundancy in the items and the chart of accounts. If you do not need your financial statements to list the different types of donations, you can set up one donation account with lots of items that record into it. Read Chapter 13 on Reports and ask your Board of Directors what level of detail they would like to see.

D. New Product and Service Feature: Category

At the time of the printing of this book, a new Products and Services feature called **Category** is being released to users in phases. (One of the advantages of QBO is that upgrades require no action on your part.) Once it is available, it will appear in the **Product/Service information** screen. Until then, you can see how it works by visiting the test drive company at https://qbo.intuit.com/redir/testdrive.

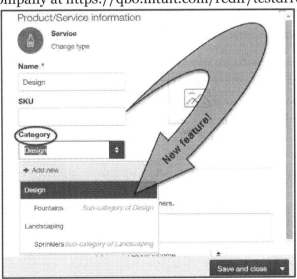

The new **Category** field provides a way of classifying your revenue and expenses. For example, if you would like a quick way to see how much money your major donors give versus foundation donors, you would set up categories called Major Donors and

Foundation Donors. Additionally, since you can search for items by category, they will save time when completing donation or expense forms.

Before we move onto Chapter 9, I would like to summarize the difference between using classes and adding new accounts or items.

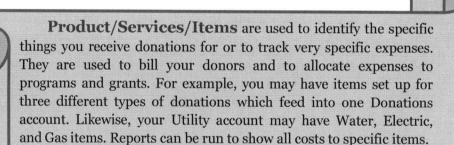

Classes	Admin				Education				Outreach			
Account	Donation		Utilities		Donation		Utilities		Donation		Utilities	
Item	Pledges	Unpledged support	Water	Electric	Pledges	Unpledged support	Water	Electric	Pledges	Unpledged support	Water	Electric

In my example above, the organization has three programs: Admin, Education and Outreach. Because each will have revenues (donations) and expenses, we need to track them via **Classes**. The revenues and expenses are shown on the financial statements as **Accounts**. Because we want more detail available that we don't need to show on the financial statements, we use **Items (Products/Services)** to track Pledged and Unpledged support and Water and Electricity.

Product/Services/Items are used to identify the specific things you receive donations for or to track very specific expenses. They are used to bill your donors and to allocate expenses to programs and grants. For example, you may have items set up for three different types of donations which feed into one Donations account. Likewise, your Utility account may have Water, Electric, and Gas items. Reports can be run to show all costs to specific items.

Account numbers are used to track revenues, expenditures, assets, and liabilities to show on your financial statements. Each item is linked to an account number, but each account may have more than one item.

There will be quite a bit of redundancy between the account numbers and the items. You can limit the number of accounts by putting the details in Items. If you need to see how much you spent on electricity, a report on the Item *Electricity* can be run without having to have a separate account on the financial statements.

Classes can be used as separate general ledgers to track the money received and spent for a particular program or fund. Account numbers are assigned classes when a transaction is recorded, so the amounts can be compiled together as individualized financial statements for each of the programs and funds.

9.   Money In—Recording Donations & Revenues

In order for your organization or church to continue to do its good work, money needs to come in the door. As responsible stewards of your donors' donations, you must implement accounting procedures and systems that will allow you to record and track the dollars while keeping the money safe. Before you learn how to enter the money received, I'll walk you through some basic internal accounting controls.

A. Accounting Controls for Receipts

If you keep in mind two basic guidelines, most of the controls I recommend will make sense.

First, no one should have access to cash and checks without other people observing them.

Second, if a person has access to the accounting system (in this case, QBO), he should not have access to the money.

This means the treasurer should be a different person than the bookkeeper, or if that is not possible, the treasurer should not have access to the bank account.

Most thefts happen when the person handling the money can adjust the books to hide their actions. I highly recommend going back to Chapter 1 to reread the **Case for Internal Accounting Controls** and **Points for the Board.**

Don't start shaking your head and saying, "But we are too small to have those kinds of controls." No organization is too small to protect both their volunteers and employees from suspicion and insure their funds from mismanagement.

In order to design controls for your organization or church, think about the way the money is received. Membership fees are paid via cash or check at meetings; a collection basket is passed around during the service; checks are received in the mail; electronic payments are made through the website; etc. Take time to walk through any scenario in which you receive money and design procedures that will not conflict with the two guidelines above.

Here are some basic steps for the most common ways of receiving money.

1.   Money Received During Meetings or Fundraisers

If your organization is large enough to have a physical location and staff, it is much easier to design basic controls over the money coming in. But even if most of the money comes in during club meetings or fundraisers, controls can still be utilized.

Basic requirements when the person recording the books is also the person collecting the money.

1.   The bookkeeper is not be a check signer.
2.   The person collecting the money must stay in plain site during the meeting or event where money is collected.
3.   A receipt book with self-duplicating pages must be utilized. If a member pays for something with cash, he should receive a paper receipt. The organization then has copies of these receipts in chronological order.
4.   At the end of the meeting or event, two people should total the checks and cash together and compare the monies received with the receipt book. They then sign a summary sheet of paper with their names and the date.

2.   Money Received During Religious Services

Most churches will pass the plate or a basket for offerings or donations during their weekly services. This money is often brought to the front of the sanctuary for the remainder of the service or is taken to another secured area of the church. If it is taken to the front of the sanctuary in full view of the congregation, it will need to be collected after the service by two people. These are usually people that will also be the "counters," i.e. they will count the money and record on a piece of paper or deposit slip how much was received.

Whether at the front of the church or in a separate room, until the dollar amount of money is recorded, the collection should be seen by at least two people. I also recommend not allowing married couples or people living in the same household to be counters together as there is more likelihood of collusion.

I like to have the members of the governing board rotate as counters with the other volunteers. It allows the board members to keep an eye on the day-to-day workings of the church.

The counters, neither of which should be the bookkeeper, will count the cash and make copies of the checks or record each of them manually. The counters fill out a summary form and sign it. The total on the summary form must match the bank deposit. The deposit will then be driven to the bank and put in the night deposit. One person can do this as there is a record of the receipts at the church. When the bookkeeper comes to work later that week, he or she will have a copy of the summary form to record for each donor's or member's offering.

If an offering envelope system is used to track contributions, the counters must:

1. Verify the money in the envelope matches the amount stated on the envelope and note it as cash or check.
2. Bring discrepancies to the team leader's attention before correcting the envelope.
3. If a check, make sure the check number is included on the envelope.
4. Complete blank envelopes with check information if check is enclosed.
5. Include any cash received in blank envelopes in the loose offering total.
6. Batch and total envelopes and deliver to bookkeeper for entry.

3.   Remote Imaging Scanner

If your organization or church receives a large number of checks, you may wish to ask your bank about an RID—Remote Imaging Device scanner. This allows you to quickly scan the checks and print out a report for your files. The scanned file is automatically sent to the bank, so the checks can be deposited immediately rather than waiting for someone to drive to it. Once the bank has the scanned image, it does not need the physical check.

Mark the original checks with a highlighter to show they were scanned and file them for future reference. The scanner should not let you send the same check twice. Beware though; if you accidentally try to deposit the scanned checks at the bank, a deposit correction fee will be charged.

By scanning the checks immediately after receiving them, there is less likelihood of someone stealing and depositing them into their own account. The scanner is also less likely to make math errors.

Banks usually charge a fee for the RID scanners, but the time savings and control features are often worth the additional expense.

4.   Money Received Through the Mail

Nonprofits often receive their donations through the mail; therefore, it is a good idea to have a post office box. This keeps anyone from stealing the checks directly out of your mailbox. However, you don't want your bookkeeper to be the one to pick up the mail. Theoretically, he could steal a check, but adjust the donor's account to look like it was received.

Designate someone without access to the accounting system to go to the post office, and then, back at the organization, have him open the mail in front of a second person. Each check should then be recorded and the summary signed by the two observers. If you have an RID scanner, scan the checks immediately, and then give the deposit report and the marked checks to the bookkeeper.

5.   Payments Received Through the Website

Now that so much is being done on the web, many organizations have found it advantageous to add a donation button to their website via PayPal® or any of many other services. It is crucial that you safeguard the link to the bank account. Many online credit card processors will require signed corporate resolutions stating you are a legal organization and the check signers have authorized the funds to go to that account. Others, like PayPal, simply use an email/password combination. This is potentially problematic as the person who has the password could reroute the appointed deposit bank account to their personal account number.

> A PayPal employee told me of a women associated with a small nonprofit who had set up its PayPal account. She had a falling out with the organization and refused to tell them the password to collect the money.

To keep this from occurring with your organization, I would recommend the account be linked to an email address administered by your organization (admin@yourorganization.org) and assigned to someone who has no access to the donors' records. This person would have the authorization to change the bank deposit account and permit transfers from the PayPal account to the bank.

PayPal allows for a secondary user with limited rights. The secondary user can only see reports, not change bank accounts. You will want this to be your bookkeeper so he can reconcile the receipts in PayPal to the cash posted into the bank. Any discrepancies should be investigated immediately.

We've covered some basic steps to protect your people and your money in the most common ways donations are received. Now make a list of all the ways your organization receives money and, for each case, ask yourself, "How can I get it to the bank and recorded in the financial statements while safeguarding the funds and my volunteers and employees?"

> These are the *minimum* steps necessary to safeguard receipts. If your organization already has more complete procedures, please follow them.

B. Entering Donations

1.   Entering Pledge, Plate, and other Simple Donations

The money you receive may be simple donations. By simple, I mean that the donor does not expect to be invoiced or given a receipt at the time of the donation. This is also the easiest way to enter receipts into QBO.

Go to *Plus, Donors, Sales Receipt* to reach the **Sales Receipt** screen.

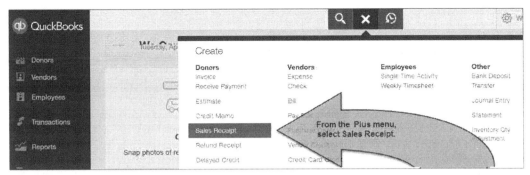

This is where all of the work you've done in setting up your lists pays off. The chart of accounts, donors/members, products/services (items), and class lists are all used to tell QBO what the source and purpose of the money coming is and where you will put it. Let's take a look at the sales receipt.

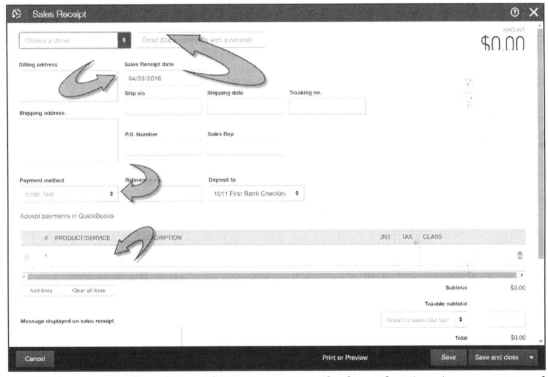

Each entry needs a donor, date, payment method, product/service, amount, and a class. A sales receipt is required for each separate donor included in that day's deposit. It is important that the person opening the mail or taking payments is documenting all of these details so the bookkeeper is able to enter data in these fields.

2.   Entering Cash and Checks Received

You are now ready to enter the money received. In the box marked **Choose a donor**, begin typing the donor's name (or code, if you didn't use last names), and the system will pull up donor names.

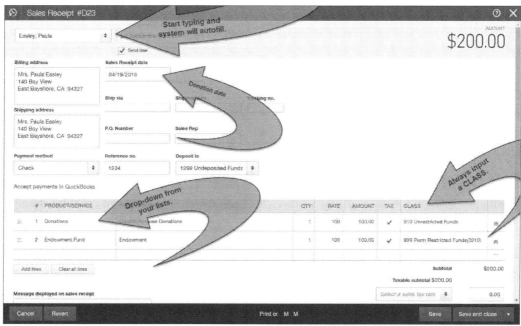

In this example, I had only typed an "e," and the system brought up all the names that started with "e." Then I selected the donor named Paula Easley. The system filled in the email, billing, and shipping addresses automatically. The **Sales Receipt date** is when the funds were received by your organization, not necessarily when you recorded them.

Select the appropriate **Payment method** (check, cash, credit card, etc.) from the drop-down menu and enter the check number if applicable. If the donor gave both cash and check in the same donation, you will need to enter it as two separate donations. Only one payment method can be selected for each receipt.

Next choose *Undeposited Funds* as the **Deposit to** account. I'll explain this in much greater detail a little later in this chapter, but for now, think of Undeposited Funds as the virtual stack of checks and money you have in a bank bag. The actual checks and cash may already have been deposited, but making this selection ensures this deposit will be batched properly in QBO. You will thank me later when it's time to reconcile the bank account, which I will tell you about in Chapter 11.

Select the appropriate **Product/Service** from the drop-down menu. If you had established a rate when you set up the service, QBO will automatically enter it.

Recall that in Chapter 8, you set up items for each type of income you expect to receive. In this example, the donor has sent in money for two separate purposes, Donations and Endowment Fund. If a service had been set up with a rate, you have the opportunity to change it on the sales receipt screen.

> If you have receipts that do not need to be tracked by donor, enter them into QBO by setting up a "Miscellaneous" donor and then enter the donations on separate lines for each donation type.

Select *Save & new* from the drop-down arrow at the bottom, and a blank sales receipt or donation screen appears ready for you to add the next donation.

> The first time you enter a donation in the sales receipt screen, you may feel a little confused with using items. (I know I did.) Just remember that items are simply the details that feed into the reports.
> Back in Chapter 8, you set up the types of donations and other receipts in items. Now you will use them on the sales receipt.
> Then, designate a class based on the program the donation is supporting, or use the unrestricted fund class.

3.   Acknowledging the Donation

After entering the donation, you may print or email it. The donation acknowledgement can be printed or sent as you are entering each one, or you can print/send them as a batch after you finish entering that day's receipts.

QBO has a convenient feature which allows you to customize the acknowledgement emailed to your donor. This is very handy as the IRS requires specific wording for acknowledgements to donors for gifts over $250. I'll go over the customization process in Chapter 16.

If you are emailing one donor at a time, you will send the email before you leave the donor receipt screen. At the bottom right corner, click the down arrow and select *Save and send*.

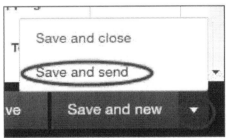

The next window allows you edit the individual donor's message on the email screen before you send it.

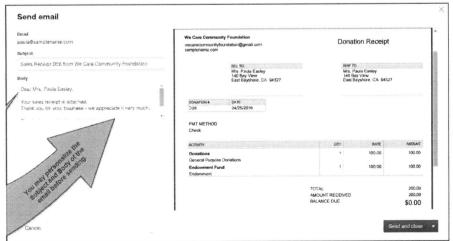

Type in your personalized message. Click *Save and send* to email the donor. If you want to send all the sales receipt emails at once, check the *Send later* block located just below the donor email address.

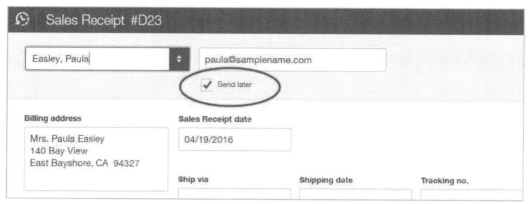

For a receipt to be included in a batch, the **Send later** box must be checked for that sales receipt. The donor email address will populate automatically if you included it during the donor set up in Chapter 7, or you can enter it here.

If you prefer to print the sales receipts, deselect the **Send later** box and go to the bottom of the sales entry screen. Click *Print or Preview*, and check *Print later*.

When you are ready to send or print, from the left **Menu,** select *Transactions, Sales*. You will then arrive at the **Sales Transactions** screen.

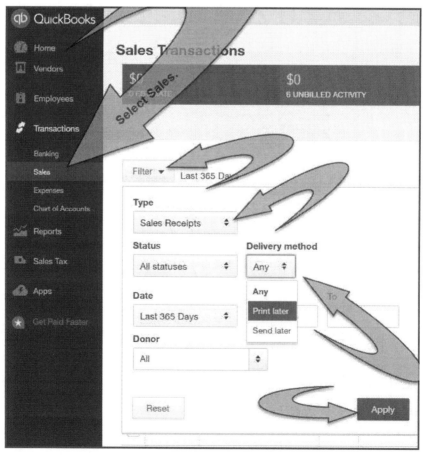

Select *Filter*. Under **Type**, select *Sales Receipts*; under **Status,** choose *All statuses*; and for the **Delivery method,** select *Print later* or *Send later*. Click *Apply*. Your donation acknowledgements you had held are now automatically sent to your donors or printed for you to mail.

I'll discuss how to customize forms and reports in Chapter 16 so your donors or members can learn about the great work you are doing.

C. Entering Cash Receipts

Let's set up a donor called **Cash** for cash donations or "loose plate" offerings that are not attributed to a specific donor.

You can add new donors directly from the **Sales Receipt** screen without having to go back to the donor list. Select the **Choose a donor** drop-down menu and then select *Add new*.

Now make the **New Donor Name** *Cash*. You do not need to input any details. Click *Save*.

The **Sales Receipt** screen will appear with **Cash** in the donor field.

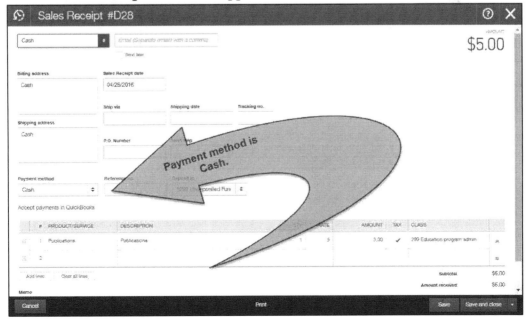

In this example, an informational pamphlet was sold. Select the appropriate **Class**, set the **Payment method** to *Cash,* and the **Item** to *Publications.* Input the amount (it can go under **Rate** or **Amount**), and *Save and close.*

D. Entering Donations from a Separate Donor Base

You do not have to track your donors through QBO. Many nonprofits and churches use internet-based donor record systems. These databases offer more flexibility in analysis and in correspondence with the donors. Some offer a download option to easily import the data into QBO. Others will require you to make a manual entry.

Without knowing which database you are using, I can't walk you through that step, but the database company will have instructions for you. I can, however, show you how to enter it manually. Start by setting up a new donor called Donor Database.

Run a report from your donor database system that totals the donations for the day, week, or month you will be entering.

Be sure to group the donations from the database to match the deposits made in the bank. For example, if you received 10 donations throughout the week and went to the bank to deposit them two different times, you will need the report to list the donations based on each day deposited.

Bring up the **Sales Receipt (Donation)** screen.

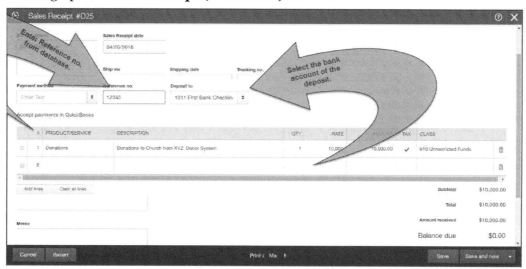

Select the customer **Donor Database** and choose the correct class (unrestricted for regular donations). Input the day these donations were deposited in the **Sales Receipt Date** box.

The **Reference No.** should be the report reference number from the donor system. You will not need to input a check number or payment method. Designate the items and amount of the first daily deposits from the donor database report and then select *Save & new.* Continue entering the amounts of the next deposit date from the report.

E. Dues & Pledges—Billing and Payment

1.   Recording Dues or Pledges as Receivables

If your organization asks its donors or members to pay dues annually or for a project, QBO can track them. If you are a religious organization with members who tithe or pledge, QBO can also help. The system uses **Invoices** to bill for **Dues or Pledges** from **Donors or Members**.

Go to *Plus, Invoice* (found under **Donors)**.

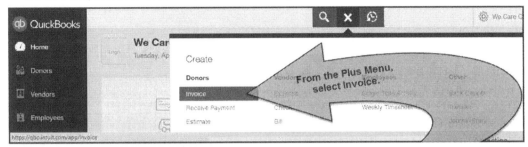

The **Invoice** screen will appear.

You will notice this looks like the **Sales Receipt** screen. Be careful to pay attention that you are on the correct entry screen. The names of the screen are always in the top left of the heading.

Enter the donor's name, today's date, due date, amount and select the appropriate Product/Service; in this case, **Annual Dues**. The system will fill in the predesignated amount. At the top of the screen is the **Online Payment** option. It should be selected if you choose to use Intuit's processing. I won't be covering that in this book as the Intuit professionals will need to set you up with this service.

Once you select *Save & new*, you will be directed back to the empty invoice screen. Continue entering dues and close. If you are entering dues received for the following year, date the dues on January 1 of the next year, otherwise keep today's date. The email and print options are the same as described earlier in this chapter in the section titled **Acknowledging the Donation**.

2.   Recording Monthly/Recurring Dues or Pledge Installments

If your members or donors make payments to you on a recurring basis (monthly, quarterly, etc.), you can enter the first period amount and have the system record the future charges using the **Make recurring** option.

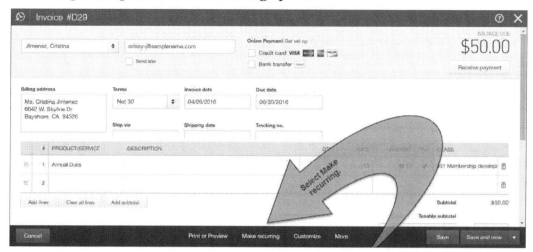

After entering the dues amount, check to make sure your invoice has the exact items (products/services) and amount you want to bill each period. Then select **Make recurring** at the bottom of the invoice entry screen. The recurring transaction will be exactly what was in your invoice.

You will arrive at the **Recurring Invoice** screen that has several options.

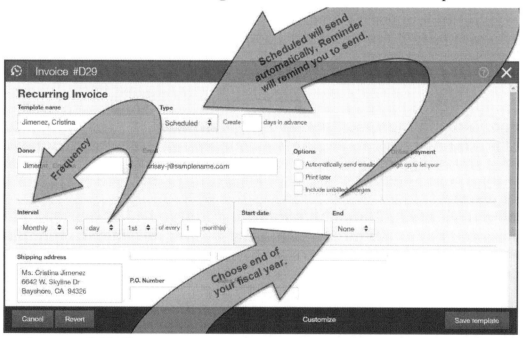

The **Type** field allows you to choose to have QBO remind you to record the entry manually (**Reminder**) or automatically record it (**Scheduled**). Choose how many **Days in Advance to Enter** into the register. I'd use seven days in advance, so you know it is coming. Select the **Interval** it should be recorded, the **Start date**, the **End date,** and. You can also select to **Automatically send emails** to the donor.

Always put a number in the **End date** or it will keep posting for eternity. I like to have them stop at the end of the fiscal year and then reset them for the new year. *Select* **Save template**.

3.   Manage Recurring Transactions

All **Recurring Transactions** are stored in a list by the same name. Go to *Gear icon, Lists, Recurring Transactions*.

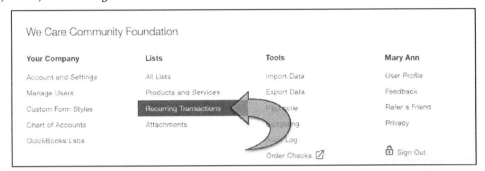

The list of **Recurring Transactions** allows you to add **New** transactions from this screen. You can also **Use**, edit or delete any recurring transaction using options in the Action column.

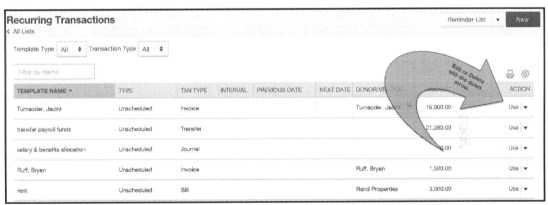

Click the downward arrow to the right of the **Use** option to get to the **Edit** and **Delete** options.

Recurring bills can be set with a **Type** of **Scheduled** or **Unscheduled**. **Scheduled** transactions will automatically post to QBO. You would only do this for transactions that retain the amount, category account and class for each period. **Unscheduled** transactions are used as needed from the Recurring Transactions list.

4.   Entering Beginning Receivable Balances

If your organization had open receivables as of the start date, you will need to enter them as invoices dated in the previous accounting year. For example, assume you had three donors with outstanding dues of $1000 each as of December 31, 2016, and you are setting up QBO with a start date of January 1, 2017. For each donor, enter an invoice dated in 2016 for $1000. This will make your beginning balances as of

January 1 correct and will give you invoices to apply payments to when the dues are received in 2016.

5.   Receiving Payments on Dues or Pledges

QBO makes receiving payments on dues easy to record. Go to *Plus, Donors, Receive Payment.*

This will then bring up the **Receive Payment** screen. Let's apply a $50 payment from Christina Jimenez from the example above.

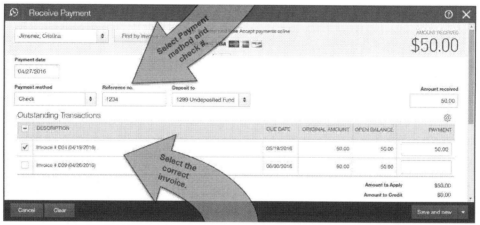

When you input the donor's name, all outstanding invoices will appear in the **Outstanding Transactions** list. In most cases, you will apply payments to the oldest invoice first. Just click on the small box to the left of the **Invoice(s)** until the **Amount to Apply** equals the payment amount received.

If a partial payment on the pledge was made, change the **Payment** amount. For example, if Christina Jimenez only sent in $25, you would change the payment to $25. Next time we pull her outstanding invoices, you will see that this invoice still has a remaining $25 due on it.

F. Receipt of Restricted Funds

When you receive money that has been restricted by the donor, you must designate the **Temporarily Restricted Class** or the **Permanently Restricted Class.** Go back to the **Sales Receipt** or donation screen.

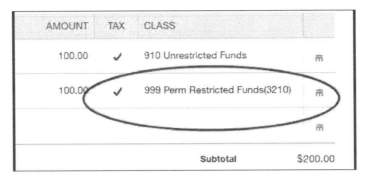

AMOUNT	TAX	CLASS	
100.00	✓	910 Unrestricted Funds	🛍
100.00	✓	999 Perm Restricted Funds(3210)	🛍
			🛍
		Subtotal	$200.00

Select **CLASS** to *Temporarily or Permanently Restricted*. If it is a grant or contract that you will need to report the related expenses, it will be set up as a sub-donor as you learned in **Chapter 6**. Let's first assume you do not need to report back to the donor.

The default descriptions from the items can be changed by typing over them. The more detail entered here, the easier it is to look up information later. You can attach documents detailing the restrictions to the donor's account through the Customer Center. If this was an endowment or other permanently restricted donation, you would select the **Permanently Restricted Fund** as the class.

In Chapter 6, you set up sub-donors for each year of a multi-year grant for the Department of Health and Human Services (HHS). Let's go back to the Donor list and learn how to apply a payment received from HHS. Select *Donors* from the left menu bar. Type *HHS* in the **Find a donor** field. The yearly grants that were created as sub-donors will appear. Select the first *sub-donor*.

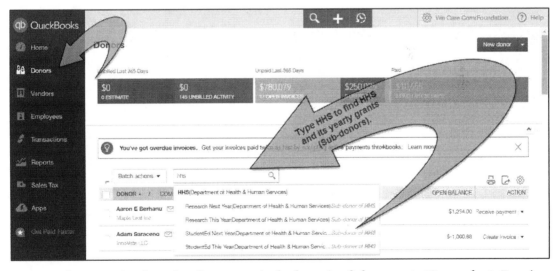

You have arrived at the first year (sub-donor) of the grant. Now select *Receive payment* to enter the check.

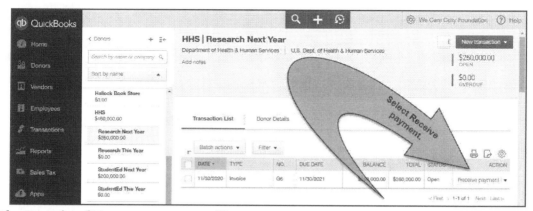

The **Received Payment** screen will appear.

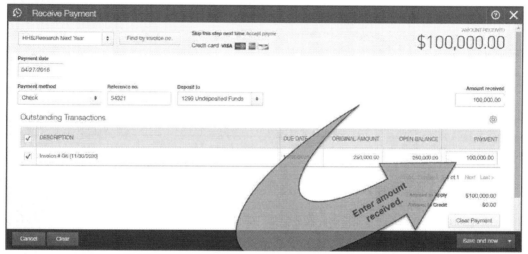

Enter the amount of the receipt next to the appropriate invoice. In this example, HHS has sent check number 54321 in the amount of $100,000. Select *Save and close* to return to the transaction list.

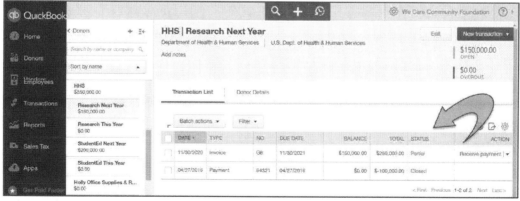

For HHS, you see the $100,000 payment and the original invoice listed with a status of **Partial**.

G. Miscellaneous Receipts

Sometimes your organization receives money for miscellaneous receipts like small fundraisers or pamphlet sales that are not related to a particular donor. For these donations, you will set up a generic customer (i.e. Carnival Fundraiser, Pamphlet Sales, or Misc.) and related items (Products/Services). The items link to specific accounts in the chart of accounts in order to record the donations in the correct line on the financial statements.

Miscellaneous receipts can be entered through **Sales Receipt** in the same way as regular donations explained earlier. For the customer name, enter the generic customer and fill out the form the same way you did cash or check receipts above.

Another option is to go to the deposit screen. Go to *Plus, Other, Bank Deposit.*

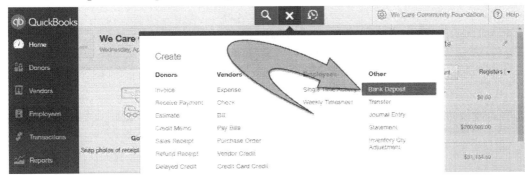

If there are outstanding deposits, they will appear at the top of the deposit screen.

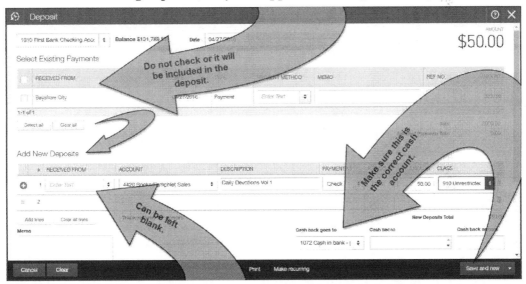

For this example, we are only depositing $50 for books sold. Ignore the Bayshore City Deposit showing in **Select Existing Payments**. In the **Add New Deposits** section below, you can enter the non-donor related income without setting up customers.

> **DO NOT** enter donations from specific donors on this screen. Donations must go through invoices or sales receipts or you will not be able to generate accurate reports by donor name.

Remember to select *Save and close* at the bottom right of the screen when done.

H. Pass-Through Collections

Your organization may take up collections for other organizations, like a local food bank or Habitat for Humanity®. A check will be sent to the nonprofit for the amount collected, so you will record them a little differently.

Let's set up a few things first. The organization the donations are to be given to needs to be set up both as a donor and a vendor. Establish a service item for pass-through donations and add to the chart of accounts an **Other Income** type account for pass-through donations and an **Other Expense** type account for pass-through payments.

When money is received, choose *Sales Receipt*.

Donor is the organization who should receive the donations. The class is unrestricted as the payment will be made to the organization on a timely basis.

Select *Pass Thru Donations* as the **Item**. If you have a description in the item, it will appear. You can delete it or add any additional information under the **Description** line. Enter the *Amount* and select *Save & close*.

The above method tracks pass-through donations assuming you usually only have one organization you are collecting for at a time. If you have several organizations you collect money for concurrently, you may wish to set up a separate class called *Pass-Through Donations* and then have sub-classes for each organization.

If you are using an RID scanner, scan all of the pass-through checks for an organization together as one deposit, and then record it as one entry instead of the individual checks. This makes it easier to keep the funds separate.

The total amount due to the other organization must now be set up as a bill to be paid. I'll walk you through that process in the next chapter.

I. Undeposited Funds

I hate to talk like an accountant, but I need to explain what QBO is doing behind the scenes for Undeposited Funds. QBO records the money coming in as revenue based on the account numbers you assigned to the items. In the accounting world, there must be two sides to each entry. Instead of recording the money straight into the **Checking** account, QBO posts the other side of the entry to the **Undeposited Funds** account. The system assumes that after you recorded the money in the accounting system, you've put that day's money in a safe or bank bag along with any other monies yet to be deposited. Think of **Undeposited Funds** as the stack of checks and money you have in that bank bag. Once the deposits are physically made, you tell QBO which checks went into each deposit.

When you are ready to deposit the money, including those through an RID scanner, go to *Plus, Other, Bank Deposit*.

This brings up the **Deposit** screen.

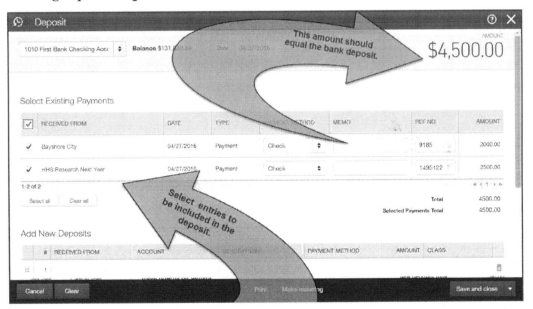

At the top, select the **Bank Account** where the deposit was made and the **Date** of the deposit. All sales receipts and payments you had previously entered, but not yet designated as deposited, will appear under **Select Existing Payments**. Choose the items for a particular deposit by clicking the box to the left of the entries included in that deposit. The total of cash and check entries should correspond with the deposits on your bank statement. If you used an RID scanner, select all the checks that were transmitted together. The top right corner of the screen will show the total of the deposit.

> The total of each deposit in the system must equal the total of each deposit submitted to the bank.

If the organization is tracking their checking account with the three subaccounts (unrestricted, temporarily restricted, and permanently restricted), the bookkeeper will need to record the donation as three different deposits—one for each subaccount.

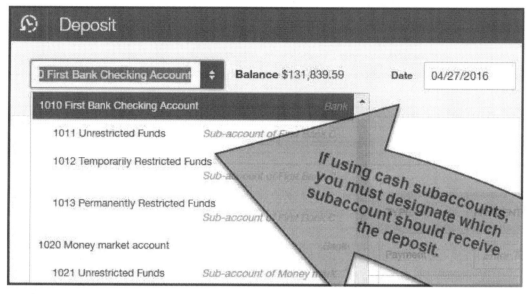

The total of all entries should also correspond to the collections totals from the sheet received from the person who collected the funds.

J. Printing a deposit slip

Select *Print* at the bottom center of the deposit screen to print a deposit slip and summary. If you have printable deposit slips, you can print a bank-ready form. The deposit forms are available from Intuit or your bank.

The first time you use a printable deposit slip, select *Setup and alignment* to test the margins and spacing.

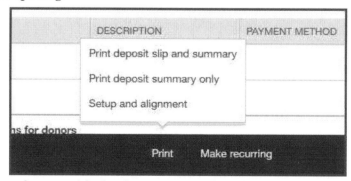

Once you are happy with the form setup, select *Print deposit slip and summary*. QBO will automatically save your deposit.

Deposit $4,500.00 saved

A **Deposit Summary** screen including all of the checks and cash you selected in the deposit screen will appear.

Deposit Summary

04/28/2016

Summary of Deposits to 1010 First Bank Checking Account on 04/28/2016

CHECK NO.	PMT METHOD	RECEIVED FROM	MEMO	AMOUNT
		Bayshore City		2000.00
1495122	Check	HHS:Research Next Year		2500.00
			DEPOSIT SUBTOTAL	4500.00
			LESS CASH BACK	
			DEPOSIT TOTAL	4500.00

Print the deposit summary and file it with the receipts document received from the financial secretary or treasurer. It will serve as your audit trail.

> Using **Undeposited Funds** makes reconciling your bank account *so* much easier. It summarizes the receipts deposited together so the total matches the deposit amount on your bank statement. Otherwise, you would have to select individual customer checks on the bank reconciliation screens until they added up to the total deposits.
> (This will be clearer in Chapter 12.)

K. Recurring Donations from Credit Cards

Organizations are increasingly encouraging donors to use credit cards to pay their pledges. Credit card receipts can be set up for online payments through a third party or through a service within QBO for a fee. You will need to research the fee structure and reports available to determine which makes the most sense for your organization. If you use a third party, you would input the receipt as we discussed above but change the **Payment Method** to the type of credit card. At the end of each month, you would record the credit card charges through a journal entry. I'll explain how to do that in Chapter 12.

If you are using the QBO service, go to the top of the **Receipt Payment** screen to see the **Accept payments online** link.

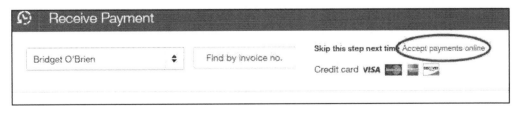

Select it and a set-up wizard will appear.

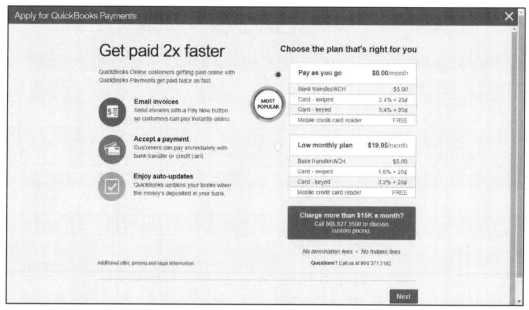

QBO processes the credit card and records the donation and the receipt into your records. Though there are fees, this process makes it much easier to reconcile the money deposited in the bank to the amount recorded in QBO.

In the next chapter we'll learn how to record the money going out.

10. Money Out—How Do I Pay the Bills?

A. Cash vs. Accrual Methods

Now that you know how to record the money coming in, it's time to work on the money going out. Before we get started, I'll need to throw a little accounting terminology at you.

There are two methods to account for expenses and revenues in the accounting world—Cash and Accrual. The cash method is the simplest. The cash is recorded in the financial statements when it is physically received and when the checks are written. The accrual method requires dating the transaction when the income was earned (i.e. when the grant was awarded) or the expense item was purchased, not necessarily when cash changed hands or a check was written.

For businesses or organizations that pay taxes or are publically held, the difference is significant. Nonprofit organizations can use either depending on their governing boards and donor or government requirements. Fortunately, QBO allows you to report the information either way.

Assume you receive an invoice from a contractor who did repairs to your office on July 31, but you didn't write him a check until August 15. If you enter the invoice with a date of July 31, you can run financial reports for July showing the expense by selecting the accrual method. If you were to run the report using the cash method, the expense would not appear until the August statements.

In case you are wondering why I'm telling you this, I'm going to have you input your bills on the accrual method so you have both options for reporting.

> The **accrual method** gives you the most accurate financial picture of your nonprofit, showing money you have earned and expenses you have incurred. The **cash basis** gives you a better idea of when the money has come in or gone out. By allowing you to run the reports either way, QBO gives you the best of both worlds.

B. Internal Accounting Controls for Paying Bills

Fraud, theft, and mistakes are as much of a concern with the money going out as they are with the money coming in. Procedures and controls need to be in place to keep phantom employees or fake vendor invoices from being paid. To assure good stewardship over your organization's money, you will need strong accounting controls as it relates to the money paid out.

> Remember the basic rule. If someone has access to the money, he should not have access to the financial records.

The bookkeeper must not be an authorized check signer. I know this sounds nearly impossible for a small organization, but, here again, you may need to utilize the members of the governing board or other volunteers.

Do not enter bills into the system without documentation and approval from someone other than the bookkeeper. This can be the executive director or treasurer. Sometimes the documentation is as simple as a bill from the utility company or a handwritten note asking the volunteer who drove someone to be reimbursed for his gas. If the expense is to be charged to more than one program, the approver should also notate this. Most importantly, all bills to be paid must be approved.

The bookkeeper will enter and code the bills into the correct expense categories and programs or grants. He will then print the checks, match them up with the approved documentation, and give them to an authorized check signer. The check signer should assure himself that the payee, address, and amounts agree to the approved documentation and sign the checks. The checks are then mailed and the documentation filed or scanned.

I recommend you use a voucher-style check. This allows a space for the payee to see what invoice was paid.

Your portion of the voucher should be stapled to the approved invoice and filed under the vendor's name. The check signer should never sign a check made out to him. A different signer is required for that.

You will want at least two authorized signers. Besides not allowing a signer to sign his own check, a signer may become unavailable and the organization will still need to pay their bills. Requiring two signatures over a certain dollar amount is another control, but be aware: with electronic scanning, banks no longer check for two signatures on the checks.

Don't forget about physical controls. Thefts do occur. A member of a cleaning crew once stole some checks from a client of mine and forged them. Keep your checks in a locked drawer or file cabinet, not just a locked office.

C. Controls for Electronic Payments

Paying bills online is a very convenient process. No more tracking down envelopes and stamps and running to the post office. However, the convenience makes it necessary to implement controls to assure all payments are recorded in the financial statements in a timely manner and no unauthorized payments are made.

> When making online payments, the bookkeeper should enter them into QBO before the association's authorized user submits the payments through the bank account or website. The bookkeeper can then give the list of payments to the authorized signer to submit. This is an especially important step to assure the cash balance is sufficient for the payments.

You may process payments electronically through QBO. This means one person can set up the vendor, enter the transaction, and send the payment electronically. While this is convenient, it does not separate the person making the entry from the person sending the money. Separate users with limited access will need to be established in the system. I'll explain how to do this in Chapter 16.

Your bank may offer bill payment through their website. If so, you will need to set up separate logins and passwords for the bill payment area and the reporting and downloading area. This is because you want to allow the bookkeeper to see the transactions and download them, while not having access to the money. Additionally, you do not want the person authorizing the payments to be able to manipulate the financial statements. Because each bank or service is different, you will need to work with their professionals to establish your logins and passwords.

If payments can be made directly through a vendor's website, the login and password combination must not be known to the bookkeeper. The bookkeeper will record the payment in QBO, but an authorized check signer should have the login and password combinations.

QBO also allows other companies to develop applications that work directly with the system. In Chapter 17, I explain Bills.com, an app to use for electronic payments.

D. Entering Bills

It's time to pay some bills. The mail has been opened, the bills approved and coded, and you are now ready to start entering. You will *enter* bills as they come in and *pay* bills when they are due.

As you have noticed in the other areas, there are several ways to access the bills area. One way is to go to *Plus, Vendors, Bill*. Clicking *Bill* will take you to a screen to start entering the invoices due.

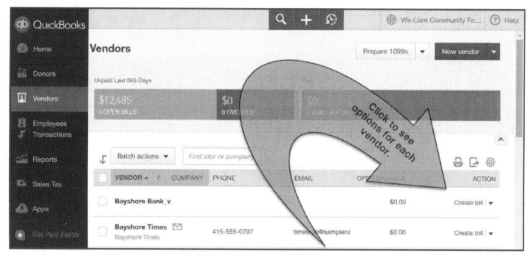

The **Vendors** tab on the left side menu bar will bring you to the **Vendor Center**.

The Vendor Center looks similar to the donor list in the Customer Center.

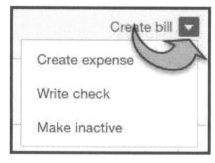

All vendors previously entered are listed. You can also create a **New vendor** using the blue button in the upper right corner of the screen.

If there are no open invoices for a particular vendor, you will see a **Create bill** link. If there are open invoices, the link will say **Make payment.**

Select the down arrow next to **Create bill** or **Make payment** for additional actions. I go over the **Create expense** and **Write check** options when we talk about paying bills later in the chapter. For now, let's focus on entering bills.

Whether you go through the *Plus* menu on the home page or click *Create bill* for a specific vendor in the **Vendor Center**, an entry screen for **Bill** will appear. If you highlight a vendor from the Vendor Center, that name will appear on the entry screen.

Once you have selected the **Vendor**, the address is automatically entered. Input the date of the invoice in the **Bill date** box. This is important in order to run reports on an accrual basis. The **Bill no.** should be the invoice number on the bill. If there is no invoice number, I like to use the date. At the top right, **BALANCE DUE** will update as you enter the details of the invoice. If you designated vendor-specific terms during setup, QBO will calculate the **Due date** automatically. If you didn't, you can use the drop-down arrow in the **Terms** field and select the appropriate date or leave it blank. Having an accurate due date helps the management of the cash flow.

The bottom half of the screen is where you will enter the individual line items of the invoice. There are two sections: **Account details** and **Item details**. You will primarily use the **Account details** section, though as I explained in Chapter 8, **Items** are useful to track the details you don't necessarily need on the financial statements.

Under **Account details**, you will enter separate lines for charges to accounts and their related classes. In the example above, the telephone bill is charged to two different programs. In the first line under **ACCOUNT,** select an account for the first item on the invoice. Start to type in the word or account number, and the drop-down menu will give you options. Next, in the **DESCRIPTION** area, explain why the money was spent. Input the dollar amount charged to the first program under **AMOUNT**.

The **BILLABLE** option is only needed if there are reimbursable expenses that can be billed back to a donor. If it was purchased for a grant or contract that needs to be tracked, select the *Sub-donor* from the **DONOR** drop-down menu. The last column is the **CLASS**. There should be a class (think program) designated for every expense item.

E. Beginning Accounts Payable Balance

If your organization has used the accrual method of accounting, you may have a balance in your accounts payable as of your start date. If so, each of the vendor invoices need to be entered into the system with an invoice date of the prior year. For example, if your beginning balance includes a $200 bill from a printing company from December of the prior year, enter it as a bill with a December invoice date. This will allow your beginning balance to reflect the correct amount in accounts payable.

F. Recurring Bills

Your organization probably has some bills that need to be paid each month, like rent, utilities, etc. QBO allows you to set up recurring bills and then reminds you to pay them. The process is similar to setting up recurring membership dues. Got to *Plus, Vendors, Bill* to bring up the **Bill** screen. Select *Make recurring* in the bottom center.

This will take you the **Recurring Bill** template. If you have just entered a bill for a vendor, the system will default to the last information entered for that vendor. You can make changes to any field before saving this template.

There are three template types relating to reminders, and they are found in the drop-down menu next to the vendor name. The first option, **Scheduled**, is the handiest. It will automatically enter the bill into your accounts to be paid. The second, **Reminder**, will add it to a reminders list that will pop up when you sign into QBO. The third option, **Unscheduled**, allows you to set up the memorized transaction but not remind you. This is used for items without a set schedule.

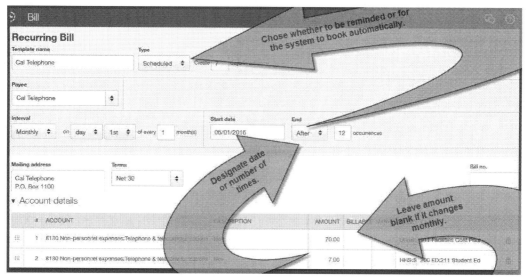

Next, the **Create X days in advance** tells QBO when to put it in the Accounts Payable list. This should be determined by how often you pay bills. If your organization pays weekly, seven days should be sufficient.

You need to determine how often you want the bill to be added. As the above example is for a utility bill, I have selected *Monthly* in the **Interval** section. I now need to let the system know the **Start date**, i.e. the date of the next invoice, and when I want it to **End**. The **End** menu gives three options: **None, By**, and **After**. The **By** option allows you to enter an end date; the **After** option goes by number of occurrences. By selecting *After* with *12 occurrences*, I am telling the system to keep generating these bills monthly until 6/1/2017.

If you pay the same amount for the bill each month, like rent, then go ahead and input the amount of rent. But for bills that vary (water or electricity, for example), leave the amount blank. Select *Save template* when you are done.

If you go a little crazy making recurring transaction, don't worry. You can always find all **Recurring Transactions** from the **Gear Icon** under **Lists**. From here, you can edit or delete any transaction template.

G. Editing and Deleting Bills

When viewing Cal Telephone, I noticed I entered the wrong amount for the November phone bill.

To remedy this situation, I need to click anywhere on the line of the highlighted bill with the error. This will bring up the bill as it was entered.

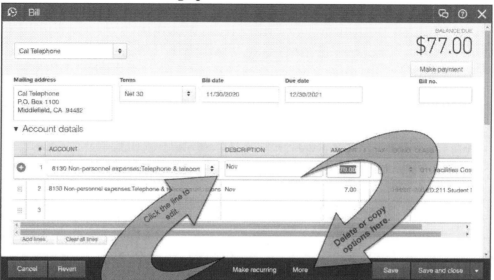

You can now edit the amounts, expense accounts, or classes. In this case, I changed the amount in line one from $707 to $70 then selected *Save and close*.

If this bill was a duplicate, you would need to delete it. At the bottom of the bill screen, select *More* and then *Delete*. A warning box will appear asking if you are sure. If you are, select *Yes*, and you will go back to the list of transactions for that vendor.

H. Paying Bills

You have entered all the bills and are now ready to cut the checks, but bills are not necessarily due at the same time. I'll show you how to select which bills you want to pay. Go to the *Plus, Vendors, Pay Bills*. The **Pay Bills** screen will list all bills due by a certain date or, if you prefer, all bills.

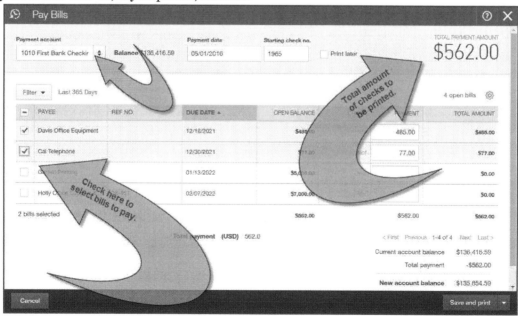

Check the **Payment account** to ascertain that the correct checking account is being charged. The default bank account is the last account used when paying bills. This can be overridden using the drop-down arrow. It will display the current system account balance (not the bank balance). **Payment date** is the date you want printed on the checks. The **Starting check no.** will default to the next check in the series from any previous printings, but can be overridden. The system will tell you how much money will be required in the top right corner.

The **Filter** option allows you to display invoices by a range of due dates and/or by vendors. If a large number of bills appears on the screen, you may want to sort them. Do this by double-clicking on the title of the column you want sorted, i.e. sort alphabetically by vender by clicking on the **Payee** title or sort by largest to smallest amounts by choosing the **Open Balance** column.

Choose the bills to be paid by selecting the small box to the left of the bill. You can choose all or some of the bills to pay. At the bottom of the screen, the system shows you the current cash balance and the impact of all the bills selected.

Once you have selected the bills you would like to pay, *Save and print*. This takes you to the **Print Checks** screen.

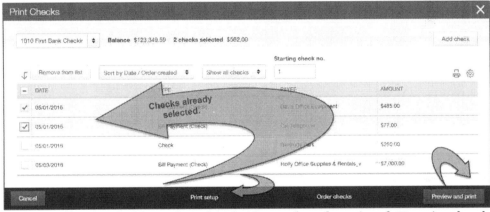

Think of this as a holding place for checks ready to be printed. To print the checks for the two bills we selected above, choose *Preview and print*. If this is the first time you are printing checks, you will be taken to a set up screen to confirm the type of check to be used.

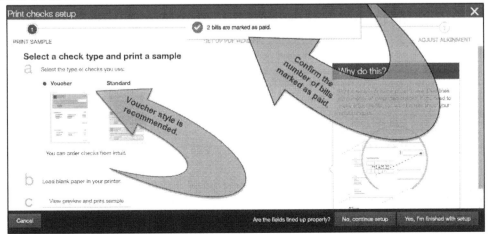

QBO will prompt you to do some test prints on a blank sheet of paper. Hold the sample up to the light over a check to see if everything is lined up before you start to print. This is also a good time to test whether you need to place checks face up or face down in your printer. I do this by placing an **X** on the blank sheet and see what side it prints on.

If the lines do not align properly, chose *No, continue setup*. A screen will appear allowing you to change margins. Run another test page, and when you are happy with the test check, select *Yes, I'm finished with the setup*. The good news is you only need to test your setup the first time you print checks. When you receive a new box of checks, I recommend doing this again, just to play it safe.

The **Print preview** screen will appear.

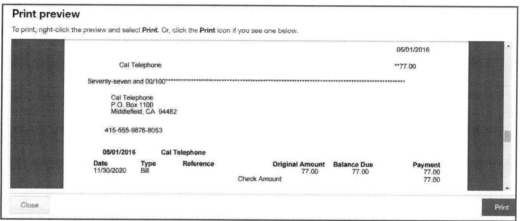

If the blank checks are ready in the printer, select *Print*. The system will bring up a dialog box asking to verify that the checks printed correctly.

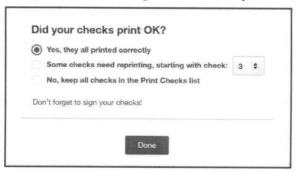

The system will default to **YES**. If the checks printed correctly, choose *Done*. If the printer jammed and the last check is unreadable, QBO makes it easy to reprint the check. Simply select *Some checks need reprinting* and choose the check number. Place new checks in the printer and click *Done* to reprint the checks.

I. Online Banking Payments

If you utilize online banking through your bank's website, you will still enter all the bills and select bills to pay as mentioned above. But on the **Pay Bills** screen, you will enter *Online Payment* in the **Starting check no.** field.

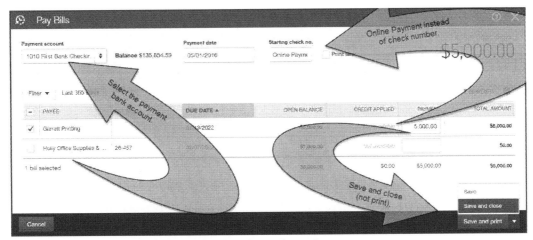

Save and close instead of **Save and print** when done.

J. Write Checks

I'm sure you have been in the situation that all of your checks have been printed, but a workman steps in and wants his check today. Rather than enter this as a bill that then needs to be paid in the future, you can write (enter) a check directly from the **Check** screen.

Go to *Plus, Vendors, Check*. The **Check** screen will appear.

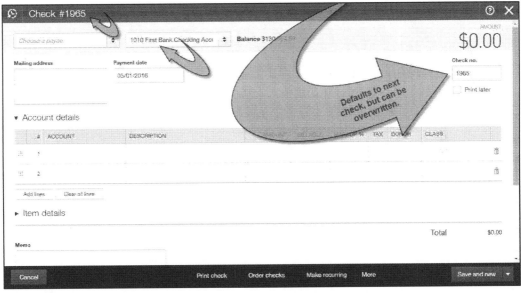

Notice this screen has similar fields to the **Bill** screen, including **Account details** and **Item details**. The check entry screen will say **Check no.** at the top followed by the defaulted next available check number. Don't worry if that isn't the check number you will be using. If you click **Print later**, you can assign a different number when you print the check.

> QBO screens can look very similar. Always check the screen title at the top left to be sure you are in the correct screen.

Payment date will default to today's date. Make sure the correct checking account is showing. The account **Balance** will show the amount QBO has recorded in the bank before you write the check.

Key in the vendor's name in the **Choose a payee** area. The options under this drop-down include all vendors, customers, and employees who have been set up previously. This will be a longer list than you saw under **Bills**, where only the vendors are listed. If the payee has been input before, scroll down until you find her name listed as a vendor.

In this example, Gertrude Park is a new vendor. When I input her name, an **Add Gertrude Park** message appears.

When you click on that message, a **New Name** box will open. From this popup screen, you have two options. You can just click *Save* to add her name only. Her other information can be added later. Use this option if you want to get names in quickly and don't need all the additional information that is tracked for vendors or donors.

> Be sure to add **Details** if the vendor may need a 1099.
> If the vendor is an independent contractor, you will need his Federal Identification Number or Social Security Number.
> There are links to the IRS publications regarding Form 1099 at
> http://accountantbesideyou.com/irs-forms.
> I also explain the difference between employees and independent contractors in detail in
> *Church Accounting—The How-To Guide for Small & Growing Churches.*

If you select *Details,* an entry menu for a new vendor, donor, or employee appears and allows you to key in all the related information. If the check is to be mailed, use the **Details** option to input the address. *Save* when done.

Either option will take you back to the **Check** screen, where you can enter the amount, the account or item it should be charged to, and the class.

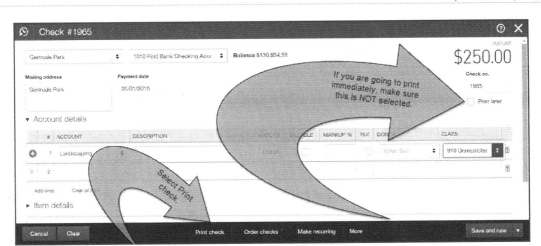

To print the check immediately, make certain the **Print later** is NOT selected. Select *Print check* at the bottom of the screen. The **Print Checks** screen will appear.

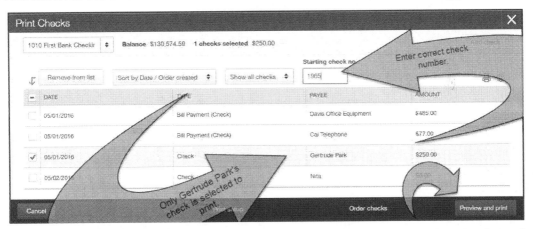

The check you are printing should be the only one selected. Put the check in the printer, type in the check number, and select *Preview and print*.

Employee and donor reimbursements can be paid through the **Check** screen. If you use the **Bill** screen to input their invoices, you will need to set up vendor accounts with a different name than their donor or employee name. One option is to put a small "v" after the name to differentiate (i.e. **Smith, J** is the donor and **Smith, J v** is the vendor account).

K. Handwritten Checks

Sometimes you may need to write a check by hand and enter it into the system later. You will do this through the **Check** option. The same fields are required for entry. The only difference is to enter a check number manually.

Deselect the **Print later** box and input the check number from the handwritten check. The rest of the information is entered as before. Then *Save and close*, and the check is recorded.

L. Bank Drafts

If you have recurring bank drafts, it is easiest to memorize them through the **Check** screen. Go to *Plus, Vendors, Check.*

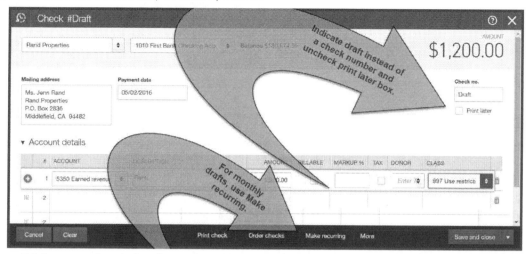

Make sure the **Print later** box is unselected and type *Draft* in the check number area. If the amount is the same for each month, go ahead and enter it. If not, leave the amount blank. Fill out the rest of the form and then click *Make recurring* just as you did for recurring bills. If an amount was entered, the system will deduct it from the cash account. If not, you will edit this check when you receive the bank statement for the amount charged. Finish by selecting *Save and close.*

M.   Entering Expenses Paid by Credit Card Manually

Some of the organization's employees may have a credit card in the organization's name. The charges need to be supported by receipts, entered into the system, and the bill paid. One of the time-saving advantages of QBO is the ability to connect to your organization's credit card company and download the transactions automatically into the system. I'll go over that in the Chapter 12, but in case you do not use that functionality, here is how to input the credit card charges manually.

There are two basic approaches. The first option is to hand the employee a copy of the bill when it arrives and require them to fill out an expense report detailing what each expense was for. The receipts are then attached to the expense report and submitted to a supervisor for approval. The approved expense report is given to the bookkeeper to enter as a bill.

The second option is to have the employee hand in receipts for approval as they use the credit card. The treasurer then knows how much cash will be needed to pay the bill when it arrives.

In QBO, credit card charges are handled a little differently than other bills. Instead of entering the charges through the Vendor Center, go to *Plus, Vendors, Expense.*

Once again, the screen is very similar to the **Bill** screen. Enter the name of the business from the credit card receipt into the **Choose a payee** field. Many of these will be new vendors, so just *Quick Add* them rather than choosing the **Detail** option as discussed earlier. If you already have outstanding bills with a particular vendor, QBO will ask you to be certain you want to enter it in this screen.

Any account set up with a credit card account type will be available from the drop-down arrow. Choose the credit card you are working with. **Payment date** will default to today and can be changed to the date on the receipt if desired. Select the type of credit card you are using from the drop-down menu of the **Payment method** box.

Next, break down the expenditure by expense account under the **Account details** section. Type in any description that may be useful. Enter the **Amount** and **Class** for each charge.

A very handy feature is the ability to scan the receipt and attach it to the entry. Scroll to the bottom to see the paperclip icon.

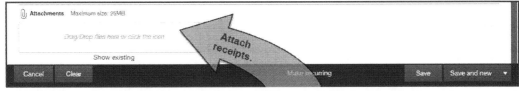

Clicking the box will bring up a menu box to select the scanned receipts you wish to attach. When you are finished, select *Save and new* to enter the next receipt or *Save and close* to finish.

Remember!
For any recurring expenses, you still need the receipts approved.

N. Paying the Credit Card Bill

When it is time to pay the credit card bill, you will use the **Check** screen. Go to *Plus, Vendors, Check*.

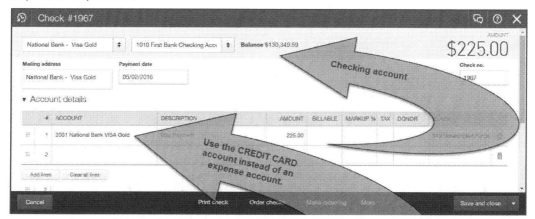

Enter the credit card vendor and select the checking account that the check or draft will come from. The **ACCOUNT** is not an expense, but the credit card account in the general ledger, usually a 2xxx series number. Click *Save and close*.

O. Credits Received from Vendors

Credits are often received from vendors or your credit card. These most often occur when you return an item. The vendor issues a credit to the account, lowering the amount due. You will need to enter this credit before you pay the vendor.

Go to *Plus, Vendors, Vendor Credit*.

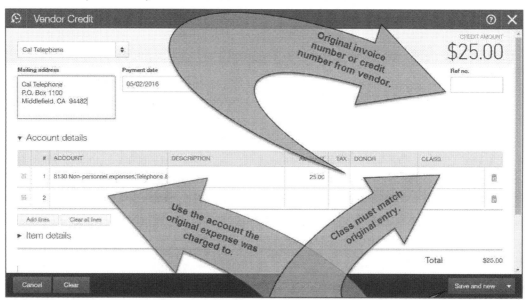

Enter the vendor's name, the credit number or the invoice number it is to be applied against, and the amount. Then enter the same expense account and class of original invoice. Select *Save and new* or *Save and close*.

If you have an open balance with this vendor, when you highlight the vendor on the **Pay Bills** screen, you will see the credit listed below the blank box.

Simply type in the amount of the credit you wish to apply and then write the checks.

If the bill has not yet been entered for the vendor, the credit will appear in a column to the right of the screen and can be applied against the new bill or expense.

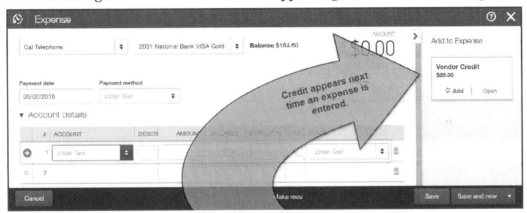

To issue a credit for a credit card, go to *Plus, Vendors, Credit Card Credit* and follow the same procedures.

This has been a long, detailed chapter. Take a break and I'll explain the payroll options in QBO and how to enter them in the next chapter.

11. Payroll

There are numerous ways nonprofits prepare their payroll. Most use an outside service that takes care of all the tax and reporting requirements and allows for direct deposits. Others use an accountant to handle it for them. Some prepare their payroll themselves.

QuickBooks offers payroll services that will link directly into your company file. This will save some data entry time, so when you are evaluating prices and services of QuickBooks Payroll and other outside services, please keep this in mind. Here is a chart showing QuickBooks Payroll options.

Please note, neither Eulica nor I are associated with QuickBooks, nor do we express an opinion on which payroll service is best suited for your organization. Similar options are available from other payroll services.

QuickBooks Payroll Subscription Levels			
Features	Basic	Enhanced	Full Service
My organization wants to:	Do payroll in house		Let the experts do it
Monthly cost	$25.00	$30.00	$99.00
Integrates with QBO	√	√	√
Easy paycheck, simply enter hours worked	√	√	√
Pay by check or direct deposit	√	√	√
Free support	√	√	√
Electronically files W-2's-year-end		√	√
Includes payroll tax forms		√	√
Intuit files & pays taxes			√
No tax penalties, guaranteed			√
Payroll set up completed			√
Free year-end forms included			√

Please note, neither Eulica nor I are associated with QuickBooks, nor do we express an opinion on which payroll service is best suited for your organization. Similar options are available from other payroll services.

> For additional information about the details surrounding payroll issues, please consider my book, *Church Accounting: The How-To Guide for Small & Growing Churches*. There are three chapters covering payroll, including the intricacies of minister's payroll, how to calculate payroll, and how to file the reports.

So now, I will walk you through the most common approach to payroll: how to record the payroll from an outside service.

A. Using Journal Entries to Record Payroll

Recording payroll can be done via a journal entry or through the **Check** screen. First I'll explain the journal entry option. If you will recall, you used the journal entry approach to record your beginning balances. You will now use it to record each period's payroll.

The first thing I like to do is design a spreadsheet for the journal entry. This is an extra step, but it assures that once I have all of the allocations completed, the entry will balance.

	A	B	C	D	E
	Description	Account	Class	Debit	Credit
6	Total Gross Pay	Salaries	Research	5,000.00	
7	Total Gross Pay	Salaries	Education	3,000.00	
8	Total Gross Pay	Salaries	Mangement	4,000.00	
9	Employer Liabilities	Payroll Tax Expense	Research	2,000.00	
10	Employer Liabilities	Payroll Tax Expense	Education	400.00	
11	Employer Liabilities	Payroll Tax Expense	Mangement	752.00	
12	Benefit Contributions Withheld	Other Withholding Liability	Unrestricted		500.00
13	Non-Direct Deposit Check	Cash	Unrestricted		1,680.00
14	Net Pay Allocations	Cash	Unrestricted		10,248.00
15	Employee Tax Withholding	Cash	Unrestricted		1,572.00
16	Employer Liabilities	Cash	Unrestricted		1,152.00
17	Totals			$ 15,152.00	$ 15,152.00

Starting from the bottom, this entry assumes the payroll service has electronically pulled the net pay ($10,248), the employee tax withholdings ($1,572), and the employer liabilities ($1,152) out of the cash account in separate amounts. It also reflects a check written to an employee that did not use direct deposit ($1,680). This is important to list separately as it will clear the bank as a check.

The Benefit Contributions Withheld ($500) went into a liability account as the organization will need to write a check to the benefit company for that withholding. The tax expenses did not have to go to a liability account because the payroll service has already withdrawn the money. If your payroll service does not pay the taxes on your behalf, you would need to record those into liability accounts and then write the appropriate checks.

> Look at your bank statement to see how the payroll service pulls the money out of your cash account. Then design your journal entry to match, which will make reconciling the bank account easier.
>
> For example, if the payroll service charges your checking account with three amounts each month—net pay, employee withholding, and payroll taxes—you will want to assure that your journal entry credits (reduces) the bank account with those three numbers separately, not one complete payroll number.

Go to *Plus, Other, Journal Entry.*

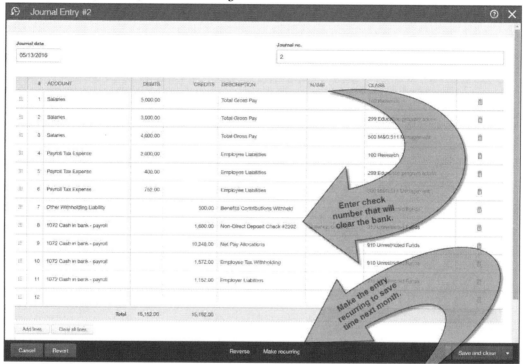

As you key in the account numbers and amounts, please note the system does not require you to use the lowest sub-account on this screen. You will need to be extra careful that you are using the correct account, especially if you are using sub-accounts to track restricted cash.

The gross pay needs to be allocated to the correct accounts and classes. If some of the payroll time should be charged to a grant or contract, select the correct **Sub-donor (grantee)** in the **Name** column for that amount. If the reports from your payroll service do not group the employees by program, ask your payroll representative if that can be arranged. Having their reports already total the dollars by program makes entering the journal entry much easier.

> All expense items, including payroll, must have a designated class. This is how the expenses are allocated to programs.

For any payroll that will not be direct deposited, record the check number in the **DESCRIPTION** to make reconciling the bank account easier. If your payroll is consistent, consider **Make recurring** to have the system record it automatically each month. You will need to edit the entry for the actual data, but it will save data entry time.

B. Entering Payroll through the Check Entry Screen

The other way to enter payroll from the outside service is through the **Check** screen. This is in lieu of the journal entry. You must be very careful that each bank draft item is treated as a separate check. Set up a vendor called **Payroll** and record the first check for the net pay.

Under the **Account details** section, you would need to record the gross pay levels by class. Employee withholdings are coded to the Payroll Withholdings account with a negative sign in front of the amount. This is to make the check equal the net pay the employees actually received.

Using the example above, you would then write three more checks—two for the other drafts and one for the non-direct deposit amount. If your payroll stays fairly consistent, use **Make recurring** and edit the checks for the following pay periods.

C. Paying the Benefit Contribution

There is one more thing to do before we finish up the payroll. We need to pay any benefit contribution that was withheld. You will do this through the **Check** screen.

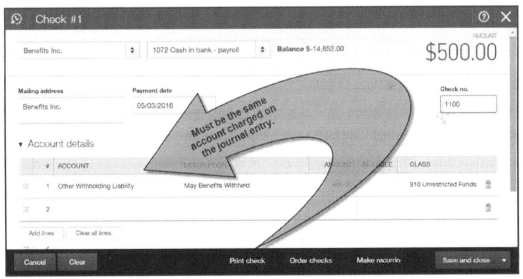

Enter the name of the benefit provider, but under **Account details**, select the liability account charged in the payroll entry. When finished, *Save and close*. This should now zero out the liability account.

I'll be adding additional resources to explain how payroll works regardless of your accounting system. Check out www.AccountantBesideYou.com periodically to see what is available.

You now know how to enter your donations and pay your bills. Next I'll show you how to reconcile your bank and credit card accounts.

12. Bank Feeds & Reconciliations

In the last few chapters, you have learned how to manually receive donations and pay bills in QBO. Next, Eulica and I will show you how to utilize QBO's **Bank Feed** function to save time in data entry and reconciliations.

A. Banking

The bank feed and bank rules features in QBO allow you to connect your bank, credit card, and payment processing accounts (PayPal, for example) to QBO. Let's take a look at the **Banking** screen in the TestDrive sample company to see what this looks like. Go to the left *Menu Bar, Transactions, Banking*.

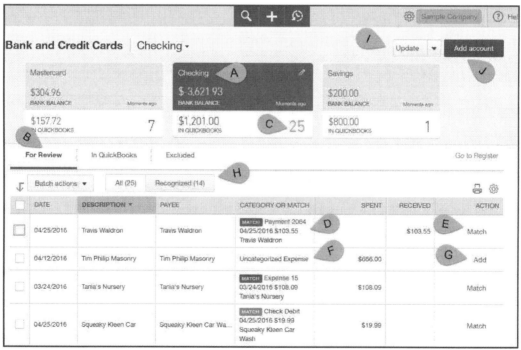

These features automate the assignment of account numbers to each transaction by using predefined assumptions and rules. For example, you may have your electrical bill automatically debited from your bank account. When QBO sees a transaction with electricity or power in the description, it will suggest that this transaction belongs to utilities.

Here you will find any connected bank, credit card, and/or payment accounts (think PayPal or Square).

A- The account currently selected is blue, and only the transactions in that account are displayed.

B- The dark blue line indicates the **For Review** tab is selected. These transactions are NOT in QBO yet.

C- There are 25 transactions for this account that require review and acceptance.

D- **Match** indicates QBO has identified what it believes is a matching payment for an existing open invoice.

E- Click *Match* if you agree that this transaction is related to a previously entered invoice and it should be added to QBO. This will apply the payment to the invoice (or the receipt to a donor invoice).

F- For any payments QBO does not recognize how to match, the system will label as an **Uncategorized Expense.** By clicking on the line, you can view the downloaded details and the related options. Select the correct account from the chart of accounts. If the amount should be split between accounts, The **Split** button will allow you to charge the expense to more than one account.

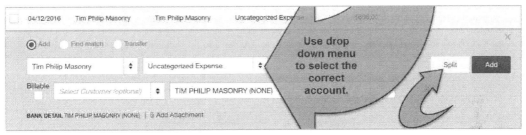

G- Back at the Banking Center screen, **Add** will record the entry after you have selected the correct category or categories for it.

H- The **Recognized** tab lists all of the matched or assigned transactions. Each should be reviewed.

I- The **Update** button brings in any new transactions. The small down arrow next to it will allow you to manage rules. I will explain how rules work shortly.

J- The **Add (Connect) account** will add a new bank or credit card account.

B. Connecting Your Accounts

Let's go back to the **Bank** screen in your QBO account. Select *Transactions, Banking.* If there are already accounts connected, you will see the **Bank** screen similar to the one we worked with in the previous section. Select *Add account.* If there are no accounts already set up, you will see a screen similar to the one below.

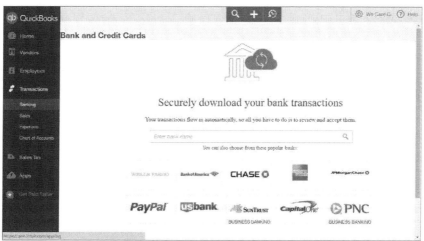

QBO has a relationship with most major banks in the US. Select the logo of your bank, if it is listed. If not, start typing in the bank name. The system will give you a drop-down list of options. If your bank is not listed, they may not have an agreement with QBO to connect your account, but I would call the bank just to make sure.

After selecting your bank, log in using your same username and password you use to access your account online on the bank's website.

This allows QBO to retrieve your account information from online banking. Every account you have at this bank will appear in the list; select any accounts used by your organization, clicking the box to the left of it.

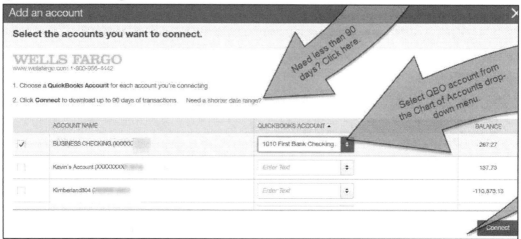

Next, choose the corresponding **QuickBooks Account** (think chart of accounts) for each account. The account may already be in your chart of accounts, or if it is new, you can create by selecting *Add new* from the drop-down menu.

You can download up to 0, 7, 30, or 90 days of checks, deposits, and other transactions. When you are done, click *Connect* to go back to the **Bank** screen.

1.   Understanding Bank Feeds

After an account is connected to your QBO Company, income and expense transactions will automatically import into the Bank area for review. They will not be entered into QBO until you match them to open invoices or chart of account numbers and accept them.

You will still create invoices (Chapter 9) for dues and pledges, and enter bills and write checks (Chapter 10). We learned in Chapters 9 and 10 how to enter these transactions manually and by recurring transactions. For example, you entered the phone bill and paid it by check. When the check clears the bank, it will download with your bank feed, and QBO will **Match** it with the check in the system.

Deposits will download as lump sums from the bank. If you have used the Undeposited Funds option and grouped your individual donations into deposits, the system should match them automatically.

If you have automatic drafts for normal recurring expenses, the system will try to "guess" the account if there isn't an invoice already set up. To take the guessing out, you can set up **Bank Rules**.

2.   Understanding Bank Rules

Bank rules are predefined conditions that tell QBO how to categorize transactions. Rules scan bank items for particular details and then assign specific payees and categories to them, saving you time matching the bank information to your accounts.

You can add and edit rules by going to *Menu Bar, Transactions, Banking*. In the upper right hand corner, you will find a box labeled **Update.** Click on the down arrow.

Select *Manage rules* to see a screen similar to this one:

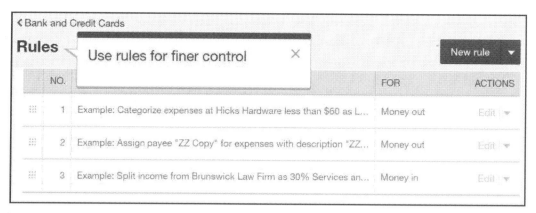

The rules are based on the text downloaded from the bank, the description, and/or the amount. Start by selecting *New rule* to see a screen similar to this one.

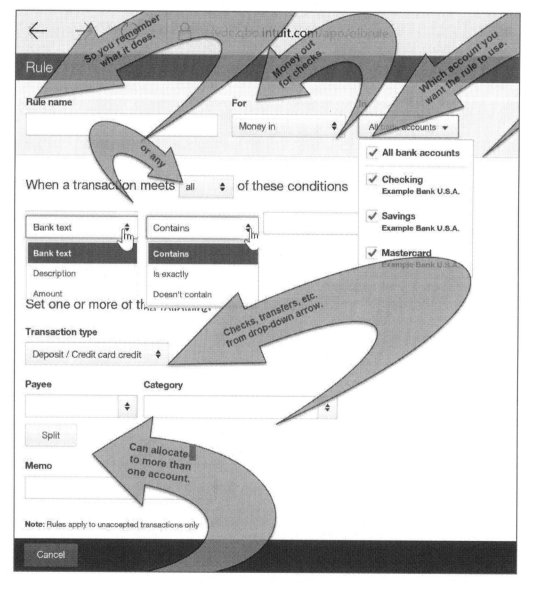

Assign a **Rule name**. Keep it simple enough to remind you what the rule does. The **For** option is **Money in** or **Money out**. If the rule is for a deposit, use Money in; if for a vendor, use Money out.

The **All bank accounts** box has a drop-down menu allowing you to select which account this rule should apply to. For example, if all checks are paid from a general operating checking account, that is the only one that should be selected for any vendor rules. If it is a rule related to credit card charges, you may want to select only the MasterCard option.

The next line defines whether the rule will be run when **all** or **any** of the conditions are met. You are allowed up to five conditions per rule. The next three boxes set the conditions. First select whether the system should look for the **Bank text, Description**, or the **Amount** from the downloaded data. Then chose whether it **Contains,** reflects **Exactly**, or **Doesn't contain** the information you key into the third box.

The **Transaction type** will tell the system whether to record it as an expense, check, transfer, or deposit. Select the **Payee** from the drop-down list and the **Category** from your chart of accounts. The **Split** button allows you to allocate the expense to more than one account.

Click *Save* when done, and the new rule will be added to your list of rules. Though the set up takes a bit of effort, it is rather easy and saves you time recording future entries

3. Posting Feed Transactions

Transactions imported from your bank account are **not** automatically posted to QBO. You must review and accept each transaction to post it. Go to the left menu and select *Transactions, Banking*.

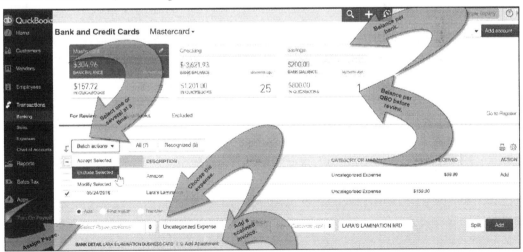

A recognized transaction will have a match—a rule has been applied, or QBO uses categories from related transactions. But the system doesn't record the match. You still must say it is okay to post. **Uncategorized Expenses** need to have the **Payee** and **Expense** assigned. You can attach a scanned invoice if desired.

A transaction may also be **Excluded** if you find that it does not belong in the accounting records at all. This may be a bank error or duplicate transaction. The three tabs on this screen show which downloaded transactions are **For Review**, **In QuickBooks**, and which are **Excluded**.

It short, you still have to pay attention! There is no autopilot. But using these features will save you lots of time once you get the hang of it.

> Working with **Bank Feeds** does not move any actual money to and from your accounts at the bank.
> The Bank Feed review process is only telling QBO what has happened in the bank account.

C. Preparing for the Bank Reconciliation

Now it is time to reconcile the bank accounts. However, rarely is there a month with only donation receipts and normal bill paying. You may have transferred cash between accounts, received an insufficient funds check from a donor, or voided a check you had written. All these will affect your bank reconciliation. So I am going to step you through a few things to do before you start the reconciliation process.

1.   Internal Controls and Bank Reconciliations

The bank statements should be received and opened by someone besides the bookkeeper. This person should review the checks paid and question any payments made to the bookkeeper or to an unknown vendor. If the bank does not send copies of the scanned checks, the reviewer should have access to the online banking program to view the checks. Paying fake vendors is a very common way to steal money, so any unusual or double payments should be investigated immediately. After verifying accuracy of the payments, the reviewer should initial the statement and give it to the bookkeeper to reconcile. The reconciliation should never be performed by anyone who has access to the cash.

2.   Cash Transfers

Most organizations have a separate investment account from the checking account. If you deposit all donations into the checking account, you will want to transfer any excess cash into the investment account. When you need the funds, you will then transfer the appropriate amount from the investment account back into the checking.

There are two ways this is usually done. A check may be written from one account and deposited into the second account. Or the transfer is made through the bank or investment company's website or customer service associate. I'll walk you through how to record each of these ways in QBO.

a)   Transfers without Writing a Check

In this first example, we will assume the money has been transferred online. Select *Plus, Other, Transfer*.

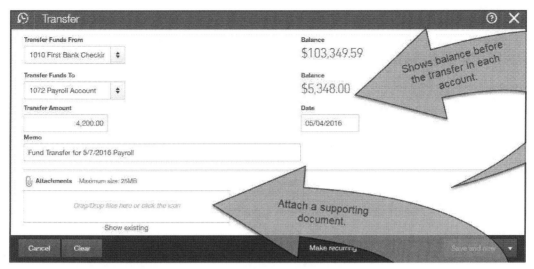

In the **Transfer Funds From** box, select from the drop-down menu the account the money was taken from. The system will show you the book balance before the transfer. Next, in the **Transfer Funds To** box, select the account the money was transferred to. Enter the **Transfer Amount** and the **Date**. In the **Memo** area, key in the reason for the transfer. If there is a supporting document you would like to have associated with this transfer, attach the file as I showed you in the previous chapter. Select *Save and close,* and your transfer has been recorded.

> At the time of this printing, you cannot assign a class to bank transfers. If you need this option, use the transfer cash via check option below.

b)   Transfer Cash via Check

If you transfer cash between accounts by physically writing a check, you will take a different approach. This method also allows you to assign classes to your transfer transactions. Go to *Plus, Vendor, Check.*

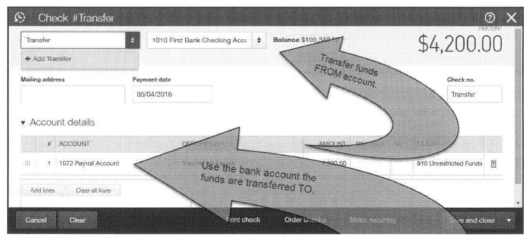

For the **Payee**, you will need to set up a vendor called Transfer. From the payee drop-down menu, type *Transfer* and click *Add Transfer*. Then, select *Details* to access the **Vendor Information** screen.

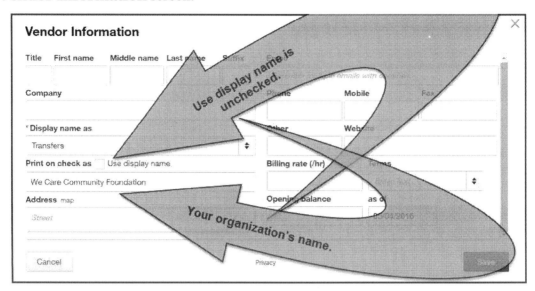

The **Display name as** *Transfers* shows up. The small box next to **Use display name** must be unchecked. Key in your organization's name in the **Print on check as** box. The other items can be left blank. Select *Save* to return to the **Check Transfer** screen (previous page).

In the **Bank Account** field, choose the account you are writing the check or transferring the money from. Now go to the bottom under **Account details**. Enter the amount of the transfer. Even though we usually select an expense account here, the drop-down menu includes the complete chart of accounts. Select the cash/bank or investment account this check will be deposited *to*, enter the related **Class,** and *Save & close.*

When you physically deposit this check, put it on a separate deposit slip. Recall that your other receipts go through Undeposited Funds and are therefore grouped together by deposit record. This transaction will not be included in the undeposited funds, but will show up in the bank reconciliation on its own.

3.   Returned Checks

Every so often you may have a check returned by the bank because a donor did not have sufficient funds in his account. You will need to take this out of the checking account in the system, record the bank fee for processing the bounced check, and invoice the donor for the original amount plus the fee.

In this example, the $50 check Ms. Jimenez wrote for dues was returned for non-sufficient funds. First, you will create an invoice to charge Ms. Jimenez for the returned check amount and the returned check fee. Go to *Plus, Donors, Invoice.* Under the **Product/Service** field, use the drop-down menu to create an item called "Returned Check – First Bank Account."

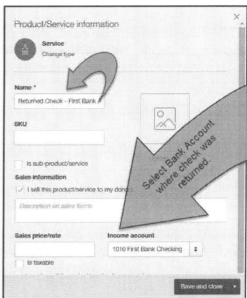

Because the item is tied directly to the bank account, you will need to create a returned check item. In the **Product/Service** details, choose the *Bank Account* instead of an **Income account**. *Save and close* when complete, and you will be back to the invoice.

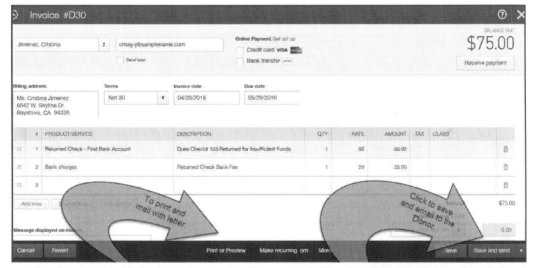

The first item of the invoice is the "Returned Check–First Bank Account" for the exact amount of the original check, and the second line is the returned check fee. You can *Print* and mail with a cover letter or *Save and send* to email this invoice to the donor email on record. Follow the regular Receive Payment step as discussed in Chapter 9 when the payment for the returned check is received.

4.   Voiding a Check

There will be times that you need to void a lost check or one made out for the wrong amount. Luckily, QBO makes this easy as you can void in the **Check** screen. *Search* using the magnifying glass icon on any screen.

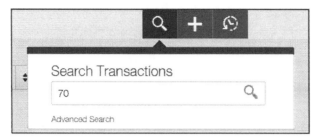

Type in the check number or vendor name and choose the transaction you wish to void. Click on the *clock icon* in the upper left corner to see a drop-down list of recent checks.

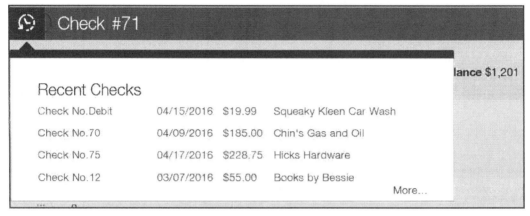

Double click on the check you wish to void to bring up the **Check** screen.

Select, *Void* from the **More** menu found at the bottom of the check screen. Never use the **Delete** option as it does not leave an audit trail. QBO will ask you if you are sure you want to void the check and will display a success message when you click *Yes*.

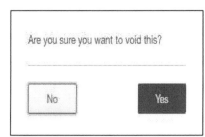

When you void the check, it records the check number in the system with an amount of $0, so there is an audit trail. After the check is voided, the screen reappears with **Voided** in the memo box and the amount as $0.

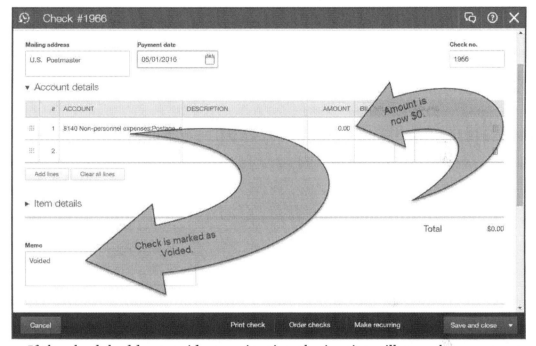

If the check had been paid on an invoice, the invoice will now show as an open accounts payable. A new check can be printed to replace the voided one from the **Pay Bills** menu. If the bill was entered incorrectly, double click on the bill line item and edit it before reprinting the check. If you do not need to reissue the check, you will need to void the original invoice as discussed in Chapter 10.

To make certain the vendor account is now correct, select *Vendors* from the side menu and scroll down to see the vendor whose check you just voided. For our example, the vendor detail for US Postmaster is showing the amount for check #1966 as $0 since it was voided.

> The system allows you to enter transactions directly into the check register, but I would like to discourage you from doing so.
> You will get more accurate and detailed reports by entering your data through the transaction screens.

D. Reconciling the Bank Account

Time to balance your checkbook, which QBO calls **Reconcile**. First, I would like you to make certain the system has recorded all of the money from undeposited funds into the checking account. Go to *Plus, Other, Bank Deposit*

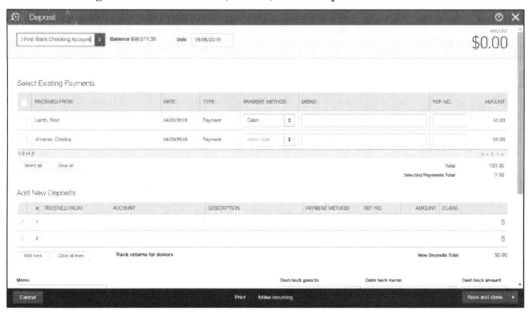

Be sure the total of the selected payments matches the deposit amount listed on the bank statement and select *Save & close*. I encourage you to check this screen each month before you begin reconciling to assure all deposits are recorded. It will save time during the reconciliation.

Next, look at your bank statement for any automatic drafts or other charges. Compare those to the check register to see if all of them were entered. If not, go ahead and enter the missing charges through the Write Check screen as we discussed in Chapter 10.

From the *Gear icon*, select *Tools, Reconcile*.

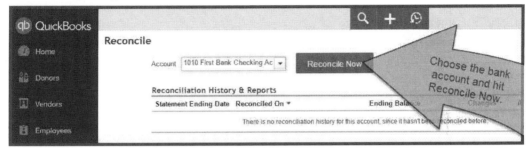

Choose the appropriate bank account. If you are using subaccounts under checking, reconcile only the parent account.

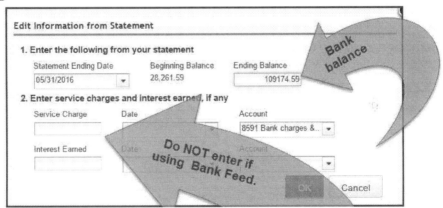

From your bank statement, you will need to enter the **Statement Ending Date** and **Ending Balance**.

Additionally, look for any service charges or interest earned on the bank statement. Enter them in their respective fields with corresponding accounts. The bank service fee on the statement should go to a bank charges expense account and interest earned should go to an interest income account. If you are using the Bank Feed function, do NOT input amounts in these fields. They have already been recorded in the system. Select *OK* to continue.

Now it's time to compare transactions you've entered into QBO to the bank statement.

The left side of this screen contains every check, bill payment, and cash transfer out of this bank account. The right side contains all deposits. Additionally, you will see zero dollar amounts for any voided transactions. Check those off as well.

You will scroll down the checks and payments side and select any of those that have cleared the bank. Notice at the top of the screen there is an option to **Hide transactions after the statement's end date**. This option displays fewer transactions on the screen to have to scroll through.

After you have selected all the payments that have cleared, look towards the bottom of the screen.

Edit Information from Statement	Beginning Balance	28,261.59
	10 Checks and Payments	37,292.00
Service Charge	6 Deposits and Other Credits	
Interest Earned		118,205.00
	Statement Ending Balance	109,174.59
	Cleared Balance	109,174.59
	Difference	0.00

You will see a line that totals the **Checks and Payments** selected. This amount should total the **Checks and Other Withdrawals, Debits, and Service Charges** on your bank statement. **Deposits and Other Credits** totals the selected deposits above. This amount should tie to the total of **Deposits, Credits, and Interest** on your bank statement. If either of these two do not match, your account will most likely not reconcile.

It's a good idea to mark each check off on the hard copy statement as you check them off in QBO. If the total payments match, you are ready to go to the deposit side. If they do not match, check to see if a payment has cleared the bank that you have not entered or if you have marked a transaction as cleared that has not. If you see a payment that has not been entered, click **Finish Later**. Enter the missing payment in the **Make Payments** or **Write Checks** screen. Once the change has been saved on the payments or checks screen, return to the reconciliation. The revised amount will appear. If it does not appear, go back and make certain you entered the correct date on the payment.

If you notice a check in your system was entered with the wrong amount, you can click on it within the reconciliation screen. The transaction screen will appear with the check data. Simply edit the amount and save. A warning may pop up. Select *Yes* and you will be back to the reconciliation screen.

The deposits listed on the bank statement should match those in your system due to using the Undeposited Funds option. If there is a receipt in the bank but not in your account, research the posting and record it on your side. If it is recorded on your books but not the bank, double check to be certain the receipt was not entered twice or entered with the wrong date. Otherwise you will need to track down the missing deposit.

Another possible reconciliation error relates to the beginning balance. When you first bring up the reconcile screen, the system shows you the beginning balance, but does not allow you to adjust it. The system has calculated the beginning balance based on the previously cleared entries in the cash account.

If the beginning balance does not match the bank statement's beginning balance, someone has probably voided, deleted, or changed a transaction that was cleared in a previous reconciliation.

For example, you pay Joe Smith $50 a week to mow the grass. He typically deposits the check the next day, and when you reconcile the bank account, you clear his checks. But one day he comes to you and says that he has lost last week's check. You void the check and issue him a new one. The only problem is, you accidentally voided a check from last month that had already cleared. This will make your beginning balance not tie to the last reconciliation.

Luckily, the **Reconciliation History & Reports** will show any changes in the bank reconciliation since the last report. Go to the *Gear icon, Reconcile,* and the report will appear.

If there have been any changes in a reconciliation, the amount of that change will appear in the list of reports in the Changes column. Simply click that line to see the details.

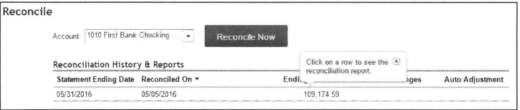

Click on the item that needs to be corrected and edit. Now go back to your reconciliation. Once you have matched everything possible with the bank statement, the bottom of the reconciliation screen should show a difference of $0. If there is a balance, you may have an error in one of your transactions. Check for transpositions (if the difference is divisible by 9, it may mean you switched two numbers around—45 instead of 54) as well as differences between the check amounts recorded by the bank and in the accounting system. If nothing works, a last resort is to select *Finish Now*. The system will offer to allow you to record an adjustment.

> Only do this for small amounts after all other options have been exhausted. What looks like a small variance could be two large mistakes that happen to offset each other.

If there is no variance, select **Finish Now**, and you will see the following screen listing the **Reconciliation History & Reports**. This list will grow as you complete bank reconciliations each month.

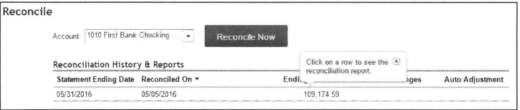

Double click the date of the report you want to view and print. Select *Print* and attach the reports to the bank statements. These should then be reviewed by someone besides the bookkeeper and filed.

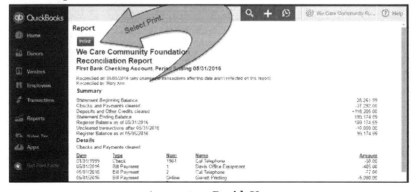

E. Credit Card Reconciliation

QBO allows you to reconcile your credit cards the same way you reconcile the bank account. First connect your credit card to download charges from the credit card company via Bank Feeds. This is a much easier way of getting all the individual charges into the system instead of keying them manually. Just like the bank accounts, you can set rules, so QBO will automatically match the expense to the correct general ledger account. Be sure to add the appropriate class!

> QBO will download the charges, but you need to be sure you have the receipts for each one. I recommend requiring each card holder to fill out a detailed expense report for his portion of the monthly credit card statement with the receipts and purpose attached.
> A supervisor should review the expense reports and receipts and approve before the bookkeeper matches the downloaded transactions into the system.

Once all of the transactions are approved and matched, they can be posted to the accounts. Simply go to *Gear, Tools, Reconcile* and change the account to the credit card account. Now reconcile the account just as you did with the bank.

F. Reconciling Petty Cash

Many organizations find it necessary to keep a petty cash account. These can take different forms; it may be a couple hundred dollars locked in a drawer, or gift cards purchased from local businesses that are used as needed.

Your organization should have written procedures and guidelines regarding the use of petty cash. One person should be responsible for maintaining the cash or cards. Receipts must be brought back to the bookkeeper in the amount of the cash expended. The fund is replenished with those receipts as the support.

I'll walk you through a typical example. Betty, the receptionist at your organization, has asked for a $200 petty cash fund. She promises to keep it in a security box locked in a filing cabinet behind her desk. People are always asking her to get donuts and coffee or office supplies at the last minute, and she doesn't personally have the funds to cover them until she can be reimbursed.

You will write a check made out to **Your Organization** to be cashed at your bank. Instead of an expense account number, you will set up a petty cash account with type marked as **Bank**. If you look at the account after you write the check, it will show a $200 balance.

At the end of the month, Betty brings you $175 of receipts and asks if she can get more money. First, verify that she has $25 of cash left. Betty should always have a combination of receipts and cash that equal $200. You will write a check for $175 and file the check voucher with the $175 of receipts under a Petty Cash file. From the **Write Check** screen, record the receipts under the **Expense** tab. Office supplies, meeting expenses, or whatever expense the receipts are for will be the expense accounts charged.

If you have purchased gift cards or prepaid credit cards, set up an account called Gift Cards with an account type of Prepaid Expenses. Each month, you should verify that the receipts and the balance of the gift cards equal the amount of the card purchases.

> Consider checking the balance of the petty cash and receipts at irregular intervals during the month. This discourages people from thinking they can borrow money they may not be able to replace at month's end.

G. Other Reconciliations

Cash is not the only thing that needs to be reconciled monthly. Some nonprofits have postage meters. The allocation of the postage expense is typically done via a journal entry. When you write the check to purchase the postage, record the amount to a prepaid asset account instead of an expense account. At the end of the month, record postage usage by going to the *Plus, Other, Journal Entry*.

Look at your postage meter usage report and allocate the postage to the appropriate classes. The total should be the amount of postage charged in your meter for the period. I recommend using the **Make Recurring** option so you will only need to change the dollar amounts each month.

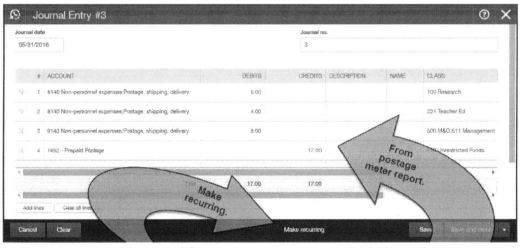

To make certain the prepaid postage amount ties to the balance in your meter, go to the chart of accounts list and compare the balance in prepaid postage to your postage balance report. If you had purchased $200 of postage and used $17, the prepaid account should show $183.

Now that you've entered all the transactions and reconciled your accounts for the month, it's time to run reports. On to Chapter 13 to learn what reports are available and what information you need to most effectively show the financial status of your organization.

13. Where Do We Stand? —Designing & Running Reports

As you were working through this book, you may have been asking yourself, "Why do I have to track the finances in such detail?" Being able to access accurate financial reports is crucial to funding the nonprofit's mission. Every entry helps paint a fuller picture for current and future donors of how well your organization is serving out its mission. In this chapter, I will explain the different types of reports specific to an organization needs, walk you through the standard QuickBooks options, and show you how to design and export customized reports.

A. Types of Reports

At a minimum, all organizations need two basic reports—the **Balance Sheet** and the **Income Statement (or Profit and Loss Statement)**. Nonprofits call these reports **Statement of Financial Position** and **Statement of Activities**. The Balance Sheet (or Statement of Financial Position) is a snapshot of what the organization owns, owes, and what is left in net assets as of a certain date. The Income Statement (or Statement of Activities) summarizes the revenues and expenses over a defined period.

So this sounds like accountant talk again, doesn't it? I'm afraid you will have to humor me a bit to assure you are comfortable with the differences and will know when to run which report. The balance sheet indicates the financial health of your organization. If assets are greater than liabilities, you own more than you owe. What is left is the net assets. Net assets are the accumulated amount of the difference between the amount owned versus owed since the organization's inception.

The income statement reflects the operations of your organization. If you want to know how much money has been donated to your organization this year and what expenses have been incurred, you would run an income statement report for the year. If you needed to know how much was donated in the last quarter, you could run the report for a three-month period.

Besides the two primary reports, you would probably like to see who your biggest donors are, who has donated how much, how your donations and expenses compare to your budgets, how much money is expected from dues, and how much you owe vendors. QBO allows you to run reports on all of this information and more. Let's walk through how to navigate the reports and see what options you have.

B. Navigating the Reports Center

Reports are very easy to access in QBO. Go to the left *Menu*, *Reports*.

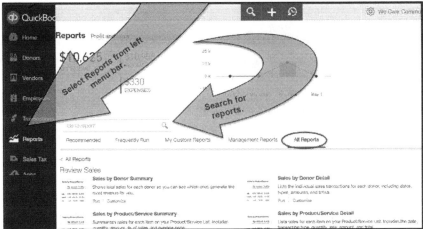

You can find a report by searching for its name in the **Go to report** field. Below that box there are five headings: **Recommended, Frequently Run, My Custom Reports, Management Reports**, and **All Reports**. QBO saves your specific reports to these various tabs. Think of these headings as file folders to help you organize your reports and get to the ones you need quickly.

Let's talk about a few of them. QBO uses an algorithm to group commonly used reports in the **Recommended** and **Frequently Run** tabs. **Management Reports** are the typical reports used by businesses. The same report may be under several different tabs.

 My Custom Reports stores the reports you have customized and saved. This saves you from having to reenter the parameters on a report the next time you wish to run it. **All Reports** lists every available report by category.

The nice thing about QBO is that the way you set parameters and formats remains consistent across all reports. So let's go over the options.

C. Defining the Parameters and Saving Customizations

From the main **Reports** screen, select the *Profit and Loss*.

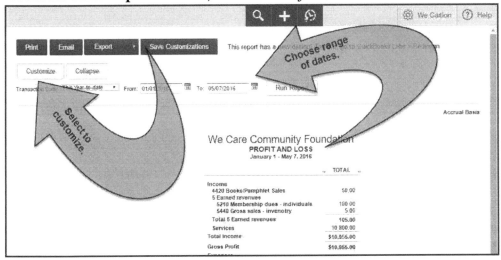

Look at the top of this report screen. You can **Print, Email, Export**, or **Save Customizations** by selecting the respective button. There is also a **Collapse** option. Report data can be "rolled up" or totaled into parent accounts. This is where the careful thought you put into the chart of accounts shows. If the report is already *collapsed*, the button will say **Expand**. Selecting *Expand* will cause the report to show each sub-account. You can click on the parent accounts individually so your report will show the details of some parents and only the summary of others.

The report will appear with a default year-to-date **Transaction Date**. This includes all transactions that you have entered so far this year. You can also change the date range displayed. For example, you may want to see information for a specific month, quarter, or the entire year. Simply change the **From** and **To** dates and select *Run Report* to refresh.

Let's play around with the **Customize** options and learn how to make some changes to reports. Select *Customize* to see the five sections of options: **General, Rows/Columns, Lists, Numbers,** and **Header/Footer.** Because these are so important, we will talk about each section individually.

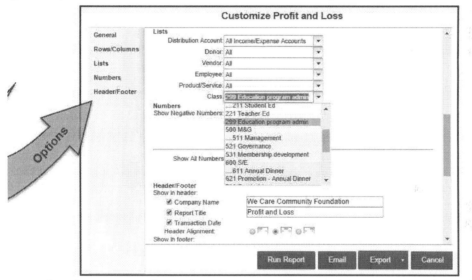

Under the **General** section, you can change the time period, including **All Dates, Today, This Week, This Week-to-date**, etc.

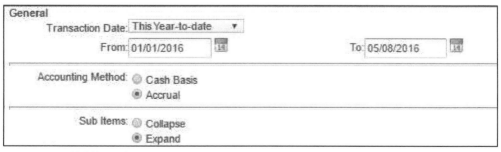

The system will fill in the dates based on your selection. For greater flexibility, you can manually type over the dates in the boxes to any range you like.

The **Accounting Method** determines whether this report will be calculated on a **Cash Basis** or **Accrual**. Recall from our previous chapters, the cash basis option will display only transactions for which cash has been received or paid out. If you have recorded dues receivable for the year, but want to run a profit and loss based on the dues actually received, select the *Cash* basis. The accrual option will display transactions based on the invoice date, not when cash was exchanged, as discussed in Chapter 10.

Sub Items gives you the option to have the reports default showing less detail **(Collapse)** or showing all the sub-accounts **(Expand)**. As I mentioned earlier, the default can be changed on the report.

Next the **Rows/Columns** section allows you to determine what columns you would like to see on the report.

The **Columns** menu is a drop-down that includes everything imaginable; *Days, Weeks, Customers, Products/Services*, etc. We'll stick with **Total Only** for now. You can decide in what order the data should **Sort By. Add Subcolumns for Comparison** gives you a wide range of comparative data, but as useful as all of these columns sound, if you select too many of them, you will have a very wide report. So play around, select a few, and see what you like.

Scrolling down the screen, **Show Rows** and **Show Columns** allows you to decide if you would like all the rows and columns to display or only the active or non-zero ones. Selecting **All** may cause your report to show accounts that have no data in them.

Lists provides drop-down menus that allow you to filter reports if you want to display information for a specific **Donor**, **Vendor**, **Product/Service**, or **Class**.

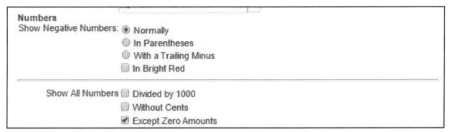

This is very useful for grant (**Donor**) or program (**Class**) reporting.

Numbers gives you the options of how to format and display amounts.

The **Show Negative Numbers** options let you decide if negatives should be shown with a minus sign, parentheses, a trailing minus sign, or in bright red. To save ink costs for printed reports, I'd recommend staying away from the colors.

The **Show All Numbers** area allows you to produce reports with the numbers rounded by 1000, without the cents showing, or omitting zero balances. Unless you are a very large organization, I doubt you'll need to round by 1000.

Header/Footer is where you will label your report.

It will default to the company name and report title, but you can type anything in the open boxes. If you don't want some of this information to show on the report, unselect the box to the left of the option.

Now you can select *Run Report* and you will see a Profit and Loss report. If you click on **Collapse**, the system will hide subaccounts and display totals by parent account. This is very handy to review for errors. Note the **Accrual Basis** in the upper right corner. If you had wanted a cash basis report, you will need to change this by selecting the *Customize* button, *General, Accounting Method, Cash Basis*.

To see the details for any line item on the Profit &Loss, click on the amount. Any field that turns blue when you hover over it can be drill downed to the details.

> I'll be referring to the ability to link to the transactions from reports as **drilling down**. In later chapters, if I tell you to drill down on a report, I mean click on the transaction in question.

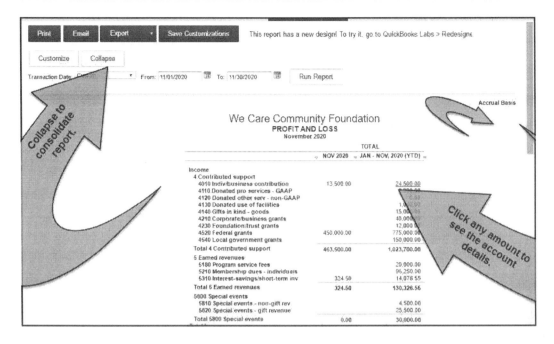

I clicked account 4010 Individual and business contribution, which total $24,500.

You can continue to click or "drill down" any of these amounts in this **Transaction Report** to be taken to the original transaction screen. That means you will be taken to the sales receipt, invoice, check, or expense screen where you entered the transaction. If there is an error, it can be fixed and saved. The system will alert you that the report needs to be refreshed. Select the *Run Report* button on the top menu, and the report will show the most updated information.

Let's look back at the top of the report.

The **Print** button allows you to print or save as a PDF. The PDF option is convenient when you want to send reports and be certain no one will change the numbers on them. It also makes the reports easier to read for people who don't use spreadsheets.

Email allows you to send the report directly from QBO. The **Export** option will create an .XLS or .XLSX spreadsheet. As QBO is designed for businesses and not organizations, many organizations prefer to export reports to a spreadsheet and then change the terminology to their own. After you become more familiar with the reports in the system, this will be an area you will want to play around with. (I'll walk you through how to do these techniques later in this chapter.)

Save Customizations allows you to memorize all of the filters and parameters of this report and will save it under the **My Custom Reports** in the Reports Center.

Note that you can add the report to a group, so different customizations can be kept together. For example, you may wish to customize a separate Profit &Loss for each of your grants. These reports may then be saved under a "Grant Group."

After we click OK, the report is now listed under **My Custom Reports** as show below.

Back to the top of the reports screen, **Customize** will take you to the Customize Transaction screen with the five sections we discussed earlier. Run Report will update the numbers for any changes in the transactions since the report was generated. Below the top bar is an area to change the date range and the columns to be shown.

> Though QBO has numerous types of reports, you will navigate around them and change the parameters in the same way.

D. Most Useful Reports

Go back to the **Reports** screen and review what types of reports are available under each of the categories. You can also search for reports by keying the name into the **Go to report** field.

I'll explain some of the reports you are most likely to need. The **Report Name** column also includes some of the customization steps needed. Play around with these reports and see what your information your organization can use.

There are reports related to the tax filings required for nonprofits (IRS Form 990). As of the writing of this book, QBO has reporting limitations. It cannot produce a report specific enough for the 990. There are work arounds to design a report that contains the information needed to complete the 990. A QBO ProAdvisor or other accounting professional may be able to assist you with this.

I want to see	Report Name	Description
Biggest Donors/Grants	Go to: Sales by Donor Summary, then *Customize, Lists, Donations for Product/ Services.* Finally, *Sort* total in descending order.	Lists donors/members in order of donation size.
Donor Contribution Summary	Go to: Sales by Donor Summary *Customize, Lists, Donations for Product/Services.*	Lists donation subtotaled by donors. Use this list to develop year-end giving statements.
Programs/Projects Report	Go to: Profit and Loss by Class *Customize, Lists, Class,* choose class or classes of your choice	Details income and expenses for an individual program.
Statement of Activities	Profit and Loss	Details income and expenses for the organization in total.
Statement of Financial Position	Balance Sheet or Balance Sheet Summary	Shows amount owned, owed, and Net Assets.

We looked at an overall Profit and Loss statement earlier, but now, let's walk through the selections for **Profit and Loss by Class** to show you how to customize your own reports. We will use this report as it will give information by each of the programs.

First, search and run the **Profit and Loss by Class** report.

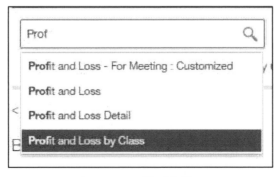

From the top of the report, click *Customize*. Change the title of the report from **Profit and Loss by Class** to **Profit and Loss by Program**.

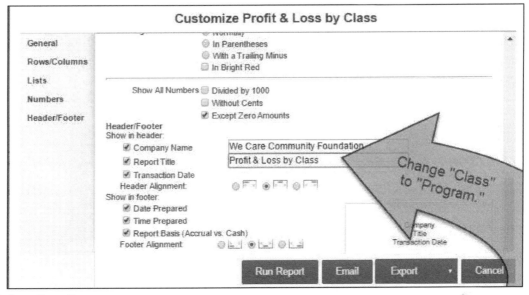

Select *Run Report*.

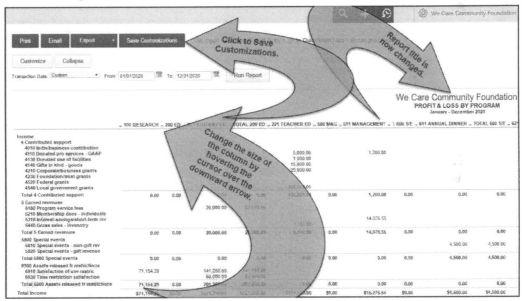

As we learned earlier, you can change the date range, header, etc. by using the buttons across the top of this screen. The **Collapse** button will hide the detail accounts. Additionally, you can change the size of the columns by hovering your mouse over the little downward arrow between the columns. When the cursor changes to a +, slide it to the left to make the column narrower or to the right to make it wider.

I collapsed the data so the report would not be so long. Looking across the columns, you see each program that was set up as a class. For each program, you can scan down the reports to see the income, operating expenses, and a net operating income line. This tells you how much you have received from regular donations and grants and the related expenses. Below the **Net Operating Income** line are the non-operating income and expenses. These are the out-of-the-ordinary expenses or revenues that may occur at your organization.

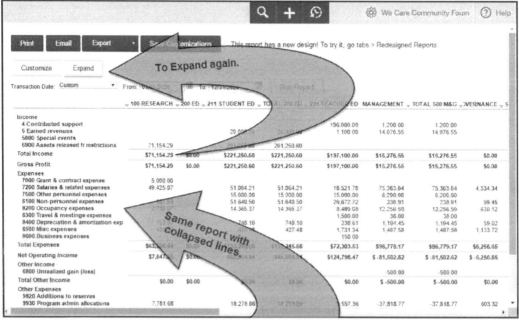

This report can be customized to show only one or some of the programs by using the **Customize** button and selecting *Classes*. If you have lots of classes, each will be in a different column, and the print would be very difficult to read.

E. Exporting Reports to a Spreadsheet

I just want to warn you, this section assumes you know Excel well enough to do basic formulas, adding worksheets, and formatting. As an accountant, I'm afraid I assume everyone uses Excel as much as I do. But if you are not familiar with the spreadsheet program, you may wish to ask for help from someone who is as you go through this section.

Once you have pulled up the report you'd like to export, select *Export, Excel (XLSX) or Excel (XLS)* from the top of the report screen. Excel XLSX is a newer format than XLS; but, newer versions of Microsoft Excel open both formats, which have the same basic functionality. Beyond that I will have to direct you to Google or the Microsoft website to learn more and decide which format works best for you.

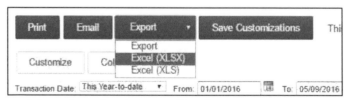

The new spreadsheet downloads immediately.

	Total 200 ED	221 Teacher Ed	500 M&G	511 Management	Total 500 M&G	521 Governance	531 Membership development ent	600 S/E	611 Annual Dinner	Total 600 S/E	621 Promotion - Annual Dinner
Income											
4 Contributed support	0.00				0.00					0.00	
4010 Indiv/business contributi	0.00				0.00					0.00	
4110 Donated pro services - G	0.00	5,000.00		1,200.00	1,200.00					0.00	
4120 Donated other serv - non	0.00	0.00			0.00					0.00	
4130 Donated use of facilities	0.00	1,000.00			0.00					0.00	
4140 Gifts in kind - goods	0.00	15,000.00			0.00					0.00	
4210 Corporate/business gran	0.00	25,000.00			0.00					0.00	15,000.00
4230 Foundation/trust grants	0.00				0.00					0.00	
4520 Federal grants	0.00				0.00					0.00	
4540 Local government grants	0.00	150,000.00			0.00					0.00	
Total 4 Contributed support	$ 0.00	$196,000.00	$ 0.00	$ 1,200.00	$ 1,200.00	$ 0.00	$ 0.00	$ 0.00	$ 0.00	$ 0.00	$ 15,000.00
5 Earned revenues	0.00				0.00					0.00	
5180 Program service fees	20,000.00				0.00					0.00	
5210 Membership dues - indiv	0.00				0.00		96,250.00			0.00	
5310 Interest-savings/short-te	0.00			14,076.55	14,076.55					0.00	
5440 Gross sales - invenotry	0.00	1,100.00			0.00					0.00	
Total 5 Earned revenues	$ 20,000.00	$ 1,100.00	$ 0.00	$ 14,076.55	$ 14,076.55	$ 0.00	$96,250.00	$ 0.00	$ 0.00	$ 0.00	$ 0.00
5800 Special events	0.00				0.00					0.00	

We Care Community Foundation
Profit & Loss by Class
January - December 2020

Profit & Loss by Class

This worksheet has all of the data from the QBO report. If you would like this report to only show the top-level (parent) accounts, you would **Collapse** the report before exporting to Excel.

Once you are in the spreadsheet, you can save space by rounding to the nearest whole dollar instead of showing the cents. To do this, highlight the entire Excel worksheet and click on the small arrow pointing to the right twice to remove any numbers after the decimal.

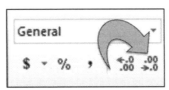

You are ready to reduce the columns to the narrowest size possible while keeping the numbers legible. Holding your cursor at the line between spreadsheet columns will change it to a bold +. You can then move the edge of the column to the right or left. Do this for each of the columns until you are happy with the result.

You can also add headings, logos, change the fonts, etc. to make the report look exactly like you want. Save the spreadsheet and note the name and place.

All reports in QBO can be exported to a spreadsheet with your customized headings and formatting. Take a few minutes and try some other reports with the sample company. Also, use the spreadsheet program to change the fonts and practice exporting. You will find this a handy tool.

F. Other Miscellaneous Reports

1.   Dues Receivable, & Donor Information

There are several other reports you will want to keep an eye on. If you have entered dues or pledges as invoices, you can search for and run the **A/R Aging**

Summary (Accounts Receivable) reports. This report lists the donors and the owed amount still outstanding.

Choose today's date and you will see how much is owed to your organization as of today. The **A/R Aging Detail** is the same report but lists the individual invoices entered by donor.

Search and run the **Customer Contact List** which can be printed, emailed, exported to Excel, or printed to PDF format. The Excel file can also be imported into other software. To print mailing labels, you will need to export the customer list and upload it to another program like Microsoft Word.

2.   Accounts Payable & Vendor Information

If you have been entering your bills as they are received, but not yet paid, you can search for the A/P Aging Summary (Accounts Payable) report. This is the accounts payable report which shows all the bills that have been entered but not yet paid and when they are due. It is a useful tool for cash-flow management. Search for the **Transaction List by Vendor** to run reports on all transactions for a particular vendor.

3.   Deposit Detail

Search for the **Deposit Detail** report to view every deposit made and the bank account it went to along with the individual transactions that made up the deposit. If the deposits on your bank account do not tie to the deposits listed in your accounts during your bank reconciliation, refer to this report to see if you put the money in the wrong account in QBO.

> The final section of the reports is **Budgets.** In the next chapter, I'll show you how to input your budgets and best utilize this powerful tool.

14. Am I Meeting My Targets? Budgeting

Planning for the future is crucial for any nonprofit. Preparing an annual budget requires an organization to consider their priorities. Because there is a limit to the donations expected to be received, there is also a limit to the services that can be offered.

> Approach the budgeting process as a way to get consensus around the priorities of your organization.

A. The Budget Process

Budgets are typically done on operating income and expenses. Income and expenses outside of normal organization operations (non-operating income and expenses, like the receipt of a bequest or repaving the parking lot) only need to be budgeted if they are substantial.

The budget process will have several steps. First you must consider if you need budgets at a top level (total organization only) or program by program. Budgeting at the program level will take more time, but will also give you more information.

You may also wish to budget by grant. QBO allows you to input class (program) budgets separate from the whole organization budget. If you prepare program budgets for all areas (including administration), this will summarize to a total organizational budget.

To begin budgeting, you need to determine what donations and other revenues can be reasonably expected. If your membership and donations have been fairly consistent over the years, you can use historical trends and tweak them for any likely changes.

For example, if dues have consistently been close to $100,000 for the last five years, you are probably safe budgeting $100,000 for next year. But if a large donor moved to another state, consider reducing the expected dues by their usual donation.

Other donations are usually budgeted based on promises to give and historical rates. This would include money received from foundations, memorials, rent, etc. Investment income can be budgeted based on expected returns of the investments. If you have $100,000 in a money market account that is currently paying 2% interest, you would budget $2000 of investment income.

For the expense budgets, I like to get buy-in from the heads of the programs. Start by printing out a report showing each program director how much money they have spent this year.

Under Reports, search for the **Profit and Loss** report and filter it for class. (You learned how to filter the reports in the last chapter.) You may email the resulting report to directors directly from this screen and include in the email a request for budget submissions.

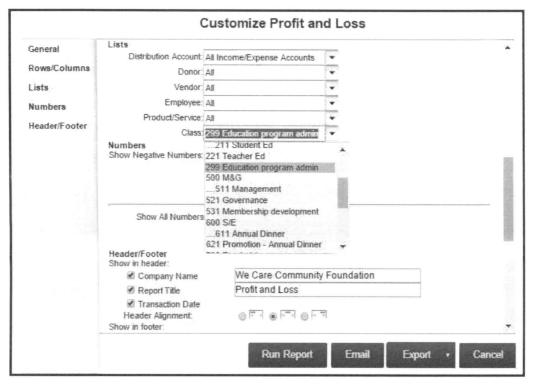

Next, ask your program heads to submit their budget proposal of expected needs, and if it is substantially different than this year, an explanation should be included. I refer to this as the wish list. Be sure to remind the directors it is not part of the budget until approved by the finance committee or governing board.

Preparing their proposal and explanation encourages the program directors to think about what they would like to do differently. The written documentation is a good resource for the governing board as they deliberate on how to divide the budget dollars. This also gives you the information to put in a class (program) budget in QBO.

Besides program expenses, your organization has facilities and other overhead expenditures. These can be calculated based on historical information or contracts. If you are allocating this expense across the programs, save yourself time by waiting until all of the direct program costs have been budgeted. Then you can do a one-time calculation to allocate the overhead based on percentage of space used, number of employees, or percentage of total costs.

For example, use a spreadsheet to estimate all of your building expenses. If you have three programs, Administration, Publications, and Education, you would add one third of the expected building expenses to each of these three budgets. You can do the same thing for salaries if you allocate people over more than one program. Some organizations use different allocation percentages for facilities costs versus supplies and administrative costs.

> Consider exporting last year's actual overhead expenses to a spreadsheet. You can use formulas that add an inflation percentage and then allocate by program. The allocation would be input into QuickBooks' budget by account.

B. Entering Your Budget

Once you have compiled all the information from the program directors, pledge cards, historical information, and anywhere else, it is time to put it all together in a budget. You will probably go through several iterations before your board decides on a final budget, so don't worry if you don't have all the information you would like.

It is very important that you are organized during the budget formation progress. Each line item should have an assigned class (program). The lines that don't have a specific program should be assigned to the Unrestricted class. The more organized you are, the easier budget entry will be.

From the *Gear* icon, select *Tools, Budgeting*.

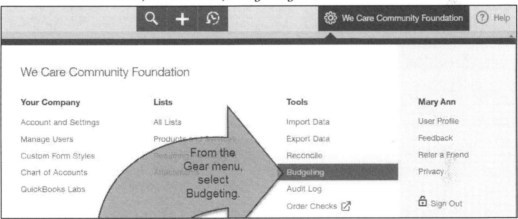

If you have never created a budget, QBO will walk you through the process. You can either create a budget from scratch or historical information you have already entered. Think of this step as creating a shell of a budget from which you can enter and adjust numbers.

The first screen explains the process QBO will take you through. Click *Next*.

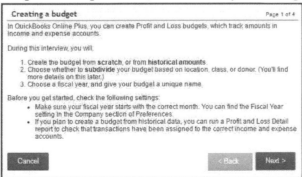

In screen 2 of 4, you will decide how to start your budget.

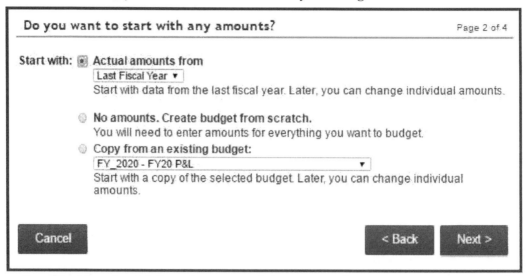

It will either be (1) based on actual income and expense accounts you have entered, (2) entered from scratch, or (3) copied from an existing budget, if you have one. The first option allows you to start your budget by having the system populate the data with the monthly amounts by account. If you are primarily using an historical approach to budgeting and have last year's data already in the system, this option is a time saver.

The second option listed is the one you will need to use if your organization is new to QuickBooks. It requires you to key in the data manually. The third option allows you to copy the data from a budget that had been set up previously. To show you the most difficult option of starting a budget from scratch, select *No amounts* and click *Next*.

On screen three, QBO allows you to subdivide your budget by Classes, or Donors.

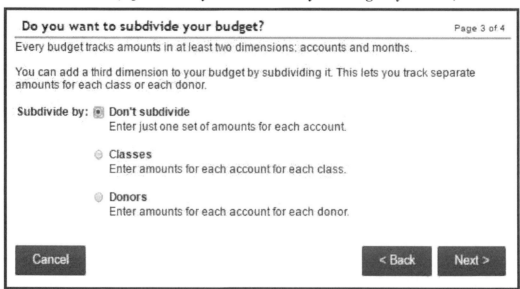

The Class and Location options will only be available if you have turned on **Track classes** and **Track locations** in **Advanced Accounts and Settings** (see Chapter 2). **Don't subdivide** is used if you are budgeting for the entire organization with one budget. The **Classes** option is needed to create a budget by **Program.** The **Donors** option is used to create a budget by **Grant**. For now, we won't worry about subdividing, so select *Don't subdivide, Next.*

Finally, you will select the fiscal year for this new budget and you name your budget.

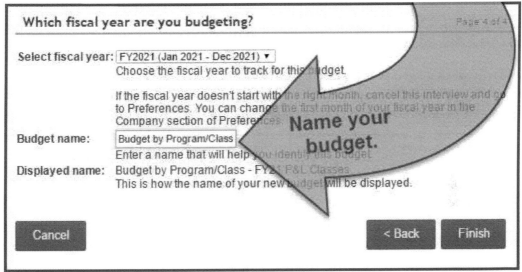

The default fiscal year corresponds to your selections in the **Preferences** we reviewed in Chapter 2. When you choose a name, remember that you may prepare more than one budget in a year, and select *Finish*.

Whether you just created your budget from scratch or are viewing a budget that has already been entered, you will view, manage, and enter amounts for your budgets in the main budget entry screen. Let's take a look at it.

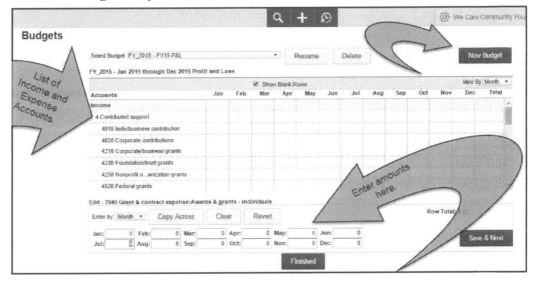

At the top of the Budgets screen, select the budget you are working on. You may have multiple budgets for the same year or budgets from previous years. Make sure they are clearly labeled so you don't get confused. Select *Rename* to change the name of the selected budget if necessary.

In the left column, you may recognize your list of income and expense accounts from your chart of accounts. Across the top of the grid are months. This example is for a Profit and Loss budget which is not subdivided by class, donor, or location.

Now let's talk about how to enter and change budget numbers. First you need to select the row for which you are entering amounts. Below, I have selected line 4010 – Individual/business contribution.

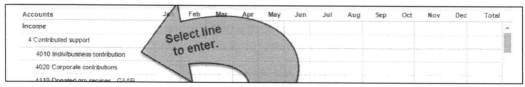

You will enter the amounts for this row in the entry fields found at the bottom of this screen.

The fields in the grid next to the selected 4010 line will populate as you enter your numbers for each month. The message just above the entry area lets you know what line of the budget you are currently entering.

Using the **Enter by** drop-down menu, you can choose to enter your budget by **Month, Quarter,** or by **Year**. By choosing **Month,** you will enter twelve separate entries. The **Quarter** option will give you four boxes to input data and then allocates the amounts evenly among the three months in each quarter. If you choose **Year,** QBO will allocate that number evenly over 12 months.

There are three buttons in the entry area to help with data entry. **Copy Across** allows you to type a number once and the system will put the same amount in all remaining months. Use this instead of the **Year** option when the first few months have a different amount than the later months. **Clear** will clear all fields. Think of **Revert** as undo for your last action. When you are done with that line of the budget, **Save & Next** will take you to the next line. When you are done entering your budget, click *Finished*.

If you need to edit any of these entries, simply highlight the line the account is on and key over the incorrect data in the entry fields. Don't forget to *Save*.

I recommend taking the time to enter your budget by month, based on historical data and current information. You'll be able to report actual versus budgeted costs by month, allowing for more accurate information. If you need it for reporting purposes, you can create separate budgets entered by quarter or year.

C. Entering Budgets by Program or Grant

Now that you have seen how the budget entry process works, we will walk through the process of entering budgets by class (for program tracking) and by donor (for grants tracking). You must create a separate budget for each.

To get stared, we will follow the same process you learned above. Go to *Gear, Tools, Budgeting, New Budget.* For this example, we will choose to create a budget from scratch by selecting *No amounts.* The first difference in this budget is that we will choose *Classes* on screen 3 of 4 of the new budget setup interview.

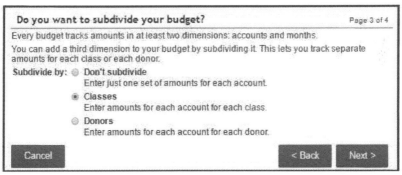

Finally, we will choose a **Budget name**. I used "Budget by Program/Class." Click *Finish* when done.

Because we chose to subdivide this budget by class, the budget entry screen has an additional section called **Show rows as**, which is found at the top of the budget grid.

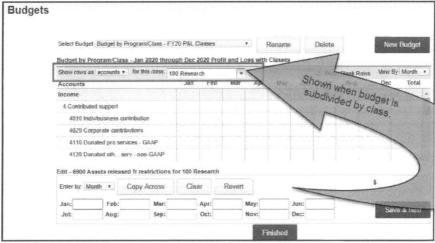

This subtle addition is a very helpful tool for budget entry. It allows you to change the left column from list of accounts to a list of classes. If you select to **Show rows as**

accounts, you will choose a class under the **for this class** drop-down menu as shown above and enter your amounts one class at a time. If you select to **Show rows as classes**, you will choose one account at a time under the **for this account** drop-down menu.

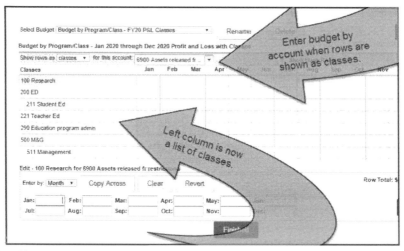

To help illustrate the difference, imagine two scenarios. The Executive Director has given you a budget for your administrative costs for the year. If all these cost go into one class, Admin, you would choose the first version, **Show rows as *accounts*, for this class *Admin***. Then you would enter each of the amounts into the accounts, and they would be summarized into the Admin class.

If she brought you a list and said, "All telephone costs should be allocated evenly across our four programs," you would choose **Show rows as *classes*, for this account *Telephone***. One quarter of the total expected telephone costs by month would then be input on the line for each of the four programs. As you enter the budgets, you can switch between the two ways of entering data.

Select *Save and next* to move to the next **Account** or **Class** listed in first column. Click *Finished* when done.

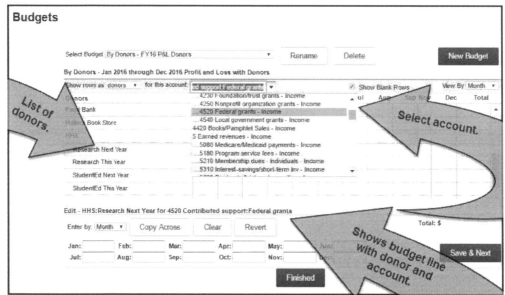

The same process is used to create a budget subdivided by Donor (used for grants). The difference is that you can enter the budget by Account or Donor (grant).

Next, we will look at how amounts entered into your budget will flow through to reports to provide useful information.

D. Budget Reports

Let's see what kind of reports we can generate once a budget is input. From the left **Menu**, select *Reports*. There are two main budget reports: **Budget Overview** and **Budget vs. Actuals**. The **Budget Overview** report shows a summary of budgeted amounts for a specific account. The **Budget vs. Actuals** report shows your budgeted income and expense to the actual amounts so you can tell whether you are over or under budget.

First let's type *Budget Overview* in the **Search** box near the top of the screen. As soon as it is selected, a **Customize Budget Overview** window will open. In this screen, make sure that the correct budget is selected. Under **Rows/Columns, Show Grid,** you must select *Accounts vs. Classes* to view your budget by class.

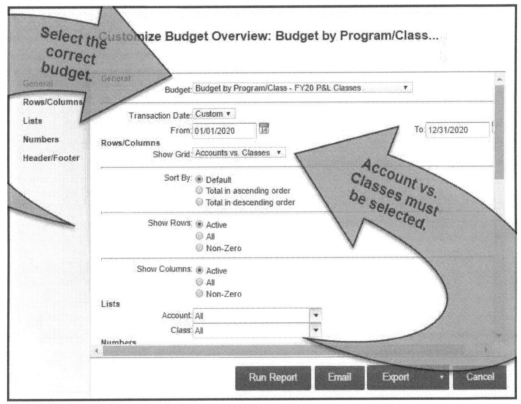

Choose one or more classes to include in your report under the **Lists, Class** drop-down menu.

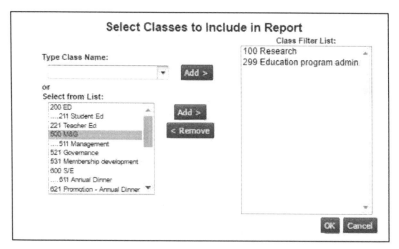

Click **Run Report** to view your report. There is a column heading for each program across the top of the report. Down the left is a row heading for each income and expense account.

We Care Community Foundation
BUDGET OVERVIEW: BUDGET BY PROGRAM/CLASS - FY20 P&L CLASSES
January - December 2020

	200 ED	211 STUDENT ED	TOTAL 200 ED	221 TEACHER ED	500 M&G	511 MANAGEMENT	TOTAL 500 M&G	521 PROMOTION - ANNUAL DINNER	700 FUNDRAISING	910 UNRESTRICTED FUNDS
Income										
4 Contributed support										
4010 Indiv/business contribution										21,000.00
4110 Donated pro services - GAAP										1,796.00
4130 Donated use of facilities										1,200.00
4140 Gifts in Kind - goods										15,000.00
4210 Corporate/business grants				25,000.00				15,000.00		
4230 Foundation/trust grants										
4520 Federal grants										
Total 4 Contributed support	0.00	0.00	0.00	25,000.00	0.00	0.00	0.00	15,000.00	0.00	39,500.00
6 Earned revenues										144,000.00
6800 Special events										
6810 Special events - non-gift rev									4,800.00	
6820 Special events - gift revenue									25,500.00	
Total 6800 Special events	0.00	0.00	0.00	0.00	0.00	0.00	0.00	0.00	0.00	0.00
Total Income	$0.00	$0.00	$0.00	$25,000.00	$0.00	$0.00	$0.00	$15,000.00	$30,300.00	$183,500.00
Gross Profit	$0.00	$0.00	$0.00	$25,000.00	$0.00	$0.00	$0.00	$15,000.00	$30,300.00	$183,500.00
Expenses										
7000 Grant & contract expense										
7040 Awards & grants - individuals		6,000.00	6,000.00							
Total 7000 Grant & contract expense	0.00	6,000.00	6,000.00	0.00	0.00	0.00	0.00	0.00	0.00	0.00
7200 Salaries & related expenses										
7210 Officers & directors salaries				20,000.00		20,000.00	20,000.00			
7220 Salaries & wages - other				70,000.00		70,000.00	70,000.00			
7230 Pension plan contributions				15,000.00		15,000.00	15,000.00			
7240 Employee benefits - not pension				10,000.00		10,000.00	10,000.00			
Total 7200 Salaries & related expenses	0.00	0.00	0.00	125,000.00	0.00	125,000.00	125,000.00	0.00	0.00	0.00
7500 Other personnel expenses										
7510 Fundraising fees									1,800.00	
7520 Accounting fees						6,000.00	6,000.00			
7530 Legal fees						24,000.00	24,000.00			
7580 Donated pro services - GAAP										1,200.00
Total 7500 Other personnel expenses	0.00	0.00	0.00	0.00	0.00	30,000.00	30,000.00	0.00	3,600.00	7,200.00
8100 Non-personnel expenses										
8110 Supplies						45,000.00	45,000.00			
8130 Telephone & telecommunications						822.00	822.00			
8140 Postage, shipping, delivery						477.00	477.00			
9170 Printing & copying						7,562.00	7,562.00			
8180 Books, subscriptions, reference						35,000.00	35,000.00			
Total 8100 Non-personnel expenses	0.00	0.00	0.00	0.00	0.00	88,861.00	88,861.00	0.00	0.00	0.00

I realize this report is too small for you to read in the book, but you can scroll through it on your screen in the QBO test drive company. As you compile your budgets, use this report to check your data entry and analyze the monthly trends.

Now, let's look at the **Budget vs. Actuals** report. Use the **Search** box and select the report. The **Customize Budget vs. Actuals** window will open. Once again, make sure that the correct budget is selected. Customize as needed and select *Run Report*.

We Care Community Foundatio

For one program

BUDGETS ACTUALS: BUDGET BY PROGRAM/CLASS - I

January - December 2020

	ACTUAL	BUDGET	221 TEACHER ED OVER BUDGET	Dollar variance
Income				
4 Contributed				
4110 Donated	5,000.00		5,000.00	
4130 Donated	1,000.00		1,000.00	
4140 Gifts in	15,000.00		15,000.00	
4210 Corpora	25,000.00	25,000.00	0.00	100.00 %
4540 Local g	150,000.00		150,000.00	
Total 4 Contrib	196,000.00	25,000.00	171,000.00	784.00 %
5 Earned reven				
5440 Gross s	1,100.00		1,100.00	
Total 5 Earned	1,100.00	0.00	1,100.00	0.00
Total Income	$197,100.00	$25,000.00	$172,100.00	788.40 %

This is a report you will want to analyze each month. Comparing your actual revenues and expenses to budgets will help your organization track its financial goals. It shows how your programs' expenses are comparing to your expectations.

The **TOTAL** column gives you the variance for the entire organization. Filter the report to each of the individual programs and email a copy to the program director each month directly from QBO.

Save each program's budget by clicking *Save Customizations* and naming the report for that program. This will allow you to send reports to program directors without having to recreate the reports each time.

Experiment with the various budget reports. Change the parameters and see what is most useful for your organization. Export the reports to spreadsheets for further analysis or to make them more aesthetically pleasing.

> We are approaching the end! You have set up the system, learned to enter transactions, run reports, and understand how budgeting works in QBO. Let's move on to the next chapter to see what needs to be done at the end of each month and year.

15. It's Month End &/or Year End—What Now?

You have entered all your transaction and reconciled your bank account. Before you print out the financial statements for the treasurer or board, let's do a review of the data.

On the next page is a checklist of things to do each month and the additional requirements for year end. You may need to add a few other things for your particular organization, but this should get you started.

As you look down the list, you will see that we have covered almost everything except allocating the fund balances. In the first chapter, I explained how QBO is designed for businesses which only have one equity account for net income: Retained Earnings. Your organization, however, has three different equity accounts: Unrestricted Net Assets, Temporarily Restricted Net Assets, and Permanently Restricted Net Assets. Additionally, you may have funds you need to track that carry forward year after year and are never closed out. In this chapter, I'll show you how to develop the funds report and how to record your net income (or loss) into the correct net assets account.

A. Month and *Year-End Checklist

Duties	Chapter	Completed
Enter all bills.	10	
Enter any vendor credits.	10	
Pay all bills.	10	
Enter any manual checks.	10	
Enter all online banking payments.	10	
Enter all bank drafts.	10	
Enter payroll.	11	
Pay any payroll liabilities.	11	
Enter any invoices required (including dues or assessments).	9	
Enter all donations.	9	
Enter any other receipts.	9	
Record postage expense.	12	
Enter credit card charges.	10/12	
Reconcile credit card bills.	12	
Reconcile bank account to statement.	12	
Charge prepaid expenses.	15	
Review Receivable Aging Report.	13	
Review Payable Aging Report.	13	
Review Statement of Financial Position (Balance Sheet).	13	
Review Statement of Activities by Class (Income Statement).	13	
Review Income Statement Comparison to Budget.	14	
*Allocate fund balances.	15	
*Set year-end closing date.	15	
*Mail 1099s and 1096.	15	
*Mail W-2s and W-3.	15	

B. Reviewing Your Transactions

The first step in closing the books for the month is to make certain everything has been accounted for correctly. To do that, let's start with the Statement of Financial Position (or Balance Sheet as it is known in the for-profit world). Go to *Reports*, and search for *Balance Sheet*. Run the report with the month-end date you are closing. Be sure to select the *Accrual* option.

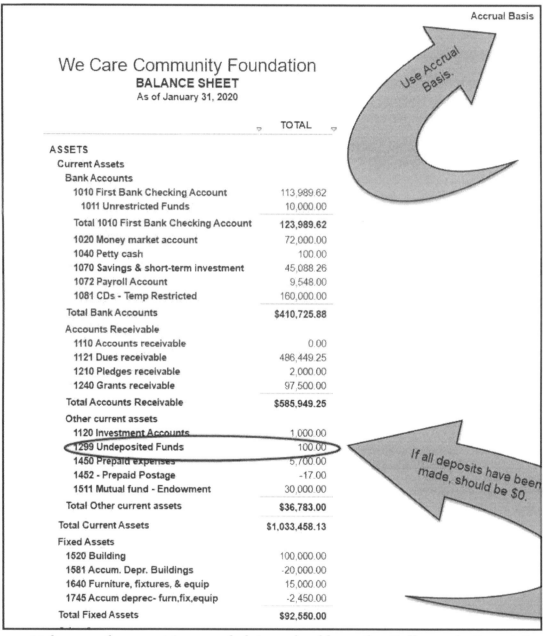

Make sure the report is expanded (you should see the **Collapse** button at the top). This report will list all the assets and liabilities for your organization. I like to print out a copy to make notes on.

At the top are the cash accounts. Check your reconciliation summaries to see that each account ties to the reconciliation you performed. If you have a petty cash account, it should tie to the amount of cash in the drawer. Investments should tie to the brokerage reconciliations. If there are any differences, investigate and correct the errors or the reconciliations.

Undeposited funds should only have a balance if a deposit has not been taken to the bank. In this example, the undeposited funds account is showing a $100.00 balance, but we know the organization has made all the deposits. Let's drill down on the account and see what is left.

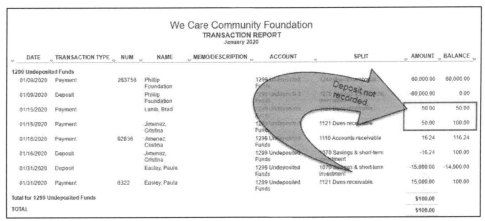

Looking through the detail, you can see the sales receipts go in and related deposit subtracted for all but three of the amounts. To correct this, go to *Plus, Other, Bank Deposit*. This gives you a list of all of the undeposited amounts.

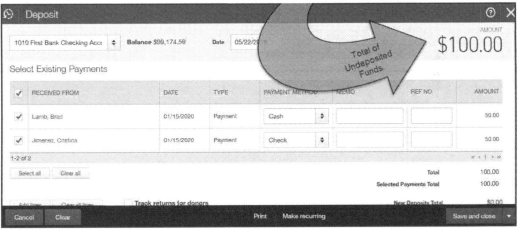

Select the receipts and change the transaction date to the date of the actual deposit. Select *Save and close*. Your balance sheet will no longer show undeposited funds as it has a $0 balance.

Next, print out the A/R Aging Report (Accounts Receivable) from the Reports Center. The date of the report should be the closing date. This report should tie to the receivable amounts. Review any outstanding balances that are overdue.

For prepaid expenses, you can drill down on the balance to see what is included. On the balance sheet above, there is only a postage account, the balance of which should match the balance in the postage meter. Other expenses paid in advance can be recorded in the prepaid account. It can be used to record property or liability insurance or items needed for a fundraising event that won't occur until next year.

A journal entry is required to move the expense out of the prepaid asset account and into an expense account (*Plus, Other, Journal Entry*). Here is an example entry.

This organization is paying various expenses in advance—copier rental, insurance, health benefits, etc.—and then charging them to the programs monthly. If the amount is the same each month, it should be memorized and automated.

To make certain the ending balance in the prepaid accounts are correct, you would need to go through the details and see what amount is leftover in each area. Set up a spreadsheet to summarize the balance by type and print it out.

	A	B	C	D
1		We Care Community		
2		Prepaid Balance		
3		11/30/2017		
4				
5				
6				
7		Property Insurance	1000	
8		D&O Insurance	4750	
9		HMO for Dec.	1250	
10		Total Acct 1450 Prepaid	$ 7,000	
11				

If you update it each month, this simple spreadsheet will save you lots of time at year end when the auditors want to know what is in the account. It will also keep you from overcharging the expense accounts.

> I recommend setting up subaccounts for insurance, postage, and any other recurring prepaid expenses. You will still need to review them on a monthly basis, but it should go much quicker.

Print out the A/P Aging (Accounts Payable) report from the **Vendors** reports for the accounts payable balance. The credit card balance will be any charges entered not yet paid.

Continue down the balance sheet this same way, documenting the balances.

> You will really impress your treasurer (or your auditor) if you hand him a package each month of the balance sheet with supporting documentation for each line of the balance sheet.

C. Allocate Fund Balances

The bottom of the balance sheet has only one equity line called **Net Income**. But you need to know how much is in your restricted versus non-restricted net assets. To do this, run a **Profit & Loss by Class** report for the same time period.

Monthly, you can review this report to see the breakout between restricted and unrestricted funds, but, at least annually, a journal entry will be necessary to reclassify the funds into their net asset accounts. I recommend having an outside accountant prepare these entries as there are particular accounting procedures relating to the release of net assets from restrictions. I won't bother you with an accounting lesson here, but if you decide to prepare the journal entry yourself, here is a basic example.

	#	ACCOUNT	DEBITS	CREDITS		NAME	CLASS
	1	3100 Unrestricted Net Assets	52,000.00				
	2	3101 Temporarily restrict net asset		52,000.00			
		Total	52,000.00	52,000.00			

QBO records all the net income into the general (unrestricted) equity account. My example reclasses the temporarily restricted balance of $52,000 from the unrestricted equity account to the temporarily restricted account.

This reduces the balance in the unrestricted net asset and increases it in the temporarily restricted net asset account.

D. Restricted versus Unrestricted Cash

Another important item to review is the restricted versus unrestricted cash. If you have used the subaccount method, you will see your restricted cash on the detail balance sheet. Otherwise, you'll need to design a report showing the cash basis of the various funds. For those of you who have used this report in the desktop version, please note that QBO handles reports differently, so it will take a few more steps.

Go to *Reports, Recommended, Budget vs Actuals* and select *Customize*. You will see a screen similar to the one on the following page.

Let's fill out this screen from the top. The budget will default to your last budget. Leave it be as we won't be using the budget data. The **Report period** needs to include ALL the data. Leave the first field blank if you can and fill in the second date field with the month-end or year-end date you are looking for. If the system requires a date in the first box, use the earliest date you have transactions in the system.

The **Accounting method** must be *Cash*. **Number format** can be your preference. Under **Rows/Columns, Show Grid,** select *Classes vs. Total*. Leave **Only accounts with budgeted amounts** unchecked as well as all the **Period Comparison** options.

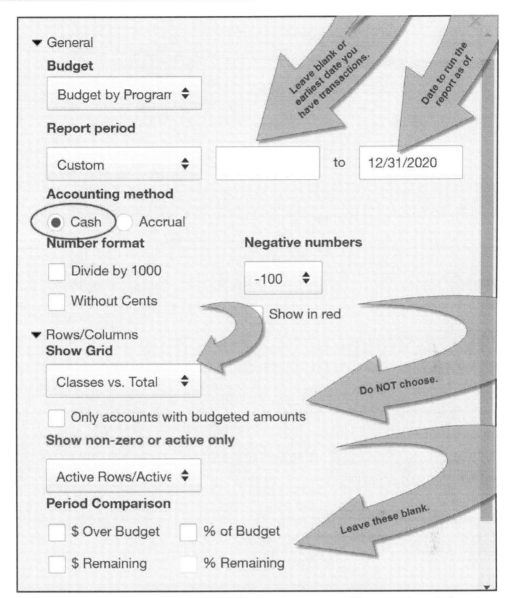

Back at the top of **Customize Report**, there is a **Filter** option. Select it to see something similar to the screen on the next page.

Select **Account**. From the drop-down arrow, you will see a variety of options. Scroll down the list until you see the individual accounts. Select all of the accounts **except** cash, investment, receivables, and payables (including payroll). Include the buildings, equity, and all the revenue and expense accounts. I'll warn you, this is a bit tedious, so be sure to save the customizations when you are through.

After you have selected all of the accounts, look for the **Class** option. Leave it unchecked. Next change the report title under the **Header/Footer** option and *Run report.*

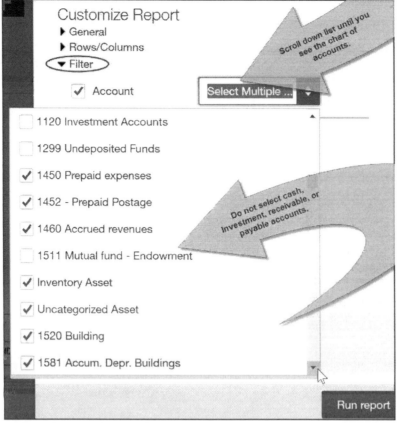

Here are the **Class** and **Header** options.

	ACTUAL	TOTAL BUDGET	OVER BUDGET
100 RESEARCH	2,861.17		2,861.17
▾ 200 ED			
211 Student Ed	48,326.08	-6,000.00	54,326.08
TOTAL 200 ED	**48,326.08**	**-6,000.00**	**54,326.08**
221 TEACHER ED	114,515.11	86,201.00	28,314.11
298 EDUCATION PROGRAM ADMIN	-3,645.00		-3,645.00
▾ 500 M&G			
511 Management	-50,749.85	-243,861.00	193,111.15
TOTAL 500 M&G	**-50,749.85**	**-243,861.00**	**193,111.15**
521 GOVERNANCE	-6,959.97		-6,959.97
531 MEMBERSHIP DEVELOPMENT	90,534.32		90,534.32
▾ 600 BIE			
611 Annual Dinner	-2,413.03		-2,413.03
TOTAL 600 BIE	**-2,413.03**		**-2,413.03**
621 PROMOTION - ANNUAL DINNER	3,253.65	15,000.00	-11,746.35
700 FUNDRAISING	19,505.23	26,700.00	-7,194.77
900 UNRESTRICTED FUNDS	10,758.00	176,300.00	-165,542.00
911 FACILITIES COST POOL	-12,390.00	-70,645.00	58,255.00
921 SALARIES COST POOL	-58,450.00		-58,450.00
996 QUASI-ENDOWMENT	29,842.10		29,842.10
997 USE RESTRICTED FUNDS	227,095.11		226,930.89
998 TIME RESTRICTED FUNDS	-60,000.00		-60,000.00
999 PERM RESTRICTED FUNDS	300.00		300.00
NOT SPECIFIED	124,637.08		124,637.08
TOTAL	**$477,020.00**	**$770,695.00**	**$ -293,675.00**

Click on the **Not Specified** amount to see a list of transactions without associated classes. Assign classes to the transactions as needed and rerun the report. The **TOTAL** on this report should match the total cash, undeposited funds, and investments on your balance sheet. If it does not, you have probably not selected all of the accounts under **Filter** properly.

The report includes budget columns you don't need, and you may want to group the funds differently. Now, we will "clean up" the report by exporting it into Excel, using the **share** icon discussed in Chapter 14. Once in the spreadsheet, delete the extra columns and group the classes together to show subtotals of unrestricted, temporarily restricted, and permanently restricted.

E. Year-End Adjusting Entries

Any year-end journal entries outside of the normal monthly entries, including the audit adjusting entries, should be recorded as of the last day of the accounting period (12/31/xx, if using a calendar year). If possible, record all regular donations and checks prior to that day (12/30/xx), so you know anything recorded on the last day of the year is an adjustment. This will allow you to run reports with and without the adjustments by changing the date.

F. Board Reports

Speaking of the governing board, I recommend you put together the following monthly reports for them and offer any more details as needed:

- Balance Sheet or Statement of Financial Position
- Budget versus Actual
- Profit & Loss by Class
- Funds Summary showing Restricted vs Non-Restricted Cash.

Additionally, you may wish to do some analysis and ratios showing:
- percentage of dues received to date
- percentage of donations received to budgeted amount.

G. Year-End Closing

After you have completed your year-end tasks, you will want to lock the data so no one can change it. This is what accountants call closing the books. In QBO, there is not a true locking of the numbers. Instead, the data is password protected and warnings are issued if you try to post something to a closed period.

A closing date needs to be designated. From the *Gear icon*, select *Account and Settings, Advanced, Accounting*.

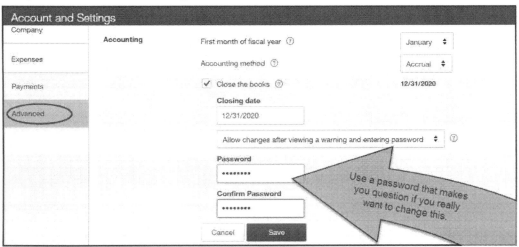

Select *Close the books* and choose a **Closing date,** entering the date of the last fiscal year or month. From the drop-down menu below it, choose to *Allow changes after viewing a warning and entering password*. This option allows you to make prior period changes but requires a password. Choose a password that makes you think to yourself, *do I really want to do this?*, like *CallAccountant*.

If you forget the closing date password, the system will let the administrator delete it in the screen above and enter a new one. So protect the administrator's password!

H. Year-End Donor Acknowledgments

Another year-end task is acknowledging the donations made by your donors and members. IRS regulations require organizations to provide acknowledgement for any donation over $250, and thanking your donors regularly for their support is always a good idea.

Additionally, you can use this communication as an internal accounting control tool and pledge reminder. As a control tool, consider sending donors who pledge or tithe a list of contributions and remaining balance quarterly. On the form should be a message to contact a designated person not involved in the bookkeeping if there is a problem with their statement. Increasing communication to thank your donors throughout the year is also a good idea.

For any discrepancies brought to your organization's attention, the designated person should meet with the bookkeeper and investigate. If the donor has made a donation that has not been recorded, the designated person will need to see if the check ever cleared the donor's bank and, if so, who endorsed it.

> The donation may have been lost in the mail, accidentally posted to the wrong donor, or the bookkeeper may have stolen the money. Regardless, this would have been hard to catch without sending out the acknowledgment letters.

Donor acknowledgment reports are designed from the **Sales by Donor Detail** report. This report will show all money received by specific donors for the designated period, whether they were entered through sales receipts or payments on invoices.

Find this report by searching the **Reports** menu and select the *Customize* button.

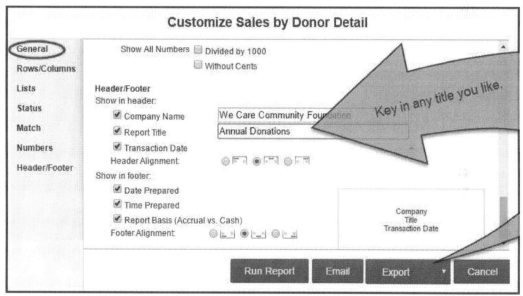

Because not all monies your organization has received are tax deductible (like dues, book purchases, tuition for example), we need to filter the report to leave those items out of the report.

Under the *Lists* option in the side bar, go to *Product/Service*, *Select Multiple* in the drop-down menu.

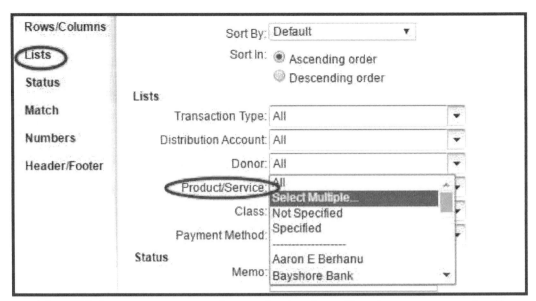

This will bring up a screen to choose the Products/Services you set up in Chapter 8. For this to work correctly, select only those items that the IRS considers deductible contributions.

For this example, I have selected *Fundraiser Support and Individual Contribution* by choosing each one individually and selecting *Add*. Click *OK* when done.

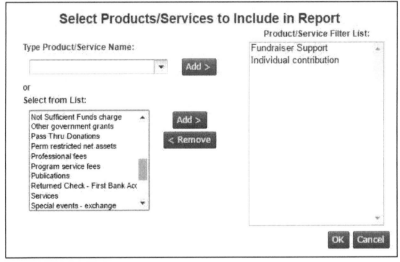

Under the **General** section, choose the Transaction Date period and select *Cash Basis* for the **Accounting Method**.

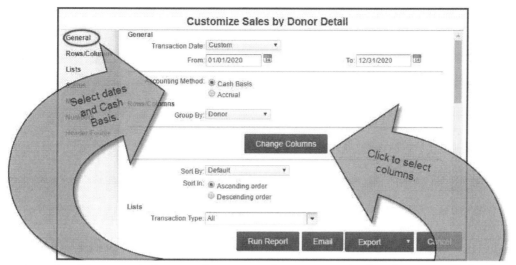

Use the **Change Columns** button to determine which columns will display on the report.

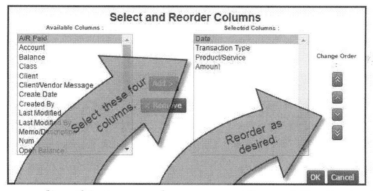

As you are sending this to your donor, you only need the **Date, Transaction Type, Product/Service,** and **Amount**. Click *OK* when done to go back to the main customize screen.

To review your report, select *Run Report*.

We Care Community Foundation
SALES BY DONOR DETAIL
January - December 2020

DATE	TRANSACTION TYPE	PRODUCT/SERVICE	AMOUNT
Bridget O'Brien			
05/31/2020	Sales Receipt	Individual contribution	125.00
Total for Bridget O'Brien			**$125.00**
Lee, Laurel			
03/05/2020	Sales Receipt	Individual contribution	125.00
03/05/2020	Sales Receipt	Fundraiser Support	300.00
03/15/2020	Invoice	Individual contribution	2,000.00
11/16/2020	Sales Receipt	Individual contribution	2,500.00
Total for Lee, Laurel			**$4,925.00**
Nicholas Anderson			
07/14/2020	Sales Receipt	Individual contribution	125.00
08/15/2020	Sales Receipt	Fundraiser Support	18.00
Total for Nicholas Anderson			**$143.00**
Various donors			
04/15/2020	Sales Receipt	Individual contribution	5,000.00
07/15/2020	Sales Receipt	Individual contribution	6,000.00
11/15/2020	Sales Receipt	Individual contribution	10,000.00
Total for Various donors			**$21,000.00**
TOTAL			**$26,683.00**

This report shows each donor and their donations in one report. You need to separate this information in order to mail it out to donors. To do this, we will export the report to an Excel spreadsheet and insert page breaks. But before doing so, remember to **Save Customizations**.

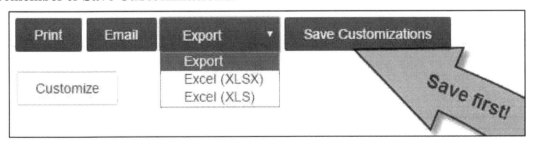

Now select *Export* to send the report to Excel to see a spreadsheet like the one on the next page.

Under the *Page Layout* tab, select the entire row with the donor name. Select *Breaks, Insert Page Break,* and a break will be inserted just above that line. Repeat this for every donor.

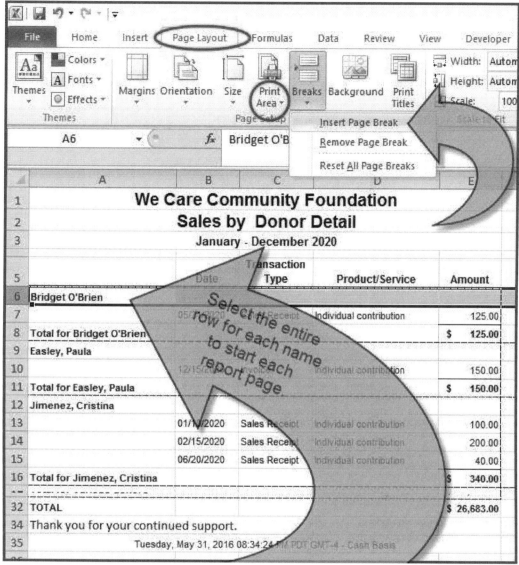

From the Excel top menu, select the drop-down arrow at *Print Area* and *Rows to repeat at the top*. A screen similar to this will appear.

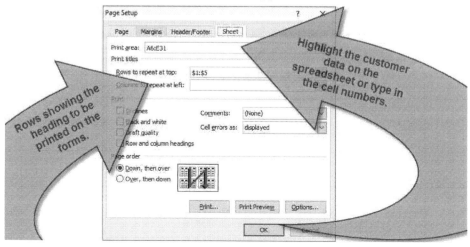

To fill in the **Print area**, click on the box next to it. Then go to the spreadsheet and highlight the rows from the first donor to just before the **Total** line. Do not include the total line in the print area.

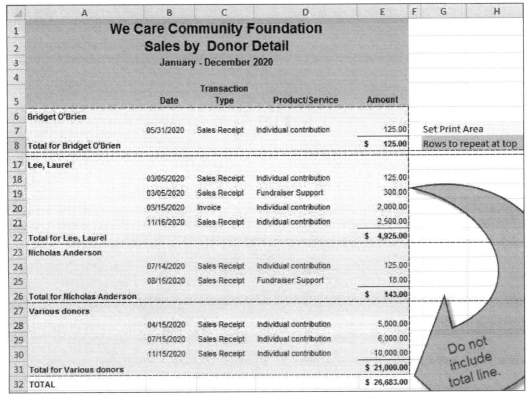

Back to the **Page Setup** box, go to **Print titles** and click on the box next to *Rows to repeat at the top*. Select the header rows from the spreadsheet you want to print on the acknowledgment form.

On the **Footer** tab of the **Page Setup** box, enter a thank you message.

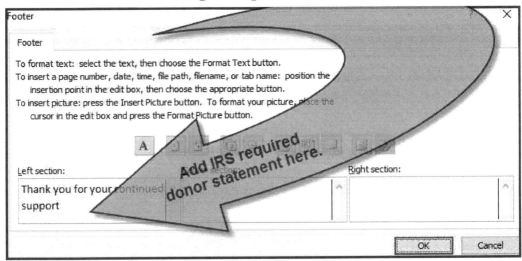

It is also a good idea to include the IRS required statement, i.e. *The donor did not receive goods or services in exchange for their donation.* (Unless they did, which has other acknowledgement rules. For details on acknowledging donor contributions, check out the IRS website or *Church Accounting—the How-To Guide for Small & Growing Churches.* Click *OK* when done.

Finally go to the top of the spreadsheet and select *File, Print, Print Preview* to view the pages of your reports.

We Care Community Foundation
Sales by Donor Detail
January - December 2020

		Transaction		
	Date	Type	Product/Service	Amount
Jimenez, Cristina				
	01/10/2020	Sales Receipt	Individual contribution	100.00
	02/15/2020	Sales Receipt	Individual contribution	200.00
	08/20/2020	Sales Receipt	Individual contribution	40.00
Total for Jimenez, Cristina				$ 340.00

Thank you for your continued support

Each donor acknowledgment will print on its own page. When you are ready, print and mail reports with a cover letter.

I. Other Year-End Requirements

1.   1099 Filings

Organizations of all types pay people for services. If these people are not employees or work for a corporation, they are considered an independent contractor. There is a link to the IRS documents regarding rules for independent contractors at www.accountantbesideyou.com/irs-forms. *Church Accounting—The How-To Guide* also details this.

Annually, the IRS requires all organizations to send a Form 1099 to independent contractors paid over $600 (as of the time of this writing). Additionally, Form 1096 must be sent to the IRS with copies of the 1099s. Please refer to the IRS website or ask your accountant for the most current filing requirements.

The good news is QBO makes it easy to print these forms but only in the Plus version. When you set up your vendors in chapter 6, the Vendor Information screen had a box labeled **Track payments for 1099**.

Before generating the 1099s, you will want to go back through your vendors and, for any that meet the IRS requirements, make sure you have selected that box.

To create 1099s, go to the left **Menu** bar and select *Vendors*. You may have already noticed the *Prepare 1099s* button next to the **New vendor** button as shown below.

Select *Prepare 1099s* to bring up QBO's 1099 Wizard. Select *Let's get started* for the first step.

Verify that your organization's Employee ID (EIN), organization name, and legal address are all correct. You can make corrections if necessary by clicking on the edit pencil to the right of *Name and address* or *Tax ID*. This information **must be correct** because it will be used on the actual IRS 1099 and 1096 forms. Select *Next* when done.

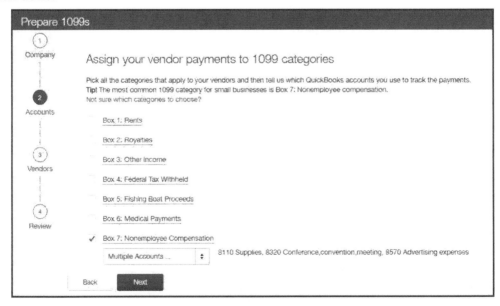

Next, pick all the categories that apply to your vendor payments which you will link to the QBO accounts you used to make payments. Each checkbox represents a box on the 1099-MISC form.

These categories are defined by the IRS. The most common 1099 category for small organizations is **Box 7: Nonemployee Compensation**. If you're not sure which category to choose, talk to your accounting professional or review the Form 1099 instructions found at IRS.gov.

In the drop-down box that appears for each category, select any of the accounts (from the Chart of Accounts) you use to track these payments in QBO. Click *Next* to see the selected vendors, tax ID numbers, and addresses.

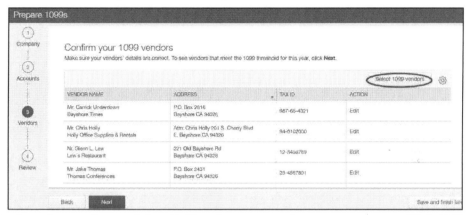

Review the vendor and details listed to assure they are accurate. Click *Edit* to the right of each Vendor if corrections are needed. Click the button *Select 1099 vendors* to add or remove a vendor from the list. Beware that making changes to your list from this screen will clear the **Track payments for 1099** check box in the vendor profile.

The **Tax ID** and the **Address** columns need to be complete and correct as they will be printed on the forms and mailed to the vendor and the IRS.

> Even if you don't have the tax ID numbers of some vendors, go through the Wizard. It will show you which vendors were paid enough to need a 1099 and how many 1099 forms you will need to order. Select **Save and finish later** and contact the vendors for any missing information. You can return to the Wizard when you have the data.

Click *Next* to view vendors whose payments meet the threshold.

Notice that even though we had selected eight vendors for 1099s, only three are displayed here. For the other five, payments made to the vendors were below the minimum required, so no 1099 is required.

Click an amount listed to open the 1099 Transaction Detail by Vendor report to see the payments that made up the total amount. You can drill down on any entry to see the transactions included for any vendor slated to receive a 1099.

We Care Community Foundation								
1099 TRANSACTION DETAIL BY VENDOR								
January - December 2015								
DATE	TRANSACTION TYPE	NUM	MEMO/DESCRIPTION	1099 BOX	ACCOUNT	SPLIT	AMOUNT	BALANCE
Holly Office Supplies & Rentals_v								
07/02/2015	Bill		student supplies	Box 7	8110 Non-personnel expenses.S	2010 Accounts payable	20,000.00	20,000.00
Total for Holly Office Supplies & Rentals_v							$20,000.00	

If you find that you need to add or edit a payment, click *Save and finish later* and make the appropriate updates in QBO. Select *Next* to print forms.

A screen will appear asking if you want to E-file or print. Intuit will walk you through the necessary steps if you choose to E-file. For this example, select *Print and mail forms*.

You will need to purchase a set of QBO compatible 1099 and 1096 blank forms to print them. These are often pricey; so if you only have a few to fill out, you may wish to order free forms from the IRS and fill them out by hand. The IRS free forms will not work with the 1099 wizard in QBO.

QBO versions of the forms can be purchased at office supply stores or from online vendors including Intuit.

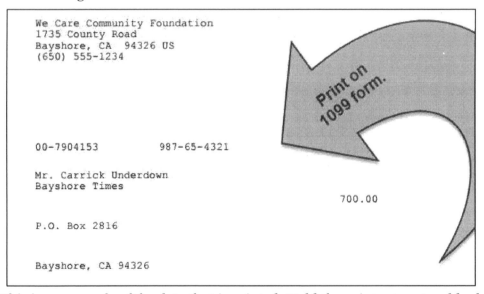

This is an example of the data that is printed. Hold the printout up to a blank IRS Form 1099 to see if the numbers fit the boxes correctly. Using the dialog box after selecting *Print, Align*, you can change the margins so the data prints on the form correctly.

2. File W-2s for Employees

From the IRS website www.irs.gov/uac/Form-W-2,-Wage-and-Tax-Statement:

Every employer engaged in a trade or business who pays remuneration, including noncash payments of $600 or more for the year (all amounts if any income, social security, or Medicare tax was withheld) for services performed by an employee must file a Form W-2 for each employee (even if the employee is related to the employer) from whom: Income, social security, or Medicare tax was withheld. Income tax would have been withheld if the employee had claimed no more than one withholding allowance or had not claimed exemption from withholding on Form W-4, Employee's Withholding Allowance Certificate.

If you are using an outside payroll service, they should prepare and possibly mail the W-2s to employees and file Form W-3, the summary transmittal, to the IRS with copies of the W-2s.

If you are not using an outside service, you will need to do this yourself from the *Employees* option on the menu bar. They are similar to what we went through with the 1099s, but for purposes of this book, I'm going to assume you are using an outside service.

> Great job! You've made it through all of the transactions for a year and know how to design and produce reports. In the next chapter, I'll go over some miscellaneous tasks that may come up.

16. What About...???

You now understand the basics of setting up your accounting system and how to run it efficiently. In this chapter, you'll learn how to account for a few unusual items, about useful system features, and how to design reports for your annual audit. You can also check www.accountantbesideyou.com for updated information and downloads to assist you.

A. How Do I Account For ...???

1.   Fundraisers

The most basic way to account for fundraisers is to have a class for each one that tracks the income and related expenses for the fundraiser. That works well if your fundraisers are a substantial portion of your organization's income and expenses (i.e. a foundation who raises money for a school through fundraisers) and you only have one or two a year. If it isn't a significant portion of your donations, then I recommend a process for tracking fundraisers that may seem a bit odd.

When you have a fundraiser, the board doesn't typically ask for the details of tickets sales versus sponsorship, etc. They want to know how much money the fundraiser netted (money in, less the money paid out). To do this, set up a parent account with an income type for each fundraiser. There can be as few as two subaccounts or as many as your system will hold. Below, I have set up a parent account for **Fundraising Income**.

NUMBER	NAME ▼	TYPE	DETAIL TYPE	QUICKF BANK E	ACTION
4200	4200 Fundraising Income	Income	Non-Profit Income		Run report ▼
4220	4220 Fundraising Event 2	Income	Non-Profit Income		Run report ▼
4221	4221 Event 2 Revenues	Income	Non-Profit Income		Run report ▼
4225	4225 Event 2 Expenses	Income	Discounts/Refunds Given		Run report ▼
4210	4210 Fundraising Event 1	Income	Non-Profit Income		Run report ▼
4211	4211 Event 1 Revenues	Income	Non-Profit Income		Run report ▼
4215	4215 Event 1 Expenses	Income	Non-Profit Income		Run report ▼

Under it are two events, and each event has a revenue and an expense title in the subaccount. The unusual thing is that I gave the expenses lines an income type. By netting the expense against the income, only the net profit from each fundraiser shows up on the financial statements.

If you would like to track the types of revenues received or detail types of expenses from a fundraiser, set up items for each (sponsorship, ticket sales, printing, advertising, etc.). Reports can then be run on the items separately.

2. Record the Sale of Merchandise

Some organizations sell merchandise related to their programs. Depending on your program and your state, there may be tax consequences. Please see a local accountant to be certain you are following all the rules.

If you maintain inventory, there are some specific ways to record the purchase of the goods and the related sales. First you need to set the company preferences to allow for inventory. From the *Gear Icon*, select *Your Company, Account and Settings, Sales.*

Click on the boxes next to *Show Product/Service column on sales forms, Track quantity and price/rate, Track inventory quantity on hand* and *Save.*

Now that you have turned these settings on, go to the *Gear Icon, Lists, Products and Services.*

Select *New* to create a new product. For this example, you will choose the **Inventory** option.

Enter the **Name** of the item you are selling. **SKUs** and **Categories** were discussed in Chapter 8. Use them as you see fit. I discourage you from using the **Initial quantity on hand.** If you already have stock, enter it as an inventory purchase in the previous year so as not to mess up your balance sheet.

Choose an **Inventory asset account,** and enter the description you would like to see on invoices in the **Sales information** box. The **Sales price/rate** should be the regular sales price, keeping in mind it can be overridden. Choose the **Income account** and select if it **Is taxable** based on your accountant's recommendations. Input the **Cost** and link the **Expense account** to your Cost of goods sold (COGS). *Save and close.*

When you receive the bill for the inventory, go to *Plus, Vendors, Bill* and type in the vendor name.

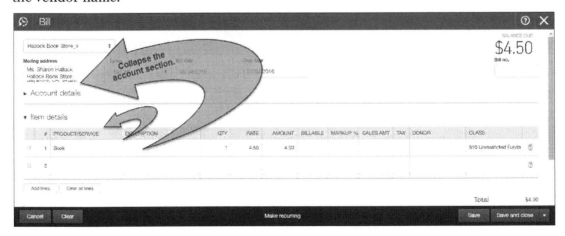

Collapse the **Account details** section and go to the **Item details.** Under **Product/Service**, choose the inventory item and fill in the quantity **(QTY)**. The system will fill in the cost. Also remember to include the **Class** (usually Unrestricted or General Fund). Click *Save and Close* and the inventory will be recorded.

When a book is sold, enter the sale through *Plus, Donors, Sales Receipt.* Select the **Book** item and the unrestricted **Class**.

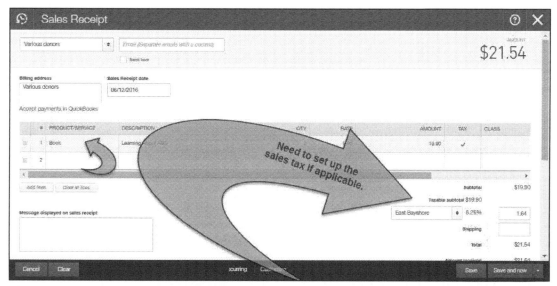

If sales tax is required, work with your accountant to set these up in the system.

Once this is saved, QBO will record the $19.90 in sales for two books and $9.00 ($4.50 x 2) in cost of goods sold (COGS), leaving a net profit on books of $10.90.

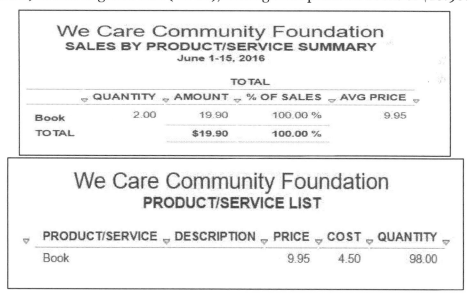

Also note the quantity has been reduced by the sale of the two books.

3.   In-Kind Donations

There are times organizations receive donations of items or professional services instead of cash. These are called in-kind donations. Typical examples of in-kind donations are computers, paintings, office supplies, legal services (this is only considered an in-kind donation if the organization would have otherwise had to pay for the service), or use of space without being charged rent.

> Every organization should have written guidelines for accepting **in-kind donations**. You do not have to accept everything that is offered. If it cannot be used or sold, do not accept it.

When you receive an in-kind gift, it is appropriate to acknowledge it. However, do not value the gift in the acknowledgement; simply thank them for the item. For the donor's tax purposes, valuation is the donor's responsibility. An exception to that rule is the donation of a car, boat, or plane received for resell. For details on how to handle this, read *Church Accounting—The How-to Guide* or call your accountant and ask how to handle tax implications and reporting of vehicle donations.

To record an in-kind donation in QBO, set up an income account titled *In-Kind Contribution* and an expense account titled *Donated Goods & Services*. If you plan to use the items donated, you can enter the transaction as a journal entry or as a sales receipt.

If you enter it as a sales receipt, you will need to set up items related to the donation. This method is useful if you have a large number of in-kind donations and would like to run an item report to see what types of goods are being received. Otherwise, it is probably easier to record it as a journal entry.

Go to *Plus, Other, Journal Entry*.

#	ACCOUNT	DEBITS	CREDITS	DESCRIPTION	NAME	CLASS
1	6800 Donated Goods and Services	100.00		Donated Computer		100 Administrative
2	4380 Contributed support:In Kind Contribution		100.00	Donated Computer		910 Unrestricted Funds

Use your best estimate to value the donation. Charge the donated goods expense line as a **DEBIT** and the in-kind contribution as a **CREDIT** for the same amount, assigning it to the appropriate program or fund. *Save and close* when you are finished.

If you are using the donated goods or services, you don't need to do anything else in QBO. However, if you sell the donated item, you will need to record the sale. Go back to the journal entry screen.

#	ACCOUNT	DEBITS	CREDITS	DESCRIPTION	NAME	CLASS
1	1010 First Bank Checking Account	100.00		Donated Computer		910 Unrestricted Funds
2	6800 Donated Goods and Services		100.00	Donated Computer		100 Administrative

Select same program as Original entry.

This time, **DEBIT** the checking account where the money received was deposited and **CREDIT** the donated goods expense. You must be certain to assign the donated good to the same program under **Class** as the original entry.

4.   Record a Mortgage

If your church has a mortgage, you will need to set up a few accounts before you get started. Go to *Gear, Your Company, Chart of Accounts* to add the following (if you haven't already):

- a Fixed Asset account to record the building or land. This may also be called Construction in Progress for a building under construction
- a Long-Term Liability account to record the loan
- a Prepaid Asset account for any escrow payments
- Expense accounts for any loan expenses.

Additionally, you will need to set up your mortgage company as a vendor.

Set up a new **Service** item (*Gear, Lists, Products and Services, New*) called **Mortgage.**

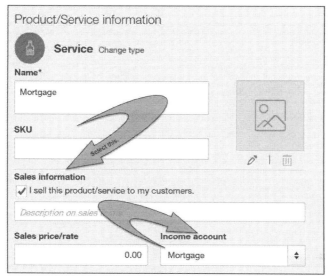

Select *I sell this product ...* and use the drop-down arrow under **Income account** to select the *Mortgage* liability account you previously set up.

When you receive the money for the loan, enter it through **Sales Receipt** (*Plus, Customers, Sales Receipt*), with the mortgage holder as your vendor.

To make loan payments, go to *Plus, Vendors, Bill*. Select the mortgage holder as the **Vendor.**

Using either the notice from the bank or an amortization schedule, split the payment between principal and interest payments. If you have an escrow, record it to the escrow account. Use *Make recurring* to remind you to book the entry each month.

You will need to adjust the principal and interest numbers each time, but it will save you entering the rest of the data.

5.   A Reserve Account on the Income Statement

Many organizations like to set up a reserve at a bank and designate an amount of money to be transferred to that account on a monthly or quarterly basis. Because the reserve account is a bank or investment account, the transfer of the funds does not show on the income statement.

If your governing board or treasurer would like to see the amount of money moved to the reserve account on the income statement of the general fund, add two accounts to your chart of accounts list: **Reserve Transfer Deposit** and **Reserve Transfer Payment**. Add the accounts by going to the *Gear, Your Company, Chart of Accounts, New*. Under **Category Type,** select the *Other Income* from the drop-down menu.

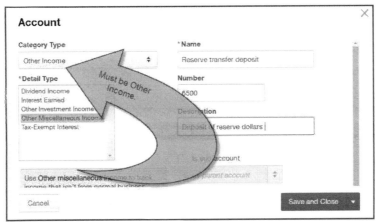

The deposit account must have an account type of *Other Income* in order to show below the operating expense line. Save this account and enter the payment account.

Next set up an **Expense** account called **Reserves Additions.**

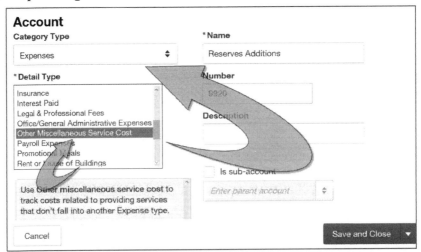

This time you will select a **Category** type of *Expenses* with a **Detail Type** of *Other Miscellaneous Service Cost* and save the entry.

When you write the check to make the transfer, instead of assigning it to the investment account, charge it to the **Reserve Transfer Payment** account. To record the check, go to *Plus, Vendors, Check* and use the general fund or unrestricted class.

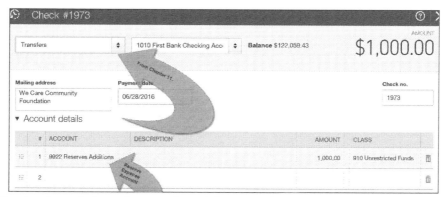

Make the deposit by going to *Plus, Other, Bank Deposit.*

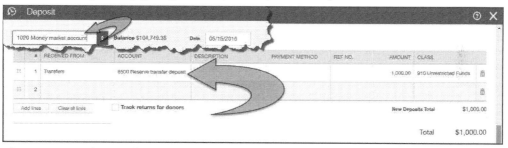

On the screen to input deposits, you will change the **Deposit to** account in the upper left corner to your investment account where the money was transferred. The **RECEIVED FROM ACCOUNT** should be the *Reserve transfer deposit* account.

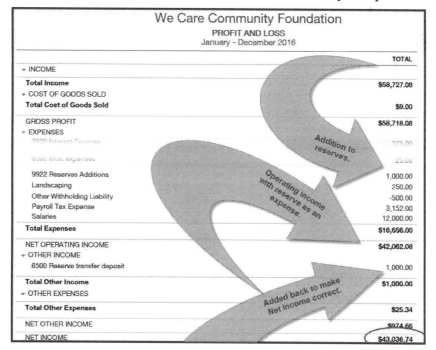

Once saved, your overall income statement will show the expense in operations and the deposit as other income.

B. How Do I???

1.   Invite and Manage Multiple Users

QBO allows you to set up and manage access for multiple users. Only a user designated as an administrator or who has been given user management permission can add a new user. QBO identifies each unique user by their email address, which also serves as their User ID.

The QBO Plus version supports up to 5 users, while QBO Essential allows up to 3 users. **Reports Only** and **Time Tracking Only** users do not account against your user limits.

Setting up users is an important process because it is where user access is controlled. Keeping in mind the importance of internal controls, I suggest you carefully consider what level access each user needs.

To add a user, click the *Gear, Your Company, Manager Users*.

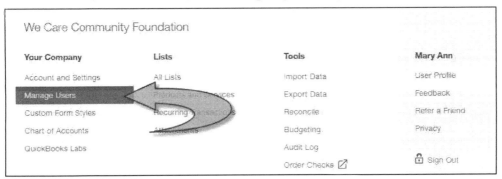

In the **Manage Users** screen, an administrator will see all users and their assigned user rights.

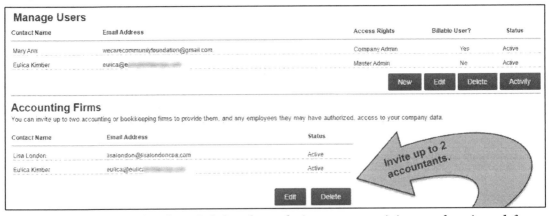

User can be added, edited, and deleted, or their system activity can be viewed from this screen. Invite up to two accountant users in the lower part. Change the user access at any time using the **Edit** button.

The **Activity** button allows you to review any user's QBO activity in the **Audit Log**. This log documents every activity performed under that user's login. Highlight the row of the user whose activity you wish to review and click *Activity*.

On your screen, you may notice some of the **Events** are listed in blue. These indicate that you can click on them to see the document that was changed.

Now let's add a new user and learn about access. Using the back arrow on your browser, go back to the **Manage Users** screen and click *New*.

An interview screen opens to start the process of adding a new user. Here you will choose the user type. In our example, we will select and look at adding the **Regular or custom user.** A **Company administrator** has full access rights. **Reports only users** do not see or enter transactions but can view most reports. You may wish to set up your board of directors as Reports only users. **Time Tracking only** users can only view and enter their own time tracking information. Select *Next* to continue through the screens.

Next we will assign user rights for the **Regular or custom user**.

QBO segregates access rights into two main functional areas: **Donors and Sales** for Money In transactions, and **Vendors & Purchases** for Money Out transactions. This allows you to segregate duties within QBO by granting access to separate people, or you may select **All** to grant full access.

Regular vs. Custom User Access	
User Access	**Access Rights**
All	These users have all of the access rights for: ☐ Donors and Sales ☐ Vendors and Purchases These users CANNOT: ☐ Add, edit, and delete employees ☐ Change preferences ☐ View the Activity Log ☐ Create, edit, and delete budgets ☐ Add, edit, and delete accounts ☐ Make deposits and transfer funds ☐ Reconcile accounts and make journal entries ☐ View all reports
Donors and Sales	These users CAN: ☐ Enter estimates, invoices, sales receipts, credit memos, and refunds ☐ Enter charges and credits ☐ Create and delete statements ☐ Receive payments from donors ☐ Fill out time sheets for anyone ☐ Add, edit, and delete donors ☐ Add, edit, and delete products and services ☐ View donor registers ☐ View donor and A/R reports These users CANNOT: ☐ Print checks, including refund checks ☐ Make bills and purchases billable to donors ☐ Add, edit, and delete accounts ☐ View bank registers ☐ Add, edit, and delete quantity on hand ☐ See total income or expense amounts on Home, Vendor, and Customer pages
Vendors & Purchases	These users CAN: ☐ Enter bills from vendors ☐ Pay bills ☐ Make bills and purchases billable to donors ☐ Write checks ☐ Enter cash and credit card purchases ☐ Add, edit, and delete vendors ☐ View vendor and A/P reports ☐ View Check Detail reports ☐ Print checks, except refund checks ☐ Add, edit, and delete products and services These users CANNOT: ☐ Add, edit, and delete accounts ☐ View bank registers ☐ Add, edit, and delete quantity on hand ☐ See total income or expense amounts on Home, Vendor, and Customer pages

Continue through the screens by clicking *Next*. Now you need to decide what kind of administrative rights you wish to assign.

Your average user will not normally need to manage users or the subscriptions.
Click *Next* and enter the user's email address and name.

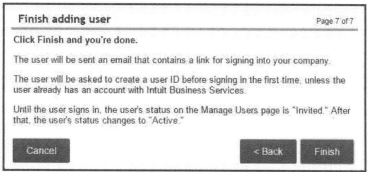

The user will receive an email invitation and will be prompted to create a password.

If the user is already a QBO user, they will use their current password. By accepting the invite, they have access to your organization's file. Click *Finish* when done.

2.   Invite an Accountant

You can invite your accountant to sign in to your company file directly. This access allows your accountant to make changes at his or her convenience. The best part is you can both work in your data at the same time. Up to two accountants can be invited for free without counting toward your current user limit. These may include your bookkeeper, accountant, auditor, or tax professional.

The process for inviting your accountant is similar to the process above. Click *Invite Accountant* in the **Manage Users** screen.

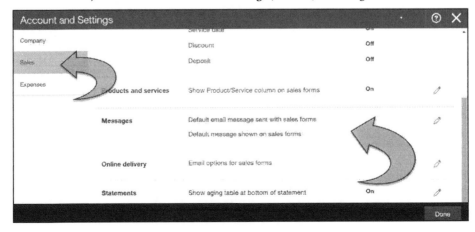

You will enter your accountant's email address.

Click *Next* and *Finish*. Now your accountant can see your data.

3.   Send a Thank You from the Receipts Screen

Thanking donors promptly is crucial for small nonprofits. You can email a donor a thank-you note directly from the sales receipt screen in QBO. It takes a bit of time to design and layout the template, but once you do, it is a huge timesaver.

From the *Gear*, select *Account and Settings, Sales, Messages*.

Double click in the *Message* section or the *edit pencil* and the **Message** template screen will open.

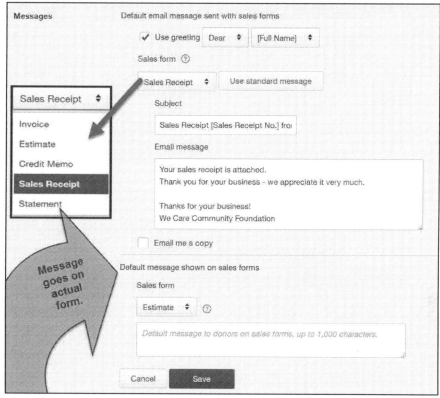

In this screen you can customize the email wording for messages that are sent with any Invoice, Estimate, Sale Receipt, or Statement. Select *Sales Receipt* and make changes to the **Greeting**, **Subject,** and **Email message**.

You can enter a **Default** message (up to 1000 characters) that will appear on the sales receipt or other sales form. Some organizations use this field to insert the motto, scripture, or the standard IRS required wording for acknowledging donations. Click *Save* when done.

You will repeat the process of creating a message for each form by selecting that form name from the drop-down menu as shown above.

4. Customize Forms

You may also want to customize forms to match your church or organization's colors. You can change the layout of your forms and select what information you want the donor or member to see.

Customizations are found under *Gear, Your Company, Custom Form Styles*. This will bring you to the **Custom Form Styles** list.

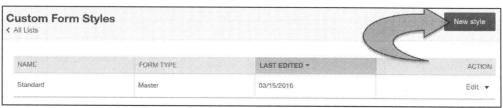

This page will list any custom forms you have created. The only form now in the list is the default form. Click *New style* to begin creating a new form.

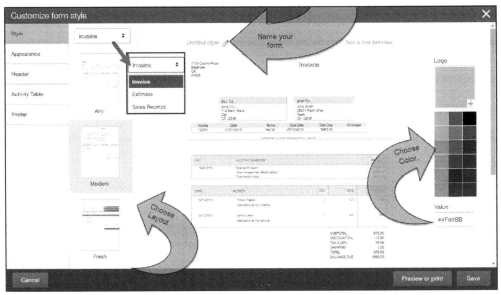

You have lots of choices to customize your forms. Notice that down the left of the screen are five headings: **Style, Appearance, Header, Activity Table,** and **Footer**. I'll walk you through each of these.

Let's begin with **Style**. That was just fun to type. Here you will select the form type to create a customized Invoice, Estimate, or a Sales Receipt. Next, name your form style, select the preset layout style, upload your logo, and pick the color scheme. The **Preview or print** button at the bottom allows you to see what the changes would look like before you save. Once you have made any changes you want to keep, be sure to select *Save*.

Click on **Appearance** in the side menu to resize and chose the placement of your logo. You can also pick a font and its size and the margins. Continue scrolling down the screen to designate if you will be using window envelopes or letterhead. If so, QBO will adjust the printing layout.

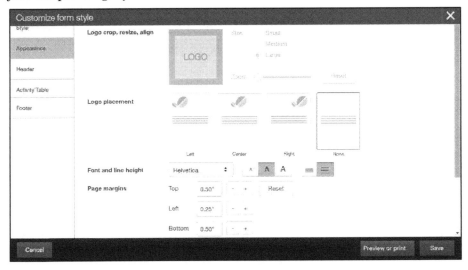

In the **Header** section, you will enter the report headings as you want them to appear on the various printouts.

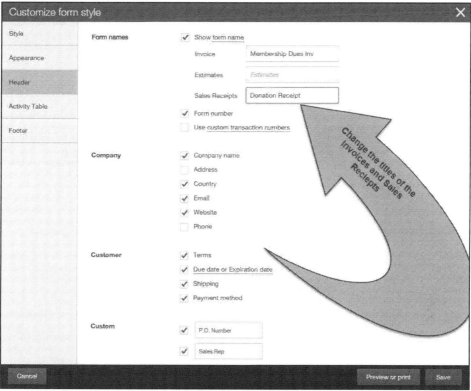

I have renamed the **Invoice** heading as **Membership Dues Inv** and the **Sales Receipt** heading as **Donation Receipt** in the example below. There is a twenty-character limit for this field, so I had to abbreviate the word Invoice (Inv).

Under the **Company** section, you can also choose how much information about your organization and the donor will appear in the header of the invoice.

The **Activity Table** section contains selections about the actual transaction.

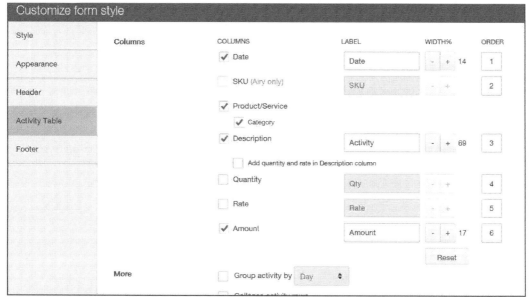

You will choose how much information about the donation or payment you want to see and how it will be displayed.

Finally, the **Footer** section allows you to enter a message to all donors. Within the footer, I suggest you enter an appropriate IRS compliant statement.

You can preview your changes at any time. Remember to *Save* when done.

5. Give Feedback to QBO

I mentioned at the start of this book that QBO is automatically updated with the latest updates and improvement to the application. Most system improvements and enhancements originate from users like you.

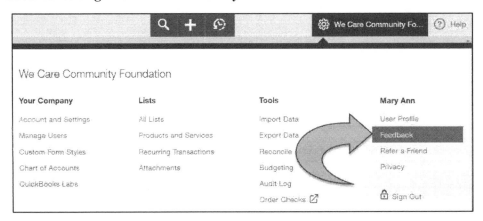

To give feedback to Intuit, go to *Gear, Profile, Feedback*. You may tell the QBO developers any ideas or bring bugs to their attention. Don't be afraid to enter your ideas. You never know what other churches or organizations may need the same thing.

QBO also likes for users to vote on what enhancements they should work on adding next.

C. What About ... ???

1. Reports I Need for an Audit

Though every audit is different, there are some basic reports your auditor will probably request. Some are financial and others are managerial. In planning for your audit, I'd recommend you gather, print, or have in an electronic file the following information as of the last day of the period being audited:

- Board Minutes
- Contracts, including employment, rent, insurance, etc.
- Accounts receivable aging detail (list of amounts due from donors)
- Accounts payable aging detail (list of amounts due to vendors)
- Payroll reports from the outside service or detail files.

Additionally, you will invite the auditor as your accountant as we learned in section 2 above of this chapter. This will give them full access to your company records to get the information they need. However, they may have questions and request documents to support your numbers in QBO.

2. Tax Stuff

Neither Eulica or I are offering any tax advice. Even though nonprofits are considered tax exempt, they may have activities that are taxable or, at least, have reporting requirements. Download IRS Publication 598 (http://www.irs.gov/pub/irs-pdf/p598.pdf) for information on unrelated business income. Additionally, ask your local accountant or tax attorney if your organization has any taxable activities.

States may also have different taxing requirements, especially with sales tax. If you sell products (like books or clothing), you may be required to collect and remit these taxes. Furthermore, some states exempt organizations and nonprofits from paying sales taxes on their own purchases or they reimburse them for the taxes paid. As every state is different, I'm afraid it is outside the scope of this book to cover them all. Again, check with your local accountant.

> You are almost done. In the next chapter, you'll learn about QBO Mobile and third party applications.

17. QBO Mobile and 3rd Party Apps

Now that we have covered the basics of QBO, I will introduce you to some tools that expand its usefulness and accessibility. QBO can be accessed from your smartphone or mobile device. Also, QBO has third party apps that work with it to help further automate and organize your work.

A. QBO from your Mobile Device

The QBO Mobile allows you to run your organization on the go! You are able to send invoices, capture receipts, or review transactions and balances from anywhere using your smartphone or tablet. The QBO app is available on both Android and Apple devices at no cost.

After the app is installed, the QBO icon will appear on your screen. Tap the icon to open it. Then sign in using the same User ID (email) and password that you use to log in on your PC.

The first time you log in, QBO want to confirm that it's really you logging into a new device. QBO will send an email to your email address with a verification code to enter.

After you check your email and enter that code, QBO opens to a screen titled **Activity**. This list contains all income and expense activity entered by any of your organzation's users up to that moment. At the top left, click the three-line menu icon to open the **Left Menu Bar.** Here you will see an abbreviated version of the menu bar from the full PC version of QBO.

Using these menus, income and expense transactions, customers, vendors, products, and services are viewed or added. Note the QBO mobile app labels your **Donors** or **Members** as customers. You **CANNOT** edit or add accounts to your Chart of Accounts using your mobile device.

First, start by viewing the Profit and Loss and Balance Sheet reports.

You can also enter invoices, income, and expense transactions. I want to show you how to enter an expense on the go. In this example below, I made a $25.34 purchase of office supplies at Staples on May 12, 2016.

Selecting *Expenses* from the left menu bar will take you to the list of expenses. Click the blue *Plus* to add a new expense.

A **New Expense** screen will open.

Enter the date, vendor, category account, amount, class, and a memo for the transaction. Take a picture of the receipt and attach to the transaction to keep the information stored together. The first time you take a picture through QBO, you will be asked to allow access to your device's camera. Tap *OK*. Then, tap *Take Photo*.

Click *Save* (top right corner) after you have entered the transaction.

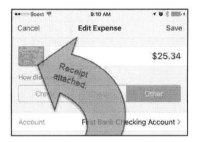

Now let's take a look back in the PC version of QBO to see what the transaction entered in the mobile device looks like. Viewing transactions entered using a mobile device is possible in real time. Back on the PC, *Search* for the transaction by date 5/12/2016.

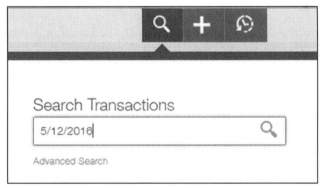

Find and *select* the transaction in the list of all transactions for that date. Here is the same transaction that was entered in the mobile device.

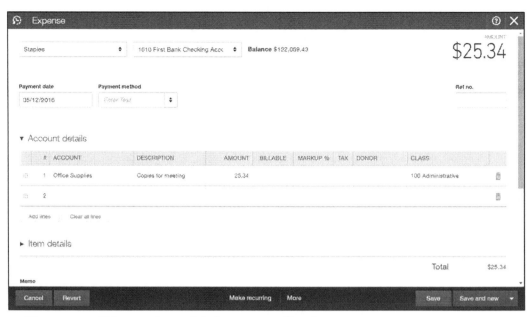

Next, you will learn about third-party applications.

B. 3ʳᵈ Party Developer Apps

Applications, referred to as apps, are created by Intuit or an approved third-party developer. They perform specific functions that are beyond the standard functionality of QBO.

The greatest benefit of using apps is that they sync seamlessly with QBO. However, only apps that you authorize have the ability to access your QBO information. Intuit makes sure that apps follow industry best practices for accessing and storing data. And you control the app's connection to QBO and can turn it off or on when you want.

You can access Apps from within your QBO company file on your computer. From the left blue menu bar, select *Apps.*

This will bring you to the QBO Apps center.

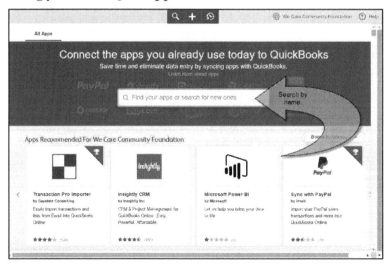

You will find apps that do anything from tracking time to accepting payments. Take some time to search the options. Each app has reviews just like those for mobile phones. You can read overview information, watch a video demonstration, and review user feedback on each app.

Some apps are free or have a basic option that is free. There is a monthly cost for others, but those usually have a 30-day free trial period. Also, you may find apps for services your organization already uses like PayPal or Square (both apps are free). Take time to explore, but I recommend you subscribe to a few apps that are truly beneficial and cost effective. Churches and organizations that use apps with QBO often find that the decrease in administrative hours outweighs the monthly cost.

Once you have decided on an app, click the *Get App Now* button. QBO and the app will sync and you will follow any set-up instructions.

I would like to give you a brief description of two Apps that may be helpful to your church or organization: **Method:Donor** and **Bills.com**.

1. Method:Donor—Donor Management Software

Method:Donor allows you to manage donors and donations all in one place. It provides a dedicated donation page link to send out to donors or include on your website. The app allows donors to make donations to your organization and then instantly syncs the information to QBO. It even sends out thank you messages and tax receipts. Method:Donor automates everything!

It also manages donor profiles, which keep track of emails, phone calls, event attendance, donation history, and more for each donor or member. This can be helpful for the management of donor information by segregating member management and fundraising duties from the accounting duties all while keeping QBO up to date. Your treasurer will thank you for this! The cost is $25 per month after a 30-day free trial.

2. Bills.com—Payment Management System

Bills.com is a business payments system that automates your accounts payable. You can pay bills via ACH, store documents, and route bills for approval. Best of all, payments automatically sync with QBO.

My favorite feature of this app is that it allows you to maintain internal controls over the bill payment process. You can set up approvers to be notified by email when a bill is ready to be approved. When approver (director or manager) receives the email, they can easily review all details and supporting information for the bill. Once a bill is approved, the treasurer will be notified that the bill is approved and can process the payment. This feature is really helpful for churches or organizations that have staff in different locations. No more chasing down approvers!

Eulica has a client that is a national organization with staff in different states that loves this program. Bills.com gets double thumbs up from treasurers. The cost is $25 per month after a 30-day free trial.

You did it!

Doesn't it feel great to realize you can set up QuickBooks for your nonprofit, enter transactions, run reports, prepare budgets, and all kinds of other useful tasks?

The system has much more functionality than Eulica and I could possibly cover in this book, so experiment, explore, and have fun with it.

We've enjoyed being the Accountant Beside You through the process. Keep an eye on www.accountantbesideyou.com for more books in the series, downloads, and seminar locations.

Appendix

A. Before You Start Checklist

Here is a list of items you will need to set up QuickBooks for your church or nonprofit.

Setting up the Organization File

Legal name and address of the organization

Federal EIN

First month of the accounting year (usually January)

Name of your organization's annual income tax form if applicable

Completing Lists and Entering Balances
Chart of Accounts:

Names, numbers, and descriptions for the Chart of Accounts

Financial statements as of the end of the prior year

Trial balances as of the QuickBooks start date

List of programs and grants (for the Class List)

Bank, credit card, and loan account numbers and data

Value of assets (original cost and accumulated depreciation)

Member and Grants Information

Donors' names, addresses, email, etc.

Grant documents

Outstanding invoices or dues as of your organization's transition to QuickBooks start date

Vendor Information

Vendor names, addresses, other contact information

List of 1099 vendors and their tax ID numbers

List of outstanding bills as of your QuickBooks start date

Other Information

Employee names and contact information

Volunteer names and responsibilities

B. Keyboard Shortcuts for QBO

Here are some useful keyboard shortcuts to help you navigate QBO efficiently.

1.   To move between fields on any screen

Press **Tab** to move forward from one field to the next.

Press **Shift-Tab** to move backward through fields.

2.   To enter dates

To change the date to...	Press
Next day	+ (plus key)
Previous day	- (minus key)
Today	T
First day of the **W**eek	W
Last day of the wee**K**	K
First day of the **M**onth	M
Last day of the mont**H**	H
First day of the **Y**ear	Y
Last day of the yea**R**	R

You can also press **Alt + down arrow** to open the popup calendar icon at the right of a **Date** field.

3.   To calculate amounts and rates

In any **Amount** or **Rate** field, you can enter a calculation. When you press **Tab**, QuickBooks Online Plus calculates the result.

You can...	Using	Example
Add	+	1256.94+356.50
Subtract	-	48.95-15
Multiply	*	108*1.085
Divide	/	89.95/.33
Group	( )	13.95+(25.95*.75)

4. To choose items in drop-down lists

a. Press **Tab** until you reach the field.
b. Press **Alt + down arrow** to open the list.
c. Press **up arrow** or **down arrow** to move through the items in the list.
d. Press **Tab** to select the item you want and move to the next field.

If you don't want to open the whole list, but just want to scroll through the items in the text box, press **Ctrl + down arrow** or **Ctrl + up arrow**.

If the list has subitems:

1. Type the first few characters of the parent item until it is selected.
2. Then you can:
   Press **Alt + down arrow** to open the list of subitems, and then press **down arrow** or **up arrow** to scroll through the subitems.
3. Press **Tab** to select the item you want and move to the next field.

5. Responding to messages

When a message pops up and the button names have underlined letters, type the letter to select the button you want.

6. Entering transactions in an account register

To select a transaction type:

1. In a new yellow transaction row, press **Shift + Tab** to select the transaction type field.
2. Press **Alt + down arrow** to open the list.
3. Press **up arrow** or **down arrow** to move through the list, or type the first letter of the transaction type you want.
4. If there are two types that start with the same letter, you can type the letter twice to select the second one. For example, type **C** once to select Check, and type **C** the second time to select Cash Purchase.
5. Press **Tab** to select the type you want and move to the next field.

Once you are familiar with the transaction types available, you can tab to the field and type the first letter to select the one you want without opening the list.

When the **Ref No.** field is selected:

- Press + to increase the Ref No.
- Press - to decrease the Ref No.
- Type **T** to enter **To Print** in the Ref No. field for a Bill Payment (from a checking account), Check, or Paycheck.

To save or edit the selected transaction:

- Press **Alt + S** to save.
- Press **Alt + E** to edit a saved transaction. This opens the transaction form.

To move between transactions within the register, selecting the **Date** field as you go:

- Press **up arrow** to select the transaction above.
- Press **down arrow** to select the transaction below.

C. Upload a Chart of Accounts

Starting out with a relevant chart of accounts is crucial to any organization. In section D, I detail my proposed charts for various types of organizations. These are for you to reference and design your own, or you can save data entry time by purchasing one at www.accountantbesideyou.com. Either way, start with these and add any accounts specific to your needs.

If you have purchased one of the chart of accounts downloads or have an Excel file with your preferred list, it is easy to upload it into QBO. (Excel must already be on your computer). Download the file and save it to your computer where you can easily find it. Now we are ready to upload the file.

In QBO, select *Chart of Accounts* from the left **Menu Bar**. In the top right corner of the **Chart of Accounts** screen, select the downward arrow to the right of the *New* button and click *Import*.

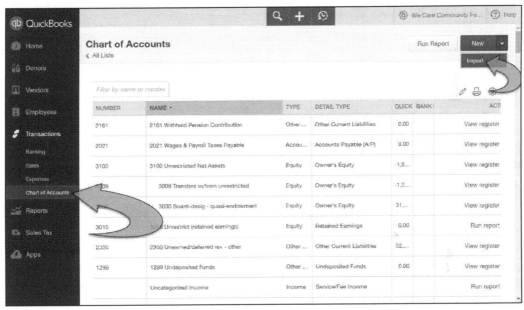

On the **Import Accounts** screen, select *Browse* to locate the file you just saved on your computer.

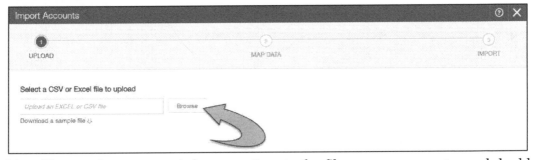

This will open the computer's browser. Locate the file on your computer and double click it.

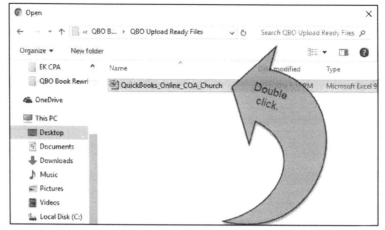

The **Import Accounts** will reappear with the Excel file listed. Select *Next*.

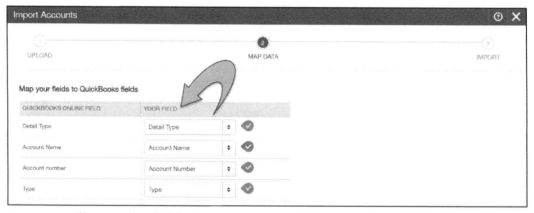

Here you will map the fields from your spreadsheet to the **QuickBooks Online Fields. Your Field** options are the headings from the spreadsheet. In other words, you are matching the spreadsheet data to the related QBO fields. Click *Next* to continue.

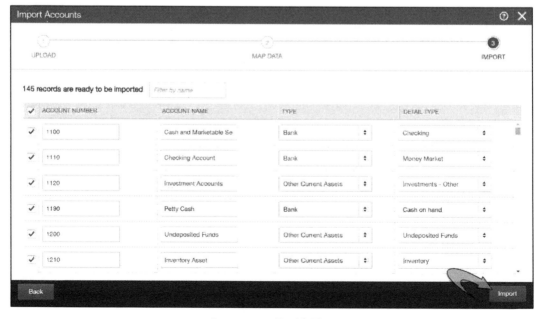

The final screen will detail how QBO will import the accounts. Scroll through the list and make any necessary changes using the drop-down arrows by each box. Unselect any accounts that you don't need by deselecting the arrows to the left of the account. When you are satisfied with the list, select *Import*.

There may be errors if any of the new accounts are already in your company file. Don't worry, duplicate accounts will not be added.

To verify the import, go to *Menu, Transactions, Chart of Accounts* and view your new Chart of Accounts.

D. Proposed Charts of Accounts

This section includes sample charts of accounts for a variety of organizations I have designed based on publically available information. None of these charts have been approved or recommended by the nonprofits listed. I used well-known organizations so you could decide which type of nonprofit might be closest to your own.

Each of these sample lists of accounts are available for purchase as a download at www.accountantbesideyou.com if you would like to save data entry time. Section C details how to upload the file.

1. For Organizations Needing a Simplified UCOA

Account	Type	Description
10000 · Cash & Invest.	Bank	
10100 · Checking Account	Bank	Rename for your bank.
10200 · Investment Accounts	Bank	Rename for your money market or savings account.
10900 · Petty Cash	Bank	For cash on hand or gift card balances
11000 · Accounts Receivable	Accounts Receivable	
11100 · Dues Receivable	Accounts Receivable	Money owed from members.
11200 · Pledges Receivable	Accounts Receivable	Promises (non-grant) to give contributions
11400 · Grants Receivable	Accounts Receivable	Promises from foundations or government to give grants
11500 · Other Accounts Receivable	Accounts Receivable	For amounts due from others not relating to grants, pledges, or dues.
11900 · Allowance for Doubtful Accounts	Accounts Receivable	Estimate of accounts receivable that will default and not be collected
12000 · Undeposited Funds	Other Current Asset	Funds received, but not yet deposited to a bank account.
13000 · Prepaid Expenses	Other Current Asset	Expenses that are paid in advance

13500 · Inventory Held for Sale	Other Current Asset	Cost of the inventory purchase, not yet sold
15000 · Furniture and Equipment	Fixed Asset	Furniture and equipment with useful life exceeding one year
15100 · Buildings - Operating	Fixed Asset	Buildings owned for current use
15500 · Facility Construction	Fixed Asset	Costs of building new facilities for use while construction is still going on
15700 · Land – Operating	Fixed Asset	Land owned for current use
15900 · Leasehold Improvements	Fixed Asset	Improvements to leased building space
16400 · Vehicles	Fixed Asset	Business automobiles and trucks, registered in the name of the business
17100 · Accum Depr - Furn and Equip	Fixed Asset	Accumulated depreciation on furniture and equipment
17200 · Accum Depr – Building	Fixed Asset	Accumulated depreciation on buildings
17300 · Accum Depr - Leasehold Imps	Fixed Asset	Accumulated depreciation on leasehold improvements
17400 · Accum Depr – Vehicles	Fixed Asset	Accumulated depreciation on vehicles
18000 · Other Assets	Other Asset	Assets used for program-related purposes other than current or fixed assets
18100 · Other Assets	Other Asset	
18700 · Security Deposits Asset	Other Asset	Deposits and other returnable funds held by other entities.(i.e. rent deposit)
18900 · Other Asset Suspense	Other Asset	Holding account for assets to ask accountant about.
20000 · Accounts Payable	Accounts Payable	
20100 · Accounts Payable	Accounts Payable	For normal operations bills due to others.
20200 · Grants Payable	Accounts Payable	Grants promised to other organizations or individuals
20300 · Credit Card	Credit Card	Enter your credit card name
24000 · Payroll Liabilities	Other Current Liability	Unpaid payroll liabilities. Amounts withheld or accrued, but not yet paid
24100 · Accrued Leave and Payroll	Other Cur. Liab.	Wages, salaries, and paid leave earned in the current period to be paid later

24200 · Accrued Expenses	Other Current Liability	Expenses incurred in the current period to be paid in future periods
25000 · Current Portion of Loans	Other Current Liability	Portion of long-term loans to be paid in the current year
25400 · Loans from Officers, Directors	Other Current Liability	Loans from officers, trustees, directors, employees, or other insiders
25600 · Short-term Notes - Credit Line	Other Current Liability	Short-term loans and notes to be paid in current year
25800 · Unearned or Deferred Revenue	Other Current Liability	Revenue received but not yet earned, refundable advances, other deferred revenue
27100 · Notes, Mortgages, and Leases	Long Term Liability	Long-term notes, mortgages payable, and capital lease obligations
27200 · Other Liabilities	Long Term Liability	Liabilities other than payroll, accounts and grants payable, deferred revenue, loans, bonds, or mortgages
27300 · Refundable Deposits Payable	Long Term Liability	Deposits and other funds held for other entities or individuals
30000 · Opening Balance Equity	Equity	Opening balances during setup post to this account. The balance of this account should be zero after completing your setup
31300 · Perm. Restricted Net Assets	Equity	Other Income
31500 · Temp. Restricted Net Assets	Equity	Other Income
32000 · Unrestricted Net Assets	Equity	Other Income
43300 · Direct Public Grants	Income	Grants from businesses, foundations, and other nonprofits
43310 · Corporate and Business Grants	Income	Grants from corporations, businesses, corporate private foundations
43330 · Foundation and Trust Grants	Income	Grants from foundations and trusts
43340 · Nonprofit Organization Grants	Income	Grants from other nonprofit organizations, churches, civic groups

43400 · Direct Public Support	Income	Contributions, gifts, donations, grants, bequests, legacies, pledges
43410 · Corporate Contributions	Income	Contributions from corporations, sponsorships
43430 · Donated Prof Fees, Facilities	Income	Donated professional services, use of facilities or equipment, utilities, rent, that meet GAAP rules for recording
43440 · Gifts in Kind - Goods	Income	Donated goods, non-cash gifts and contributions, donated inventory
43450 · Individ. & Busin. Contributions	Income	Contributions from individuals, businesses, direct mail, telethons, including any portion of dues that is greater than the value of member benefits received
43460 · Legacies and Bequests	Income	Bequests, legacies, planned gifts, deferred giving, gift agreements
43480 · Volunteer Services - Non-GAAP	Income	Donated services that do not meet GAAP rules - volunteer, non-professional services
44400 · Government Contracts	Income	Contracts to provide services to local, state, and federal governments
44500 · Government Grants	Income	Grants from local, state, and federal governments
44800 · Indirect Public Support	Income	Contributions received through federated fundraising agencies - United Way, CFC, etc.
44810 · Affiliated Org. Contributions	Income	Contributions received from a parent organization, subordinate, or another organization with the same parent
44820 · United Way, CFC Contributions	Income	Contributions from United Way, CFC, and other fundraising federations
45000 · Investments	Income	Revenue from investments in cash, securities, and property
45020 · Dividend, Interest (Securities)	Income	Dividends received from security and bond investments
45030 · Interest-Savings, Short-term CD	Income	Interest received from savings, CDs, and other short-term investments
45050 · Other Investment Revenue	Income	Revenue from other types of investments
46400 · Other Types of Income	Income	Revenue from program-related sales, advertising, etc.

46410 · Advertising Sales	Income	Sales of advertising space in publications, etc.
46420 · Inventory Sales	Income	Gross sales of inventory held for re-sale
46430 · Miscellaneous Revenue	Income	Revenue from occasional or non-material activities
47200 · Program Income	Income	Program service fees, member dues and assessments
47220 · Member Assessments	Income	Assessments of members that compare reasonably with the benefits provided, whether used or not
47230 · Membership Dues	Income	Member dues that compare reasonably with membership benefits available, whether used or not
47240 · Program Service Fees	Income	Participant fees, admissions, royalties, tuition, registration fees, and other program-related income
47500 · Rental Income	Income	Revenue from rental of assets
47700 · Rev Released from Restrictions	Income	Revenues earned and released from restrictions, satisfaction of donor restrictions (for use by accountant)
48400 · Securities	Income	Revenue from sales of securities
49000 · Special Events	Income	Fundraising special events, dinners, carnivals, raffles, bingo, other gaming
49010 · Special Event #1	Income	
49011 · Special Event #1 Revenue	Income	Revenues raised for Special Event # 1
49012 · Special Event #1 Retail Value	Income	Funds raised for the retail value of the goods or services given.
49013 · Special Event #1 Cost of Event	Income	Record costs of the special event here if not substantial to the entire organization.
49020 · Special Events # 2	Income	
49021 · Special Even #2 Revenue	Income	
49022 · Special Event # 2 Retail Value	Income	
49023 · Special Event # 2 Costs	Income	
50700 · Cost of Sales - Inventory Sales	Cost of Goods Sold	Costs related to sales of program-related inventory - supplies, materials, direct and indirect labor, not marketing or distribution

60300 · Awards and Grants	Expense	Program-related awards, grants, benefits, individual assistance
60900 · Business Expenses	Expense	Expenses of creating and maintaining the organization's business entity
60920 · Business Registration Fees	Expense	Permits, registrations, licenses, moving, royalties, bank charges, credit card fees
60930 · Fines, Penalties, Judgments	Expense	Fines, penalties, judgments, fines, late payment fees
60940 · Taxes - Not UBIT	Expense	Taxes other than unrelated business income tax
60950 · UBIT	Expense	Taxes on unrelated business income
62100 · Contract Services	Expense	Fees for outside services
62110 · Accounting Fees	Expense	Outside (non-employee) accounting, audit, bookkeeping, tax prep, payroll service, and related consulting
62120 · Donated Prof Fees – GAAP	Expense	Donated services that meet GAAP rules - professional
62130 · Fundraising Fees	Expense	Outside (non-employee) fundraisers and fundraising consultants
62140 · Legal Fees	Expense	Outside (non-employee) legal services
62150 · Outside Contract Services	Expense	Outside contractors (non-employee) for projects, consulting, short-term assignments for internal organization activities
62160 · Volunteer Services - Non-GAAP	Expense	Donated services that do not meet GAAP rules - volunteer, non-professional
62800 · Facilities and Equipment	Expense	Expenses related to office, storage, and other space
62810 · Depreciation and Amortization	Expense	Depreciation and amortization
62820 · Depr and Amort - Non-allowable	Expense	Depreciation and amortization not allowable for government grants
62830 · Donated Facilities	Expense	Donated use of facilities, utilities, rent, equipment
62840 · Equip Rental and Maintenance	Expense	Rental and maintenance of office, program, and other equipment
62850 · Janitorial Services	Expense	Janitorial expenses and cleaning supplies
62860 · Mortgage Interest	Expense	Interest, points, and other fees on mortgages

62870 · Property Insurance	Expense	Insurance on property (not investment) owned by the organization
62880 · Real Estate, Personal Prop Tax	Expense	Taxes on real estate and personal property
62890 · Rent, Parking, Utilities	Expense	Office and parking space, storage, basic utilities
65000 · Operations	Expense	Expenses related to providing program services and maintaining operations
65010 · Books, Subscriptions, Reference	Expense	Books, subscriptions, reference materials, periodicals for use
65020 · Postage, Mailing Service	Expense	Postage, parcel delivery, local courier, trucking, freight, outside mailing services
65030 · Printing and Copying	Expense	Printing, copying, duplicating, recording
65040 · Supplies	Expense	Supplies, materials, food and beverages, plaques, medicines
65050 · Telephone, Telecommunications	Expense	Telephone equipment and service, telegraph, internet access, fax, conference calls
65060 · Website/Technology Costs	Expense	Website maintenance and technology costs
65100 · Other Types of Expenses	Expense	Expenses listed on line 43 of Form 990
65110 · Advertising Expenses	Expense	Advertisements in outside publications, websites, etc.
65120 · Insurance - Liability, D and O	Expense	Non-employee or property insurance - liability, malpractice, directors
65130 · Interest Expense – General	Expense	Interest on loans and leases, other than interest attributable to rental property or mortgages on facilities
65140 · List Rental	Expense	Mailing list rentals
65150 · Memberships and Dues	Expense	Dues and memberships for civic, service, professional, or other organizations
65160 · Other Costs	Expense	Miscellaneous, small, or non-recurring expenses
65170 · Staff Development	Expense	Staff continuing education, training, development
66000 · Payroll Expenses	Expense	Payroll expenses
66100-Salaries & Wages	Expense	Gross pay to employees

66200-Payroll Taxes	Expense	Employer's payroll taxes (FICA, Medicare, FUTA, SUTA)
66300-Medical Benefits	Expense	Medical benefits paid on behalf of employees
66400-Other Benefits	Expense	Any other benefits paid on behalf of employees
68300 · Travel and Meetings	Expense	Expenses related to travel, meetings, conferences
68310 · Conference, Convention, Meeting	Expense	Conducting, or sending staff to, program-related meetings, conferences, conventions
68320 · Travel	Expense	Hotels, airfares, local transportation, car rentals, taxis, per diems, meals
80300 · Additions to Reserves	Expense	Increases or decreases in board-designated net assets
70100 · Reserve Transfer Deposit	Other Income	Use this to record the deposit into the reserve account.
70400 · Other Changes in Net Assets	Other Income	Prior year adjustment (use by accountant)
70600 · Unrealized Gains and Losses	Other Income	Unrealized change in value of investments and other assets
80000 · Ask My Accountant	Other Expense	To be discussed with accountant
80100 · Capital Purchases	Other Expense	Capital purchases made through a grant
80110 · Grant Capital Purchase – Land	Other Expense	Land purchased through a grant
80120 · Grant Capital Purchase – Bldg	Other Expense	Buildings purchased through a grant
80130 · Grant Capital Purchase – Equip	Other Expense	Equipment purchased through a grant
80140 · Grant Capital Purchase- Vehicle	Other Expense	Vehicles purchased through a grant
80200 · Payments to Affiliates	Other Expense	Payments to affiliated organizations - dues to state or national parent organizations
80400 · Program Admin Allocations	Other Expense	Management and program administration allocations to programs

2. For a Religious Organization

Account	Type	Description
1100 · Cash and Marketable Securities	Bank	
1110 · Checking Account	Bank	Rename with your bank name
1120 · Investment Accounts	Bank	Rename with your investment account name
1190 · Petty Cash	Bank	For cash or gift cards held at the church
1300 · Accounts Receivable	Accounts Receivable	Unpaid or unapplied customer invoices and credits
1310 · Pledges Receivable	Accounts Receivable	Unpaid pledges by members
1320 · Accounts Receivable	Accounts Receivable	Monies due from others.
1330 · Sales Tax Receivable	Accounts Receivable	Only necessary if your state reimburses sales taxes paid
1200 · *Undeposited Funds	Other Current Asset	Funds received but not yet deposited to a bank account
1210 · Inventory Asset	Other Current Asset	Costs of inventory purchased for resale
1400 · Prepaid Assets	Other Current Asset	
1410 · Prepaid Insurance	Other Current Asset	Record the future periods portion of the insurance paid here
1420 · Prepaid Postage	Other Current Asset	Postage Meter Balance
1500 · Property, Building, and Equip	Fixed Asset	
1510 · Land	Fixed Asset	Land owned by the church (put address or plot number here)
1520 · Building	Fixed Asset	Put address here
1530 · Computers	Fixed Asset	
1540 Furniture and Equipment	Fixed Asset	Furniture and equipment with useful life exceeding one year
1550 · Vehicle	Fixed Asset	
1580 · Accumulated Depreciation	Fixed Asset	Only needed if you record depreciation
1900 · Other Assets	Other Asset	
1910 · Other Assets- Suspense Account	Other Asset	Use this if you aren't sure which asset account to post to

2100 · Accounts Payable	Accounts Payable	Money owed to others
2150 · Credit Card	Credit Card	Add a subaccount for each credit card
2200 · Unearned Revenue/Prepaid Pledge	Other Current Liability	
2210 · Unearned Revenue/Prepaid Pledge	Other Current Liability	Record pledges received before the pledge period here
2300 · Accrued Liabilities	Other Current Liability	
2400 · Payroll Liabilities	Other Current Liability	Unpaid payroll liabilities. Amounts withheld or accrued, but not yet paid
2410 · Wages Payable	Other Current Liability	Only needed if not using an outside service
2900 · Mortgage Payable	Long Term Liability	
3000 Opening Balance Net Assets	Equity	System account. Should be $0
3100 Unrestricted Net Assets	Equity	General Fund
3200 · Temp. Restricted Net Assets	Equity	Fund balances of temporarily restricted funds
3300 · Perm. Restricted Net Assets	Equity	Endowments and other permanently restricted funds
4100 · Pledges/Offerings	Income	Normal donations
4110 · Plate Income	Income	Cash from the plate not designated to a member
4120 · Pledges Income	Income	Pledge commitments
4130 · Unpledged Support	Income	Money received from a member not pledged
4140 · EFT Offerings	Income	Electronic Funds Transfers of Donations
4150 · Special Collections-Operating	Income	Use for special collections for church operations
4200 · Fundraising Income	Income	Design a subaccount for each significant fundraiser
4210 Fundraising Event 1	Income	Income from annual fundraiser
4211 · Event 1 Revenues	Income	
4215 · Event 1 Expenses	Income	
4220 Fundraising Event 2	Income	
4221 · Event 2 Revenues	Income	
4225 ·Event 2 Expense	Income	

4300 Other Operating Income	Income	Money or goods received for services offered by the church
4310 · Donation, Gift, Bequest Income	Income	
4320 · Wedding, Funeral, & Memorials	Income	
4330 · Flowers	Income	
4380 · In-Kind Contribution	Income	Receipt of goods or services instead of money
4390 · Other Miscellaneous Income	Income	
4400 · Income -Other Operating Areas	Income	
4420 · Books/Pamphlets Sales	Income	
4430 · Cemetery Plots	Income	
4490 · Other Income-Other Operating	Income	
4500 · Investment Income	Income	Record interest, dividend and investment gains and losses in the subaccounts
4510 · Interest Income	Income	Interest from money market or bank accounts
4520 · Realized Gain/Loss – Investment	Income	Money from dividends or stock. From your brokerage account statements
4530 · Unrealized Gain/Loss-Investment	Income	Change in the market prices. Data is on your brokerage statements
4800 Net Assets Released	Income	Used to reclassify dollars that are no longer restricted
5999 · Cost of Goods Sold	Cost of Goods Sold	Costs of items purchased and then sold to customers
6000 · Facilities-Utilities	Expense	Water, electricity, garbage, and other basic utilities expenses
6100 · Facilities-Other	Expense	
6105 · Rent Expense	Expense	Facility rental expense
6110 · Church Building Repairs & Main	Expense	
6120 · Grounds Maintenance	Expense	
6130 · Custodial Supplies	Expense	
6140 · Insurance	Expense	Includes all insurances except payroll related
6150 · Building and Property Security	Expense	Building and property security monitoring expenses
6160 · Pastor Housing Expense	Expense	
6161 · Pastor Housing	Expense	

Repairs & Main		
6190 · Misc, Facilities	Expense	
6300 · Administrative Expenses	Expense	
6310 · Office Supplies	Expense	Office supplies expense
6320 · Postage and Delivery	Expense	Postage, and delivery services
6330 Telephone Expense	Expense	Telephone and long distance charges, faxing, and other fees
6340 Printing Expense	Expense	Printing and copying expenses
6350 · Software and Technology	Expense	Software, website, and computer support
6360 · Advertising and Promotions	Expense	
6370 · Conventions and Conferences	Expense	Costs for attending conferences and meetings
6372 · Dues and Subscriptions	Expense	Subscriptions and membership dues for civic, service, professional, trade organizations
6380 · Financial Fees	Expense	Any charges for financial services-payroll processing, credit card discounts, etc.
6381 · Bank Service Charges	Expense	Bank account service fees, bad check charges, and other bank fees
6382 · Professional Fees	Expense	Payments to accounting professionals and attorneys for accounting or legal services
6390 · Miscellaneous Administrative	Expense	
6400 · Payroll Expenses	Expense	Payroll expenses
6500 · Employee Benefits	Expense	
6560 · Other Payroll Tax Expense	Expense	
6600 · Program Expenses	Expense	Use for expenses that do not fall into other categories
6610 · Worship Program Expense	Expense	Use only if the expense doesn't fall in another account
6620 · Youth Program Expenses	Expense	Use only if the expense doesn't fall in another account
6630 · Adult Education Program Exp	Expense	Use only if the expense doesn't fall in another account
6690 · Other Program Expense	Expense	Use only if the expense doesn't fall in another account
6700 · National Church Allocation Exp.	Expense	For charges, dues, etc. owed to a supervising organization
6800 · Donated Goods and Services	Expense	Offset account for the receipt of goods or services instead of money
6900 · Reserve transfer	Expense	Record payment of transfer to

payment		reserves here
5000 · Other Income-Non-Operating	Other Income	Income received not from normal operations of the church
5020· Capital Campaign	Other Income	
5030 Endowment Donations	Other Income	
5040· Specific Bequests	Other Income	
5080 Sale of Fixed Assets	Other Income	
5090 · Misc. Other Inc.-Non-Operating	Other Income	
5010 · Specific Gifts Restr. -Non-Operating	Other Income	Specific gifts received for designated non-operating purposes
5100 · Special Collections Pass Thru	Other Income	Use this account to record donations received for other charitable organizations
5800 · Reserve Transfer Deposit	Other Income	Deposit of reserve dollars
7100 · Payments of Donations to Others	Other Expense	Use to pay pass-through donations to other organizations
7200 · Extraordinary Repairs	Other Expense	For large repairs outside the normal operations
7300 · Capital Expenditures	Other Expense	
7400 · Capital Campaign Expenses	Other Expense	
7500 · Grant Expense	Other Expense	Only for unusual expenses specifically required by a grant
7600 · Interest Expense	Other Expense	Interest payments on loans, credit card balances, or other debt
7700 · Depreciation Expense	Other Expense	Depreciation on fixed assets
8000 · Ask My Accountant	Other Expense	To be discussed with accountant

3. For Associations

Chart based on recommendations from the ASAE (American Society of Association Executives):

Account	Type	Description
1000 · Cash	Bank	
1010 · Checking account	Bank	Rename for your account
1020 · Impress accounts	Bank	Payroll, etc.
1030 · Savings account	Bank	Rename for your account
1040 · Cash Equivalents	Bank	Money Market accounts
1050 · Cash on hand	Bank	Petty cash or gift cards held
1100 · Investments	Bank	
1110 · Certificates of Deposit	Bank	
1120 · Mutual Funds	Bank	
1130 · Commercial Paper	Bank	
1140 · Corporate Bonds/Notes	Bank	
1150 · Government Bonds	Bank	
1160 · Common Stocks	Bank	
1200 · Accounts Receivable	Accounts Receivable	
1210 · Dues	Accounts Receivable	Members, chapters, related organizations, etc.
1220 · Products and Services	Accounts Receivable	Exhibitors, registrations, resale, materials, etc.
1230 · Contributions/ pledges	Accounts Receivable	Members, foundations, corporations, etc.
1240 · Grants	Accounts Receivable	Government, foundations, corporations
1250 · Accruals	Accounts Receivable	Interest, etc.
1260 · Current portion long-term	Accounts Receivable	Notes, etc.
1300 · Inventories	Other Current Asset	
1310 · Inventories	Other Current Asset	Supplies, resale materials, etc.
1400 · Prepaid Expenses	Other Current Asset	
1410 · Prepaid Expenses	Other Current Asset	Meetings trade shows, conventions, insurance, rent, etc.
1500 · Other Current Assets	Other Cur. Asset	

1510 · Other current assets	Other Current Asset	Deposits, advances to employees
1600 · Property and Equipment	Fixed Asset	
1610 · Land	Fixed Asset	
1620 · Buildings – Operating	Fixed Asset	Buildings owned for current use
1630 · Building improvements	Fixed Asset	
1640 · Furniture and Equipment	Fixed Asset	Furniture and equipment with useful life exceeding one year
1650 · Leased Equipment	Fixed Asset	
1660 · Vehicles	Fixed Asset	
1680 · Accumulated Depreciation	Fixed Asset	Land, buildings, equipment, and vehicles
1800 · Other Assets	Other Asset	Assets other than current or fixed assets.
1870 · Security Deposits Asset	Other Asset	Deposits and other returnable funds held by other entities (rent deposit, etc.)
2010 · Accounts Payable	Accounts Payable	
2015 · Credit Card	Credit Card	rename with your card provider
2020 · Payroll liabilities	Other Current Liability	Unpaid payroll liabilities. Amounts withheld or accrued, but not yet paid
2030 · Accrued expenses	Other Current Liability	Rent retirement, salaries, taxes, vacation
2110 · Notes payable – current	Other Current Liability	
2120 · Mortgage payable – current	Other Current Liability	
2310 · Capital lease obligation – Curr	Other Current Liability	
2410 · Deferred dues	Other Current Liability	
2510 · Deferred revenue	Other Current Liability	Grants, registration, subscriptions, etc.

2710 · Notes payable	Long Term Liability	
2720 · Mortgage payable	Long Term Liability	
2730 · Capital lease obligation	Long Term Liability	
2820 · Deferred subscriptions	Long Term Liability	Amounts received for future fiscal periods
2910 · Deferred rent credit	Long Term Liability	
2999 · Other Liabilities-suspense	Long Term Liability	Liabilities to discuss with your accountant.
3000 · Unrestricted Net Assets	Equity	Other Income
3010 · Unrestricted	Equity	
3011 · Undesignated/operating	Equity	
3012 · Board designated	Equity	Contingencies, future programs, etc.
3300 · Temp. Restricted Net Assets	Equity	Other Income
3310 · Purpose Restricted	Equity	
3320 · Time Restricted	Equity	
3600 · Perm. Restricted Net Assets	Equity	Other Income
3610 · Endowment	Equity	
3999 · Opening Balance Equity	Equity	The balance of this account should be zero after completing your setup
4010 · Dues	Income	Members, chapters, related organizations, etc.
4110 · Initiation fees	Income	
4210 · Special assessments	Income	
4510 · Registrations	Income	Regular, associate, exhibitor, etc.
4610 · Exhibitor fees	Income	
4710 · Supplementary activities	Income	
4800 · Fundraiser	Income	
4810 · Fundraiser income	Income	
4820 · Fundraiser expenses	Income	
5100 · Advertising	Income	
5200 · Subscriptions	Income	
5300 · Reprints	Income	

5400 · Video	Income	And other visual materials
5500 · Royalties	Income	
5550 · Certification	Income	
5600 · Mailing Labels	Income	
5700 · Management fees	Income	Related entities, etc.
5800 · Administrative fees	Income	Insurance program, etc.
5900 · Commissions	Income	
6000 · Grants	Income	Government, foundation, corporate and individual
6110 · Contributions	Income	Cash, property, services
6210 · Sponsorships	Income	
6220 · Endorsements	Income	
6230 · Interest	Income	
6240 · Dividends	Income	
6250 · Rent	Income	
6260 · Gain on sale of investments	Income	
6270 · Gain on disposal	Income	
6280 · Miscellaneous	Income	
7000 · Personnel costs	Expense	
7050 · Salaries and Wages	Expense	Payroll expenses
7070 · Payroll taxes	Expense	FICA, FUTA, state unemployment, etc.
7090 · Benefits	Expense	Health, life & disability insurance, etc.
7095 · Retirement	Expense	Pension, etc.
7120 · Parking	Expense	
7130 · Professional development	Expense	Staff education, etc.
7410 · Mortgage interest	Expense	
7420 · Rent Expense	Expense	
7430 · Maintenance	Expense	
7440 · Repairs	Expense	
7450 · Property Taxes	Expense	
7460 · Utilities	Expense	
7520 · Audio visuals	Expense	
7530 · Awards-plaques	Expense	
7540 · Meals	Expense	
7550 · Entertainment	Expense	
7560 · Equipment rental	Expense	
7570 · Exhibit hall	Expense	
7580 · Hotel	Expense	
7590 · Cancellation insurance	Expense	
7610 · Speakers	Expense	

7620 · Tours	Expense	
7710 · Travel	Expense	Board, committees, staff, etc.
7720 · Professional fees	Expense	Audit, legal, consultants, outside services
7730 · Computer supplies & maint.	Expense	
7740 · Reproduction	Expense	
7750 · Depreciation	Expense	
7760 · General insurance	Expense	Liability, office, etc.
7770 · Loss on disposal	Expense	
7780 · Office supplies	Expense	
7790 · Postage	Expense	
8010 · Printing	Expense	
8020 · Taxes	Expense	Federal and state income, sales, etc.
8030 · Reference materials	Expense	
8040 · Dues to other organizations	Expense	
8999- Ask My Accountant	Expense	

4. For a PTA

Account	Type	Description
1100 · Cash &Marketable Securities	Bank	
1110 · Checking	Bank	Enter your bank name here.
1120 · Money Market/Savings	Bank	Enter your bank name here.
1130 · Petty Cash	Bank	
1300 · Accounts Receivable	Accounts Receivable	
1310 · Pledges Receivable	Accounts Receivable	Pledges not yet received.
1320 · Member Dues Receivable	Accounts Receivable	Dues owed by members not yet received.
1200 · Undeposited Funds	Other Current Asset	Money entered into the system, not yet deposited in the bank.
1400 · Other Current Assets	Other Current Asset	Prepaid expenses (Postage, Insurance, etc.)
1900 · Other Assets	Other Asset	Assets other than current or fixed assets
2100 · Accounts Payable	Accounts Payable	
2150 · Credit Card	Credit Card	Rename for credit card company or user
2200 · Other Current Liabilities	Other Current Liability	
2210 · Due to National	Other Current Liability	
2220 · Due to State	Other Current Liability	
2500 · Other Liabilities	Long Term Liability	
2520 · Other Long Term Liabilities	Long Term Liability	
2510 · Long Term Debts to Business	Long Term Liability	
3000 · Opening Balance Equity	Equity	Do not post to.
3100 · Unrestricted Net Assets	Equity	
3200 · Temp. Restricted Net Assets	Equity	
3300 · Perm. Res. Net Assets	Equity	

4100 · Membership Dues	Income	
4200 · Donations	Income	
4300 · Fundraisers	Income	
4310 · Fundraiser #1	Income	
4311 · Fundraiser #1 Income	Income	Income from Fundraiser #1
4315 · Fundraiser #1 Expense	Income	Expenses for Fundraiser #1
4320 · Fundraiser #2	Income	
4321 · Fundraiser #2 Income	Income	
4325 · Fundraiser #2 Expense	Income	
4400 · Community Sponsored Grants	Income	
4600 · Other Income	Income	Miscellaneous Income received.
4700 · Interest Income	Income	
5100 · School Programs	Expense	
5200 · Scholarships	Expense	
5300 · Membership Promotion	Expense	
5350 · Newsletter& Publicity	Expense	
5360 · Gifts & Awards	Expense	
5400 · Council Dues	Expense	
5450 · Convention & Meetings	Expense	
5460 · Officers Reimbursements	Expense	
5510 · Supplies	Expense	
5520 · Administrative Expenses	Expense	
5525 · Bank Fees and Charges	Expense	
5530 · Outside Contract Services	Expense	
5540 · Other Expense	Expense	
8000 · Ask My Accountant	Expense	

5.   For a Civic Club

Account	Type	Description
1100 · Cash & Invest.	Bank	
1110 · Checking	Bank	Enter your bank name here.
1120 · Money Market/Savings	Bank	Enter your bank name here.
1130 · Petty Cash	Bank	
1300 · Accounts Receivable	Accounts Receivable	
1310 · Member Dues Receivable	Accounts Receivable	Dues owed by members not yet received.
1320 · Other Receivables	Accounts Receivable	Amounts due from others not for dues.
1200 · Undeposited Funds	Other Current Asset	Money entered into the system, not yet deposited in the bank.
1400 · Other Current Assets	Other Current Asset	Prepaid expenses (Postage, Insurance, etc.)
1500 · Furniture and Equipment	Fixed Asset	Furniture and equipment with useful life exceeding one year
1900 · Other Assets	Other Asset	Assets other than current or fixed assets
1910 · Security Deposits Asset	Other Asset	Deposits and other returnable funds held by other entities
2100 · Accounts Payable	Accounts Payable	
2150 · Credit Card	Credit Card	Rename for credit card company or user
2200 · Other Current Liabilities	Other Current Liability	
2210 · Due to National	Other Current Liability	
2220 · Due to State/Council/etc.	Other Current Liability	
2500 · Other Liabilities	Long Term Liability	
2520 · Other Long Term Liabilities	Long Term Liability	
2510 · Long Term Debts to Business	Long Term Liability	
3000 · Opening Balance Equity	Equity	Do not post to.

3100 · Unrestricted Net Assets	Equity	
3200 · Temp. Restricted Net Assets	Equity	
3300 · Perm. Restricted Net Assets	Equity	
4100 · Membership Income	Income	
4110 · Membership Dues	Income	
4120 · Meals/Guarantee Assessment	Income	
4130 · Membership Fees (Induction)	Income	
4140 · Fines	Income	
4200 · Donations	Income	
4300 · Fundraisers	Income	
4310 · Fundraiser #1	Income	
4311 · Fundraiser #1 Income	Income	Income from Fundraiser #1
4315 · Fundraiser #1 Expense	Income	Expenses for fundraiser # 1
4320 · Fundraiser #2	Income	
4321 · Fundraiser #2 Income	Income	
4325 · Fundraiser # 2 Expenses	Income	
4400 · Community Sponsored Grants	Income	
4600 · Other Income	Income	Miscellaneous Income received.
4700 · Interest Income	Income	
5100 · Programs Expenses	Expense	
5110 · Program Expenses	Expense	Rename or add accounts for specific costs related to your group's programs.
5200 · Scholarships	Expense	
5300 · Membership	Expense	
5310 · Council/National Dues	Expense	For dues paid to an umbrella organization.

5320 · Magazine Subscriptions	Expense	Cost of Subscriptions for Members
5330 · Dues to Umbrella Organization	Expense	
5340 · New Member Processing Fees	Expense	
5350 · Newsletter& Publicity	Expense	
5360 · Gifts & Awards	Expense	
5400 · Delegate & Travel Expenses	Expense	
5410 · District Convention/Gathering	Expense	
5420 · National/International Convention	Expense	
5430 · Gifts & Flowers	Expense	
5440 · President's Gifts	Expense	
5450 · Social Activities	Expense	
5460 · Officers Reimbursements	Expense	
5470 · Installation	Expense	
5500 · General & Administrative	Expense	
5510 · Supplies	Expense	
5520 · Meals/Guest	Expense	
5521 · Meals/Members	Expense	
5525 · Bank fees and charges	Expense	
5530 · Insurance	Expense	
5540 · Taxes	Expense	
5570 · Outside Contract Services	Expense	
5580 · Other Expense	Expense	
8000 · Ask My Accountant	Expense	Put here if you don't know where to charge something.

6.   For a Boy Scout Troop

This is based on the Boy Scouts of America (BSA) budget worksheet.

Account	Type	Description
1100 · Cash and Reserve Funds	Bank	
1110 · Checking	Bank	Enter your bank name here.
1120 · Reserve Fund	Bank	Enter your bank name here.
1130 · Petty Cash	Bank	
1300 · Accounts Receivable	Accounts Receivable	
1310 · Member Dues Receivable	Accounts Receivable	Dues owed by members not yet received.
1320 · Due from Fundraiser	Accounts Receivable	Moneys owed to troop for fundraisers (popcorn, etc.)
1330 · Other Receivables	Accounts Receivable	Amounts due from others not otherwise accounted for.
1200 · Undeposited Funds	Other Current Asset	Money entered into the system, not yet deposited in the bank.
1400 · Other Current Assets	Other Current Asset	Prepaid expenses (postage, insurance, etc.)
1510 · Furniture and Equipment	Fixed Asset	Furniture and equipment with useful life exceeding one year
1520 · Building	Fixed Asset	Use if the troop owns the building
1900 · Other Assets	Other Asset	Assets other than current or fixed assets
2100 · Accounts Payable	Accounts Payable	
2150 · Credit Card	Credit Card	Rename for credit card company or user
2200 · Other Current Liabilities	Other Current Liability	
2210 · Due to National	Other Current Liability	
2220 · Due to Council	Other Current Liability	
2500 · Other Liabilities	Long Term Liability	
2520 · Other Long Term Liabilities	Long Term Liability	
3000 · Opening Balance Equity	Equity	Do not post to.
3100 · Unrestricted Net Assets	Equity	
3200 · Temp. Restricted Net Assets	Equity	
3300 · Perm. Restricted Net Assets	Equity	
4100 · Membership Income	Income	
4110 · Registration Fees	Income	Fees collected for registration

4120 · Troop Dues Collected	Income	
4130 · Activity Fees	Income	Money received for campouts & outings. Use classes to match revenue &expenses.
4200 · Donations	Income	
4300 · Fundraisers	Income	
4310 · Fundraiser #1	Income	
4311 · Fundraiser #1 Income	Income	Income from a Fundraiser
4315 · Fundraiser #1 Expense	Income	Expenses for Fundraiser
4320 · Popcorn Sale	Income	
4321 · Popcorn Sale Income	Income	
4325 · Popcorn Sale Expense	Income	
4600 · Other Income	Income	Miscellaneous Income received.
4700 · Interest Income	Income	
5100 · Registration Fees Paid	Expense	
5110 · Unit Insurance	Expense	
5111 · Insurance for Cub Scouts	Expense	
5112 · Insurance for Boy Scouts	Expense	
5113 · Insurance for Varsity Scouts	Expense	
5114 · Insurance for Venturers	Expense	
5115 · Unit Liability Insurance Fee	Expense	
5150 · Boys Life Subscriptions	Expense	
5200 · Program Materials	Expense	
5210 · Activities	Expense	
5220 · Campout/Outing Expenses	Expense	Campground fees, food, etc.
5230 · High Adventure Camps Expenses	Expense	Use with a class for the total cost of the trip. To tie money received to money paid out by member, use Customer:Job.
5250 · Literature	Expense	Merit Badge pamphlets, etc.
5260 · Training Materials	Expense	
5300 · Awards, Badges, and Prizes	Expense	
5350 · Food and Refreshments	Expense	For meetings and award dinners.
5400 · Trips and Transportation	Expense	
5500 · General & Administrative	Expense	
5520 · Service Projects	Expense	
5530 · Bank Fees and Charges	Expense	
5550 · Equipment	Expense	
5570 · Building Maintenance	Expense	Cost to maintain the Scout Hut.
5600 · Other Expenses	Expense	
5900 · Scholarships	Expense	
8000 · Ask My Accountant	Expense	

7.   For a Girl Scout Troop

This chart of accounts was based on a Girl Scout Troop Financial Report.

Account	Type	Description
1100 · Cash & Invest.	Bank	
1110 · Checking	Bank	Enter your bank name here.
1120 · Money Market/Savings	Bank	Enter your bank name here.
1130 · Petty Cash	Bank	
1300 · Accounts Receivable	Accounts Receivable	
1310 · Member Dues Receivable	Accounts Receivable	Dues owed by members not yet received.
1320 · Due from Fundraiser	Accounts Receivable	Moneys owed to troop for fundraisers (cookies, etc.)
1330 · Other Receivables	Accounts Receivable	Amounts due from others not otherwise accounted for.
1200 · Undeposited Funds	Other Current Asset	Money entered into the system, not yet deposited in the bank.
1400 · Other Current Assets	Other Current Asset	Prepaid expenses (postage, insurance, etc.)
1510 · Furniture and Equipment	Fixed Asset	Furniture and equipment with useful life exceeding one year
1520 · Building	Fixed Asset	Use if the building is owned
1900 · Other Assets	Other Asset	Assets other than current or fixed assets
1910 · Security Deposits Asset	Other Asset	Deposits and other returnable funds held by other entities
2100 · Accounts Payable	Accounts Payable	
2150 · Credit Card	Credit Card	Rename for credit card company or user
2200 · Other Current Liabilities	Other Current Liability	
2210 · Due to National	Other Current Liability	
2220 · Due to Council	Other Current Liability	
2500 · Other Liabilities	Long Term Liability	
2520 · Other Long Term Liabilities	Long Term Liability	
3000 · Opening Balance Equity	Equity	Do not post to.
3100 · Unrestricted Net Assets	Equity	
3200 · Temp. Restricted Net Assets	Equity	
3300 · Perm. Restricted Net Assets	Equity	

4100 · Membership Income	Income	
4110 · G. S. Registration Fees	Income	Fees collected for registration
4300 · Fundraisers	Income	
4310 · Fall Product	Income	
4311 · Fall Product Income	Income	Income from Fall Product
4315 · Fall Product Expense	Income	Expenses for Fall Product
4320 · Cookie Sale	Income	
4321 · Cookie Sale Income	Income	
4325 · Cookie Sale Expense	Income	
4330 · Money Earning Projects	Income	
4331 · Money Earning Project Income	Income	
4335 · Money Earning Projects Costs	Income	
4400 · Juliette Low World Friendship	Income	Donations to the JLW FF
4600 · Other Income	Income	Miscellaneous Income received.
4700 · Interest Income	Income	
5100 · G.S. Registration Fees Paid	Expense	
5200 · Program Supplies	Expense	
5210 · Crafts	Expense	
5220 · Publications	Expense	
5300 · Awards and Insignia	Expense	
5350 · Food and Refreshments	Expense	For meetings and award dinners. Put camping food with campout expenses.
5400 · Trips & Transportation	Expense	
5500 · General & Administrative	Expense	
5510 · Money Earning Costs	Expense	
5520 · Service Projects	Expense	
5530 · Bank Fees and Charges	Expense	
5540 · Overnight Camping	Expense	Campground fees, food, etc. Use classes to match revenue by outing to expenses.
5550 · Equipment	Expense	
5600 · Other Expenses	Expense	
5700 · Juliette Low World Payments	Expense	Payments to the JLW FF
5900 · Scholarships	Expense	
8000 · Ask My Accountant	Expense	Put here if you don't know where else to.

8. For a Private School

Chart based on the North American Montessori Teachers Association (NAMTA) recommendations.

Account	Type	Description
1100 · Cash & Marketable Securities	Bank	
1110 · Checking	Bank	Enter your bank name here.
1120 · Money Market/Savings	Bank	Enter your bank name here.
1130 · Petty Cash	Bank	
1300 · Accounts Receivable	Accounts Receivable	
1310 · Student Receivable	Accounts Receivable	Dues owed by members not yet received.
1330 · Other Receivables	Accounts Receivable	Amounts due from others not otherwise accounted for.
1200 · Undeposited Funds	Other Current Asset	Money entered into the system, not yet deposited in the bank.
1400 · Other Current Assets	Other Current Asset	Prepaid expenses (postage, insurance, etc.)
1510 · Furniture and Equipment	Fixed Asset	Furniture and equipment with useful life exceeding one year
1520 · Building	Fixed Asset	Use if the building is owned
18000 · Marketable Securities	Other Asset	Investments in stocks or bonds, singly or in mutual funds
18700 · Security Deposits Asset	Other Asset	Deposits and other returnable funds held by other entities
1900 · Other Assets	Other Asset	Assets other than current or fixed assets
1910 · Security Deposits Asset	Other Asset	Deposits and other returnable funds held by other entities
2100 · Accounts Payable	Accounts Payable	
2150 · Credit Card	Credit Card	Rename for credit card company or user
2200 · Other Current Liabilities	Other Current Liability	
2500 · Other Liabilities	Long Term Liability	
2520 · Other Long Term Liabilities	Long Term Liability	
3000 · Opening Balance Equity	Equity	Do not post to.
3100 · Unrestricted Net Assets	Equity	
3200 · Temp. Restricted Net Assets	Equity	

3300 · Perm. Restricted Net Assets	Equity	
4100 · Tuition	Income	
4110 · Application Fees	Income	Fees collected for registration
4200 · Donations	Income	
4210 · General	Income	
4220 · Annual Giving	Income	
4300 · Fundraisers	Income	
4310 · Fundraiser #1	Income	
4311 · Fundraiser #1 Income	Income	Income from Fall Product
4315 · Fundraiser #1 Expenses	Income	Expenses for Fall Product
4320 · Fundraiser #2	Income	
4321 · Fundraiser #2 Income	Income	
4325 · Fundraiser #2 Expenses	Income	
4600 · Other Income	Income	Miscellaneous income received.
4700 · Interest Income	Income	
6100 · Payroll Expenses	Expense	
6110 · Salaries and Wages	Expense	
6120 · Payroll Taxes	Expense	Employer taxes-FICA, FUTA, etc.
6130 · Employee Benefits	Expense	
6140 · Professional Development	Expense	
6150 · Faculty Financial Assistance	Expense	Tuition discounts, etc. to employees.
6200 · Classroom Expenses	Expense	
6210 · Books	Expense	
6220 · Educational Materials	Expense	
6230 · Classroom Supplies	Expense	
6240 · Services	Expense	
6280 · Donated Classroom Time	Expense	
6300 · General & Administrative	Expense	
6310 · Postage and Printing	Expense	
6320 · Insurance	Expense	
6330 · Equipment Maintenance	Expense	
6340 · Audit	Expense	
6350 · Website and Technology	Expense	
6360 · Telephone	Expense	
6390 · Miscellaneous	Expense	
6400 · Facilities	Expense	
6410 · Mortgage	Expense	
6430 · Utilities	Expense	
6440 · Maintenance and Supplies	Expense	
6450 · Building Repairs	Expense	

6460 · Property Tax	Expense	
5100 · Scholarships	Other Income	Money donated for scholarships. Needs a temporarily restricted class.
5200 · New Building Fund	Other Income	Needs a temporarily restricted class.
7100 · Capital Account	Other Expense	
7110 · Major Repairs	Other Expense	
7120 · New Furniture and Fixtures	Other Expense	
7130 · New Building	Other Expense	
7200 · Scholarships Granted	Other Expense	
8000 · Ask My Accountant	Expense	Put here if you don't know where to charge something.

Acknowledgements

I have enjoyed working with Eulica on this book. Her breadth of knowledge and experience is amazing and, more importantly, her extreme work ethic and patience with me borders on sainthood!

Huge thanks to our husbands, Kevin and Skip, for putting up with cold dinners and frequent conversations centering around the exciting topic of nonprofit accounting. Eulica also wishes to thank her daughters, Kiana and Kandace, for their support.

I'd especially like to thank our editor, Susan Sipal, who had been encouraging me to write this book for some time and our various early readers for their input and suggestions.

If you liked the book, you can help other churches and nonprofits find out about us by posting reviews on Amazon, Barnes & Noble, and your favorite social media sites. If you would have other topics you'd like covered, please contact us through AccountantBesideYou.com. Our blog posts usually come from reader suggestions.

Happy Accounting!

Index

Made in the USA
Middletown, DE
15 February 2017